THE ROUGH GUIDE

Website
Directory

There are more than two hundred Rough Guide
travel, phrasebook and music titles, covering
destinations from Amsterdam to Zimbabwe,
languages from Czech to Vietnamese, and musics
from World to Opera and Jazz

**ROUGH
GUIDES**

www.roughguides.com

Rough Guide Credits

Text editor: Jo Mead
Series editor: Mark Ellingham
Production: Julia Bovis, Katie Pringle

Publishing Information

This second edition published October 2002 by
Rough Guides Ltd, 80 Strand, London WC2R 0RL.

Distributed by the Penguin Group

Penguin Books Ltd, 80 Strand, London WC2R 0RL
Penguin Putnam, Inc., 375 Hudson Street, New York 10014, USA
Penguin Books Australia Ltd, 487 Maroondah Highway,
PO Box 257, Ringwood, Victoria 3134, Australia
Penguin Books Canada Ltd, 10 Alcorn Avenue,
Toronto, Ontario, Canada M4V 1E4
Penguin Books (NZ) Ltd, 182–190 Wairau Road,
Auckland 10, New Zealand

Printed in Spain by Graphy Cems.

© Angus J Kennedy, 2002
400pp, includes index
A catalogue record for this book is available from the British Library.
ISBN 1-84353-011-2

THE ROUGH GUIDE

Website Directory

written by
Angus J Kennedy & Peter Shapiro

Contents

Contents

Contents

Contents

Introduction

Find it
without losing your mind

Barring total deforestation of the world, it would be physically impossible to list, let alone review, every Website currently floating around the ether; in fact, this book lists less than one-tenth of one percent of all the information available on the World Wide Web. Therefore, the art of **finding something** pinned up on the world's biggest scrapboard is, without doubt, **the most valuable skill** you can glean from your time online. If you know how to use the Net to find an answer to almost anything quickly and comprehensively, you'd have to consider yourself not only useful but pretty saleable too. Most people, including many Net veterans, simply **bumble their way around**. Yet it's a remarkably basic skill to master. So read this section, then get online and start investigating. Within an hour or two you'll be milking the Net for all it's worth. It might turn out to be the best investment you'll ever make!

Find it

How it works

The Net is massive. Just the Web alone houses well over two billion pages of text, and many millions more are added daily. So you'll need some serious help if you want to find something. Thankfully, there's a wide selection of search tools to make the task relatively painless. The job usually entails keying your **search terms** into a form on a Web page and waiting a few seconds for the results.

Over the next few pages we'll introduce you to **search tools** that can locate almost anything: on the Web; linked to from the Web; or archived into an online Web database, such as email addresses, phone numbers, program locations, newsgroup articles and news clippings. Of course, first it has to be put online and granted public access. So just because you can access US government servers doesn't mean you'll find a file on DEA Operative Presley's whereabouts.

Your weapons

There are three main types of Web search tools: **search engines**, **hand-built subject directories** and **search agents**. Apart from the odd newspaper archive, they're usually free. Because they're so useful and popular, there was a trend towards tacking other services onto the side and building themselves into so-called **portals**, **communities** and **hubs**. More recently, that trend has begun to reverse with the launch of several skeletal search tools free of fancy overheads. Irrespective of which you use, ignore the quantity of froufrou and concentrate on the quality of the results. The next few pages discuss each category in detail and show you how to torture them for answers.

Search engines

The best way to find just about anything online is to start with a **search engine**. The good thing about search engines is they can search through the **actual contents** of Web pages (and file servers), and not just descriptions. The better search engines can rifle through **billions of Web pages** in a fraction of a second. You simply go to the search engine's Website and submit **keywords**, or search terms, into a simple form. It will query its database and, almost instantly, return a list of results or "**hits**". For example, if you were to search on the expression "Rough Guide Website Directory", here's what might come up on top:

1. Welcome to the Rough Guide Website Directory
The Rough Guide Website Directory is the ultimate guide to the World Wide Web, complete with a 2500+ site directory.
www.roughguides.com/web/index.html/

In this case the top line tells us the name of the page or site, followed by a description excerpted from the page and then the page's address. If it suits, click on the link to visit the site.

Tip: don't just click on a result, and then hit the Back button if it's no good. Instead, run down the list and open the most promising candidates in new browser windows. It will save you tons of time. Do this by holding down the **Shift key** as you click.

The reason it's so quick is **you're not searching the Web live**. You're merely searching a database of Web page extracts stored on the search engine's server. This database is compiled by a program that periodically "crawls" around the Web looking for new or changed pages. Because of the sheer size of the Net and a few factors relating to site design, it's not possible for the crawlers to find every site, let alone every word on every page.

Nor is it possible to keep the database completely up to date. That means you can't literally "search the Web" – you can only search a snapshot taken by a search engine. So, naturally, different search engines will give you different results depending on how much of the Web they've found, how often they update, how much text they extract from each page and how well they actually work.

So, which search engine?

There are dozens of search engines, but only a few are worth trying. In fact, you'll rarely need more than one. But since you'll be using it often, make sure it's up to speed. You'll want the **biggest, freshest database**. You'll want to **fine-tune your search** with extra commands. And you'll want the most hits you can get on one page with the most **relevant results on top**. Right now, that's **Google**.

Google http://www.google.com

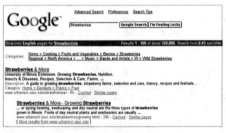

This completely free service has an uncanny knack of getting it right in the first few hits, both from within its search engine database and its association with the **Open Directory**. It also provides local cache access to pages that have disappeared since its crawl or are otherwise unavailable. Click on "cached" to see how this works. Use it when you can't get a link to load.

If Google falls short, try **All the Web** and **AltaVista**. They're also big, fast, clutter-free and can deliver a long page of relevant hits. Next up is **Northern Light**, which is worth a shot. It's also big, but not so fast or user-friendly despite its curious system of organizing hits into folders.

All the Web http://www.alltheweb.com

AltaVista http://www.altavista.com

Northern Light http://www.nlsearch.com

As for the rest? Just because an engine isn't the biggest or best doesn't mean it's worthless. Even the smallest engines can find unique hits. Still, unless you're after extra hits, you're unlikely to need them. Of course, they might improve:

Excite http://www.excite.com

HotBot http://hotbot.lycos.com

Lycos http://www.lycos.com

If you notice some engines give identical or very similar results it might be because they share technologies. **AOL**, **HotBot** and **MSN**, for example, currently use the **Inktomi** system. Another option to consider is the BBC's recently launched search engine (http://www.bbc.co.uk) which gives priority to UK sites. As of press time, it hadn't been working long enough to give it thorough consideration.

But if you seriously need **more results**, rather than visit several engines in turn, query them simultaneously using an agent such as **Copernic**. You can tell how each engine ranks from the results. For more detailed analysis, see:

Search Engine Watch http://www.searchenginewatch.com

Search Engine World http://www.searchengineworld.com

Search Engine Showdown http://www.searchengineshowdown.com

Find it

Search Lore http://www.searchlore.org

They keep tabs on all the finer details such as who owns what, how they work and who's currently biggest. Essential reading for budding Webmasters.

Limitations

Search engines aren't the be-all and end-all of what's on the Web. **They're only as good as their most recent findings**, which might be just a small proportion of what's actually there and possibly months old. So just because you can't find it through a Web search doesn't mean it doesn't exist. If you're after something brand-new, they're not always the best choice. You might be better off searching **Usenet** (see p.20) or a news service.

How to use a search engine

OK, get this right and you'll find anything. The trick is to think up a **search term** that's unique enough to get rid of junk results but broad enough not to miss anything useful. It will depend entirely on the subject, so be prepared to think laterally!

One search won't fit all – read the instructions

Although most search forms look alike, the mechanisms behind them differ. That means you might have to adjust your search terms slightly, depending on the engine, to get the best results. The same applies to online stores, encyclopedias, newspaper archives and anything else you can search. It also means some engines work better than others.

While the easiest way to learn is to dive straight in, at some point pause and read the instructions. You should find a link to a FAQ, Search Tips or Help section on the front page. The main things to glean are how to **create a phrase,** how to **search on multiple phrases** and how to **exclude certain words.** A few minutes' study could save hours of weeding through poor results.

A typical search

Let's start with a complex example. Suppose we want to search for something on one of the esteemed authors, *Angus Kennedy*. Let's see how you'd do it in **All the Web**.

If you were to enter:

angus kennedy

it would return all pages that contain "angus" **or** "kennedy" **or both.** That means there'd be lots of pages about Angus cattle and JFK. We don't want to sift through those, so let's make sure the pages contain **both words.** In Raging Search, and most other search engines, you can use a **plus sign (+)** to state that the page **must contain a word**. So let's try:

+angus +kennedy

That's better. All the pages now contain both words. Unfortunately, though, there's no guarantee that they'll be next to each other. What we really want is to **treat them as a phrase**. A simple way to do this is to enclose the words within quotes, like this:

"angus kennedy"

Now we've captured all instances of Angus Kennedy as a phrase, but since it's **a person's name**, we should look for *Kennedy, Angus* as well. So let's try:

"angus kennedy" "kennedy, angus"

As with the first example, we now catch pages with **either or both phrases**. Now suppose we want to narrow it down further and exclude some irrelevant results, for example others with the same name. Our target writes books about French literature, so let's start by getting rid of that pesky Rough Guide author. To

exclude a term, place a minus sign (-) in front. So let's ditch him:

"angus kennedy" "kennedy, angus" - "rough guide"

That's about all you need to know in most instances. These rules should work in most engines, as well as the search forms on individual sites. However, there are exceptions.

Variations - such as Google

Google makes searching easier by including all the search terms. Which means you don't have to add the **+** sign. So searching on: *angus kennedy* would search for pages containing "angus" **AND** "kennedy." If you want to search for pages containing either, do two separate searches or use the Boolean operator "OR": *angus OR kennedy*.

Many engines also have a **dropdown menu** with the options of "any of the words", "all the words" or "the exact phrase". If the meaning of that isn't instantly obvious, try it.

To tune your searches further, look for an "advanced search option," or refer to the instructions. Observe how the engine interprets **capitals**, dashes between words, brackets, wild cards, truncations and the **Boolean** operators such as AND, OR, NEAR and NOT.

In particular, watch out for **stop words**. These are words that are normally ignored. In Google, for example, single letters are ignored unless you place a

Tip

You'll be using your favourite engines often, so drop their addresses onto your browser Links bar. But rather than save the front page, favour the one with advanced options. At All the Web, for example, click on "Advanced search" to bring up an assortment of tuning boxes, including the friendlier **100 hits per page option**. At Google and Raging Search, click on "Preferences" and "Customize" respectively to increase the default number of hits per page. You can then save the front page, as your preferences will be stored in your cookies.

"+" sign in front of them. So to search for Angus J Kennedy, you'd enter: *"angus +j kennedy"*

Translations

If your results include foreign language sites, Google and Altavista can roughly translate them into English or another preference. Just click on "translate".

Can't find it?

If search engines can't find something it doesn't mean it's not on the Web. It just means their trawlers haven't visited that site yet. So you'll have to turn to another, maybe fresher source. Read on.

Subject directories

It's sometimes more useful to browse a range of sites within a topic or region rather than throw darts into the entire Web. For this you should turn to a **subject directory**. These aren't compiled by trawling the Web, **they're put together by human beings**. Everything is neatly filed under various categories, like a phone directory or library, making it easy for you to drill down to what you're after. This is particularly useful if you're looking for a listing of services in an area such as your home town.

You usually have the choice of browsing directories by **subject group** and sometimes by other criteria such as **entry date or rating**. Often you can search the directory itself through a form rather like a search engine. Unlike search engines, directories don't keep the contents of Web pages but instead record titles, categories, and sometimes comments or reviews, so adjust your search strategy accordingly. Start with broad terms and work down until you hit the reviews.

Find it

General directories

The Internet doesn't have an official directory, but it does have several broadly focused directories that will help you on your way to most subject areas. The best **general directories** are:

About.com http://www.about.com
Open Directory http://dmoz.org
Yahoo http://www.yahoo.co.uk

Yahoo is the closest the Net has to a central directory. If the Web has seven wonders, it would probably be the first. Apart from the massive site directory it also has loads of added extras

such as national and metropolitan directories, regional TV listings, weather reports, kids' guides, seniors' guides, yellow pages, sport scores – plus outstanding news and financial services. You should spend at least one session online exploring its reaches. Chances are you'll be back there every day.

The Open Directory is a relatively recent project, compiled by about 37,000 volunteers and served through several sites including Google. While it lacks Yahoo's armada of added services, its directory is better maintained in many areas. It pays to look at both.

About.com deserves a special mention, because unlike most broad directories its topics are presented by expert guides. This makes it an excellent jumping-off point if you need a helping hand. If you like this approach, **Suite101** (http://www.suite101.com) attempts the same tack.

There's no shortage of alternatives which might prove useful if the above fail, such as:

AltaVista http://www.altavista.com
Excite http://www.excite.com
LookSmart http://www.looksmart.com
Lycos http://www.lycos.com

But broad subject directories aren't always the best at digging up everything within a category or giving you expert guidance. For that you need a specialist directory – or, as the suits call them, **vortals**.

Specialists

Whatever your interest, you can bet your favourite finger it will have several dedicated sites and another that keeps track of them all. Such **specialized directories** are a boon for finding new, esoteric or local interest pages – ones that the major directories overlook. How do you find a specialist directory? You could go straight to Google with a very specific search, but in this case it would make more sense to seek a helping hand. Try **About.com** first. It maintains specialist directories on most common interests. Next, try Yahoo and the Open Directory. If there's more than a couple of Web directories on the subject they'll put them in their own section. You might also glean something from consulting a directory that specializes in listing specialist directories such as:

Complete Planet http://www.completeplanet.com
Directory Guide http://www.directoryguide.com
GoGettem http://www.gogettem.com
Search Bug http://www.searchbug.com
Search Engine Guide http://www.searchengineguide.com

Find it

Search IQ http://www.zdnet.com/searchiq
Webdata http://www.webdata.com

Specialist sites often maintain a **mailing list** to keep you posted with news and, in some cases, run **discussion lists** or **bulletin boards** so you can discuss issues with other visitors. If you

feel you can contribute to the site, email the Webmaster. That's how the Web community works. Of course, you'll find thousands of specialist sites all through the pages that follow.

Search agents

Search agents, or **searchbots**, gather information live from a limited number of sites – to find new information, compare prices or stock, or combine the results from several search engines, for example. **Shopping agents** (see p.304) like PriceWatch and Shopper.com scan online stores for the best deals.

Metasearch sites that query multiple search engines and directories simultaneously, such as Metacrawler, Vivisimo, Dogpile, Mamma and Ixquick, are close to useless. You'll get better results in less time by going directly to Google.

You'll find the same goes for the bewildering layers of **search aids** built into Internet Explorer and Windows. Click on IE's **Search** button, or **Search (Find) on the Internet** from the Windows Start menu, and a search form will appear on the left-hand side of your browser. Click **Customize** to choose from an impressive array of search engines, directories, email databases, maps and more. It looks promising, but again you'll probably get better value at the source. Only use Apple's metasearch agent, **Sherlock**, if you feel you need a handicap.

But all is not lost. For serious research, try **Copernic** (http://www.copernic.com). It's a free standalone program that can query hundreds of search engines, directories, Usenet archives, shops and email databases at once. It filters out the duplicates, displays the results on a single page in your browser and even retrieves them automatically for offline browsing.

There are also dozens of ways to monitor search engines, individual sites and newsgroups for changes. For example, **Spyonit** (http://www.spyonit.com) can notify you by email, pager, SMS or ICQ whenever your search term comes up on an auction, TV listing, directory or search engine. And **Tracerlock** (http://www.tracerlock.com) will let you know when your keywords come up on AltaVista, Usenet or the online personals.

For more on searchbots, see BotSpot (http://bots.internet.com).

Lists, picks & weblogs

If you're merely browsing for pleasure rather than looking for something in particular, you might like to try the sites dedicated to listing, ranking or reporting sites that are new, "cool" or popular. They come in many guises, from the top 100 busiest sites in various categories to daily doses of extreme weirdness. **Weblogs**

("blogs") are generally kept like diaries, with daily postings on whatever's attracted the author's interest over the last 24 hours. To find hundreds, run a search on "Weblog" at Dmoz.org. For some light entertainment, shuffle through the following selection:

100 Hot Websites
http://www.100hot.com
http://www.hitwise.com
Attempts to rank the hundred most visited Websites each week, overall or by category, in several countries.

Cruel Site of the Day
http://www.cruel.com
Something horrid daily.

Losers.org
http://www.losers.org
A list you don't want to make.

MemePool
http://www.memepool.com
Daily Weblog from multiple authors, archived by subject. A great source of interesting links.

Netsurfer Digest
http://www.netsurf.com/nsd/
Subscribe to receive weekly site updates and reviews.

Portal of Evil
http://www.portalofevil.com
At least three guaranteed jaw-droppers from the Web's outer limits daily. Not for the squeamish.

Useless Pages
http://www.go2net.com/useless/
http://www.worstoftheweb.com
The sludge festering at the bottom of the Net.

Yahoo's picks
http://www.yahoo.com/picks/
http://dir.yahoo.com/new/
What's new and cool, according to the staff of the world's biggest Web directory.

Finding stuff

Although a general search engine or directory might not instantly strike gold, they'll often point you in the right direction. As you get more familiar with the run of the Net, you'll gravitate toward specialist sites and directories that index more than just Web pages, add their own content and shine in specific areas. What's best depends largely on what you're after. When you find a useful site, **store it in your Favorites or Bookmarks**, so you can return. Here's how to:

Find someone's email address

Not as simple as you might think. When you're given an email address it's private unless you instruct someone to list it in a directory or make it public in some other way. So if you're looking for a long-lost friend's email address, there's no guarantee you'll find it. Nevertheless, it's worth trying the **email directories**. The biggest directories are:

Bigfoot http://www.bigfoot.com

Find it

Internet Address Finder http://www.iaf.net
WhoWhere http://www.whowhere.com
Yahoo PeopleSearch http://people.yahoo.com

These get most of their data from Usenet postings and visitors, so while they're not in any way comprehensive, they're pretty vast databases – and growing by the day. If these fail, try searching on your quarry's full name in a search engine or Deja.com. Alternatively, if you know where they work, search their company's Web pages, or (an old standby of detective agencies) **ring up and ask**. For other tips, see:

FAQ on finding email addresses:
http://www.qucis.queensu.ca/FAQs/email/finding.html/

Yahoo's email search directory:
http://dir.yahoo.com/Reference/Phone_Numbers_and_Addresses/
Email_Addresses/

ICQ email directory: http://www.icq.com/search/email.html/

Find local information

You'll sometimes want to find sites that cater to a very specific region. Say, for example, you want to look up film screenings across your city or select a honeymoon suite in Tamanrasset. Although it might seem logical to use a local search engine to find local sites or information, it's often not the most efficient method. Always start your searches with Google and then move on if that fails: most small local search engines simply aren't very good. Directories, however, can be another matter. Try Yahoo and the Open Directory and see what's listed in the region. Don't make it too narrow as it might be filed under the country, state or province rather than the town or suburb. Then drill down from the broad region into your area of interest. These should lead you to the major specialist directories in your area of interest. For a directory of regional directories, see:

Search Engine Colossus http://www.searchenginecolossus.com

Find a local business or phone number

While online residential and business telephone directories can be kept more up to date than their paper equivalents, they're not usually as easy to browse. Apart from the phone companies' offerings you'll also find a raft of private directories in competition. Some even deliver a book as well. If you haven't been exposed to their advertising, don't expect too much. Investigate a few of the following major services and see what they offer, and keep your eye out for advertisements in your local press. They should come looking for you, not vice versa.

192 Enquiries http://www.192enquiries.com
192.com http://www.192.com
BT Directory Enquiries http://www.bt.com
Scoot http://www.scoot.co.uk
Yellow Pages http://www.yell.com

To find a phone number in almost any country:

World Pages International Directories http://global.wpz.com

Find answers to the most common questions

Where else would you look for answers to the most Frequently Asked Questions than the repository for Usenet FAQs? If the answer's not in http://www.faqs.org try Usenet itself. For more information on using Usenet, see *The Rough Guide to the Internet*.

Find out what others think on Usenet

You want to, but you don't know how. You want one, but you don't know which one. You have one, but you can't get it to work. You want more than just a second opinion. You want a forum on the subject. That's Usenet.

There's no better place to find opinions and personal experiences than Usenet, but it's a lot of text to scan. Although it's sorted into subject bundles, if you had to find every instance of discussion about something it could take days. And if it was tossed around more than a couple of weeks ago, the thread might have expired.

With **Google Groups** (http://groups.google.com), though, not only can you scan close to all Usenet now, but you can get a fair chunk of its history as well. You can pursue entire threads and profile each contributor. Which means you can follow a whole discussion, as well as check out who's who and how well they're respected. And on top of that you can identify which groups are most likely to discuss something and then join the group. You'll get to the bottom of even the most obscure subject.

However, since moving over from Deja.com, the archive has become a little less friendly to navigate. It would pay to read the Help page.

Find computer help

Enter a couple of unique phrases from your error or computer problem into Google Groups. Try both the Usenet and Web searches. If your question isn't answered in the archives, join a relevant newsgroup and post it there.

Find games, hints, and cheats

Try one of the big games sites such as the **Games Domain**
(http://www.gamesdomain.com), **Gamespot** (http://www.gamespot
.com), or **Happy Puppy** (http://www.happypuppy.com), or search
through Usenet as explained above. Stuck on a level? Look for a
walkthrough or ask in Usenet.

Find a product review or an online shop

See Shopping (p.302).

Find product support

Whenever you buy anything substantial, see if the company has
a Website offering **follow-up support** and **product news**. If
it's not on the accompanying literature, try putting its name
between www and .com and if that doesn't work, look it up in
any of the search directories.

Most companies offer some kind of online product support
and registration, but if you want advice from other users, go to
Usenet.

Find the latest news, weather, finance, sport, etc

Apart from hundreds of newspapers and magazines, the Net carries several large **news-clipping archives** assembled from all
sorts of sources. Naturally there's an overwhelming amount of
technology news, but there's also an increasing amount of services dedicated to what you would normally find on newsstands –
and it's often fresher on the Net. They occasionally charge, though
usually only for the archives. For pointers, check under News,
Fashion, Finance, Weather and so forth. The best place to start
would be **Moreover** (http://www.moreover.com), where you can
search or browse headlines from over 1500 newsfeeds and then

link to the story. **Yahoo Daily News** (http://dailynews.yahoo.com) is also good.

Find out about a film or TV show

See Film (p.122) or Television (p.327) or try the entertainment section of any major directory for leads to specialist sites. The **Internet Movie Database**, for example, is exceptionally comprehensive and linked to Amazon in case you're tempted to order the video.

Find the latest software

See Computing and Tech News (p.91).

Find health support

Start by searching the Web. Try Yahoo for listings of organizations and so forth, and then Google for mentions on Web pages. Chances are they'll refer you to useful mailing lists and discussion groups. If not, try Google Groups to see if, and in which groups, it's being discussed on Usenet. Ultimately, though, you'd like to join a mailing list.

Find a mailing list

The best place to find mailing lists is through a well-worded Web search (that includes "mailing list" and the topic), or through the small list directories at:

List Universe http://www.list-universe.com
Liszt http://www.liszt.com
PAML http://www.paml.net

If that's not satisfactory, try Google Groups and check the FAQs from groups with hits.

Find something you've forgotten

Don't give up if you can't remember where you saw that hot tip last week. Just open Internet Explorer's History and search the cache. So long as it hasn't been deleted, you should even be able to recall it offline.

Find advice

If all else fails – and that's pretty unlikely – you can always turn to someone else for help. Use Deja.com or Google Groups to find the most appropriate newsgroup(s). Summarize your quest in the subject heading, keep it concise, post, and you should get an answer or three within a few days. Alternatively, try a mailing list or one of the free "expert" advice services such as:

Abuzz http://www.abuzz.com

AllExperts http://www.allexperts.com

Finding the right Web address

You're sure to come across a **Web link or address that won't work**. It's common and usually not too hard to get around. Many of the addresses in this book will be wrong by the time you try them. Not because we're hopeless – they just change. That's the way of the Net. The most useful thing we can do is show you how to find their new homes.

Error codes

When something goes wrong, your browser will **display a page with an error message** – or nothing will happen no matter what you try. To identify the source of the problem, get familiar with the types of errors. Different browsers and servers will

Find it

return different error messages, but they'll indicate the same things. As an exercise, identify the following.

Incorrect host name

When the address points to a nonexistent host, your browser should return a page headed "Cannot find server" and reading "The page cannot be displayed." Test this by keying: http://www.rufgide.com

Illegal domain name

If you specify an **illegal host name** or **protocol**, your browser should tell you. Try this out by keying http://wwwrufguide and then http:/www.ibm.com (noting the single slash before the www). Internet Explorer should automatically detect the latter error, and correct it.

File not found – 404 error

If the **file has moved**, **changed name** or you've overlooked **capitalization**, the server will tell you the file doesn't exist, or send you back to the front page. It differs between servers. Test this by keying a valid address with a bogus path, such as: http://www.bbc.com/bogus/ and http://www.cnn.com/bogus/

Busy host or host refuses entry

Occasionally you won't succeed because the server is either **overloaded with traffic** or it's temporarily or permanently **off-limits**. This sometimes happens when a site is heavily promoted or makes the news. It's a bit hard to test, but you'll come across it sooner or later. You might find foreign sites less busy when the locals are sleeping.

When nothing works

Now that you're on speaking terms with your browser, you're set to troubleshoot that problem address. First check your **connection**. Try another site, like: http://www.yahoo.com

If that works, you know it's not your connection. If you can't connect to any Website, **close and then reopen your browser**. It might only be a software glitch. Otherwise, it's most likely a problem with your Net connection or proxy server (if you're using one).

Check your mail. If that fails, log off then back on. Check it again. If your mailer connects and reports your mail status normally, you know that the connection between you and your ISP is OK. But there still could be a problem between it and the Net or with your proxy server. Check you have the right proxy settings and if so, disable them. If it still doesn't work, **ring your ISP** and see if there's a problem at their end or diagnose it yourself.

To do this, test a known host – say www.yahoo.com – with a **network tool** such as **Ping**, **TraceRoute** or **NetMedic**. If this fails, either your provider's connection to the Net is down or there's a problem with your **Domain Name Server**. Get on the phone and sort it out.

If you've verified that all connections are open but your browser still won't find any addresses, the problem must lie with your **browser setup**. Check its settings and reinstall it if necessary.

When a page won't display

You'll sometimes find that a page or frame inside a page instantly comes up blank. You can tell if your browser hasn't tried to fetch the page because it happens too quickly. In this case hit the **Refresh** button. If that doesn't work, reboot your browser and re-enter the address. Failing that, open **Internet Options** and clear your Temporary Internet Files or browser cache. Finally, if you're still having problems and it appears to be related to Internet Explorer security, such as the acceptance of an ActiveX control at an online banking site, check your security settings within Internet Options, disable **Content Advisor**, and consider adding the site to your Trusted sites.

When one address won't work

If only **one address fails**, you know its address is wrong or it has server problems. Now that you're familiar with error messages you can deduce the source and fix that address.

Web addresses disappear and change all the time, often because the address has been simplified, for example from: http://www.netflux.com/~test/New_Book/htm/ to http://www.newbook.com. Sometimes they'll leave a **link to the new page** from the old address, but that too might be out of date. Since the Web is in a constant state of construction, just about everything is a test site in transit to something bigger and more glorious. Consequently, when a site gets serious, it might change hosts and discard the old address.

If you're convinced the address is fine then try it later, perhaps even days later. It might be down for maintenance or experiencing local problems. If you can reach it on another machine but not yours, the problem might lie with your **Windows Hosts** file – especially if you've ever installed any browser acceleration software. If so, first get rid of the offending program properly through the **Add/Remove** applet in Windows Control Panel. Then locate the file called **Hosts** in your Windows folder. It will have no file extension. Open it with Notepad and remove any lines not starting with **#** except for the **localhost** entry. Then save the file and exit.

Finding that elusive address

The error messages will provide the most helpful clues for **tracking elusive addresses**. If the problem comes from the host name, try **adding** or **removing the** www **part**. For example, instead of typing http://roughguides.com try http://www.roughguides.com. Other than that you can only guess. It may only be that the host is busy, refusing entry or not connecting, so **try again later.**

If you **can connect to the host but the file isn't there**, there are a few further tricks to try. Check capitalization, for instance: book.htm instead of Book.htm. Or try **changing the file name extension** from .htm to .html or vice versa, if applicable. Then try **removing the file name** and then each subsequent directory up the path until finally you're left with just the host name. For example:

    http://www.roughguides.com/old/Book.htm/
    http://www.roughguides.com/old/book.htm/
    http://www.roughguides.com/old/book.html/
    http://www.roughguides.com/old/
    http://www.roughguides.com

In each case, if you succeed in connecting, try to locate your page from whatever links appear.

If you haven't succeeded there's still hope. Try **submitting the main key words** from the site's address or title into **Google**. If Google knows the site but it's not available, you can still access Google's copy by clicking on "cached." Failing that, try searching on related subjects, or scanning through one of the subject guides like **Yahoo** or the **Open Directory**.

By now, even if you haven't found your original target, you've probably discovered half-a-dozen similar if not more interesting pages, and in the process figured out how to navigate the Net.

Directory

Amusements

Looking for a chuckle or perhaps to extend your lunchbreak into the late afternoon? Click through the following directories to enter a whole new dimension of time-wasting:

Humour Sites

Ranks.com http://www.ranks.com/home/fun/top_humor_sites/
Open Directory http://dmoz.org/Recreation/Humor/
Yahoo http://dir.yahoo.com/Entertainment/Humor/

If you have a high bandwidth connection or are blessed with abnormal patience, you might like to investigate the world of online animation. Offerings range from clones of old school arcade games to feature-length Flash cartoons from renowned cartoonists such as the creators of Ren & Stimpy (http://www.spumco.com). Peruse the galleries and links from:

About Animation http://animation.about.com
Animation http://dmoz.org/Arts/Animation/
Flashkit http://www.flashkit.com
Flazoom http://www.flazoom.com
Shockwave http://www.shockwave.com

Ali G Translator
http://www.webdez.net/alig/
Make yourself comprehensible to the Staines massive.

Amused.com
http://www.amused.com
Online headquarters of the easily amused, featuring everything you need to waste several weeks at work. For even more time-wasting opportunities, try **9 to 5 Café** (http://www.9to5cafe.com).

Assassin
http://www.newgrounds.com/assassin/
Waste a few excess celebrities.

Amusements

Bert is Evil
http://www.fractalcow.com/bert/
Sesame Street star exposed in photo shocker.

Bilbana
http://www.tv4.se/lattjo/kojan/bilbanan.asp/
Shockwaved online Scalextric.

Brain Candy
http://www.corsinet.com/braincandy/
Riddles, jokes, insults and general wordplay.

Burn Maker
http://toy.thespark.com/burn/
Convert weak platitudes into powerful vitriol.

Caption of the Day
http://www.cdharris.net/dailypics
Prepare for your upcoming appearance on *Have I Got News for You* here.

Cartoon Bank
http://www.cartoonbank.com
Every cartoon ever published in *The New Yorker*.

Comedy Central
http://www.comedycentral.com
Download full South Park episodes, listen to comedy radio and see what's screening across the network. More of a station promo than a source of laughs.

Comic Book Resources
http://www.comicbookresources.com
http://www.bigpanda.net
http://www.zapcartoons.com
http://www.cartoon-links.com
http://www.geocities.com/Area51/Aurora/2510/greatest_comics/
Comic and cartoon sites, shops, fanfare – and the hundred greatest? And if you're really serious about your comics, check out Sequential Tart (http://www.sequentialtart.com), a Webzine about the industry.

Complaint Letter Generator
http://hugin.sigusrl.org/~pakin/complaint
Punch in a name for an instant dressing-down.

Dean & Nigel Blend In
http://www.deanandnigel.co.uk
Witness the gentle art of urban camouflage.

Dobe's Punny Name Archive
http://www.eskimo.com/~dobe/
Thousands of unwise baby names.

Down the Pub
http://members.aol.com/downthepub/
Chained to your desk but jonesing for a pint of bitter and a discussion about David Beckham? Point your browser to this virtual pub.

The Elizabethan Curse Generator
http://www.tower.org/insult/insult.html/
Curse with grace and elegance, thou prating fen-sucked rudesby.

Amusements

Extra Bad
http://www.extrabad.com
Bitter and twisted cartoons, plus the excellent Virtua Fighter parody, Rest Home Fighter.

Face Generator
http://www.dhuk.co.uk/other/face-generator.htm
Customize your emoticons.

Funny Forwards
http://www.ilovebacon.com
http://humor.inept.net
http://www.collegehumor.com
http://www.mrjoker.net
http://www.millerinc.com
http://www.goofball.com
Most of the sight gags that arrive in your inbox courtesy of your caring friends will wind up in these, or similar, archives sooner or later. Usually before you see them. Don't go near the galleries if you're a bit sensitive.

Gary Duschl's Gumwrapper Chain
http://www.gumwrapper.com
If only you had so much ambition.

Guess the Dictator or Sit-Com Character
http://www.smalltime.com/dictator.html
Pretend to be Emperor Bokassa from the Central African Empire or Nash Bridges and stump the computer.

The Guys vs The Girls Burping Contest
http://burpcontest.com
The ultimate battle of the sexes, with hundreds of MP3 files of catastrophic belches.

Horrorfind
http://www.horrorfind.com
A helpful hand into the darkness.

Hot or Not?

http://www.hotornot.com

One of the biggest Web stories of the past couple of years. Post a picture of yourself or someone else, and then the site's visitors rate your attractiveness on a scale of 1 to 10. So popular it has spawned a string of spoofs, such as:

http://www.amigothornot.com
http://www.amigeekornot.com
http://www.amifuglyornot.com
http://www.amipotornot.com
http://www.amiallyourbase
ornot.com

If you'd rather rate buildings than people, check out Archibot's Hot Or Not (http://www.archibot.com /ratings/index.html).

Am I Annoying or Not?

http://www.amiannoyingornot.com

To sort by rating, see: http://log.waxy.org/hot/

To instantly create your own custom "Am I" page: http://www.iamcal .com/ami/

In the 70s/80s/90s

http://www.inthe70s.com
http://www.inthe80s.com
http://www.inthe90s.com

Re-enter the landscape that wallpapered your childhood memories.

The Insanity Test

http://www.funny-funny-pictures.com/insanity

Try not to laugh.

Internet Conspiracy Generator

http://www.westword.com/extra/conspire.html/

Are you really that desperate for pub conversation fodder?

The Internet Squeegee Guy

http://www.website1.com/squeegee/

Your monitor's looking a bit dusty.

Joke Index

http://www.humor.com
http://www.humordatabase.com
http://www.humournet.com
http://www.jokecollection.com
http://www.jokeindex.com
http://www.looniebin.mb.ca
http://www.tastelessjokes.com
http://www.twistedhumor.com
http://www.uselessjokes.com
So many jokes it's not funny.

Japanese Engrish

http://www.engrish.com
Copywriters wanted, English not a priority.

Jester: the Online Joke Recommender

http://shadow.ieor.berkeley.edu/humor/
It knows what makes you laugh.

LASCO Fittings

http://www.lascofittings.com/BarCode-EDI/
Everything you ever wanted to know about the bar code ... and a lot more.

Liebography

http://www.liebographytv.com
Guerilla media at its best. Every month this site posts a new mocku-mentary of a celebrity, deliberately misusing footage from American cable channel A&E's Biography series.

Misc Games

http://www.pastor2youth.com/gamesindex.html
An archive of "fun" Christian games.

National Lampoon

http://www.nationallampoon.com
Daily humour from the satire house that PJ built. Not what it was in the '70s, as you'll see from the vault.

Random Name Generators

Generator of Random Bandnamesx
http://www.irz.com/robin/bandnameprogram/

Get a Gangsta Name
http://www.jasonschock.com/gangsta/

Gorm's Viking Name Converter
http://gorm.com/name/

Hobbit Name Generator
http://www.chriswetherell.com/hobbit

Louis Farrakhan African Name Generator
http://www.fadetoblack.com/namegenerator/

Metal Gear Solid Name Generator
http://www.buzzsite.com/goodies/MGSnamegen/

New York Times Random Log-in Generator
http://www.majcher.com/nytview.html

Random Old School Hip Hop Name Generator
http://www.fat-lace.com/articles/issue4/namegenerator/
namegenerator.html/

The Sopranos Nickname Generator
http://www.rickmelfi.com/sopranos.html

Upper West Side Manhattan
Chinese Restaurant Name Generator
http://www.novia.net/~matt/chinese/restaurant.html/

What's Your Pokéname?
http://pizza.sandwich.net/poke/pokemon.html/

The Work Nickname Generator
http://users.snip.net/%7Ecbravo/v2/fun.htm

The true champion of name generation, however, is the Wu-Tang Clan:
WuName (http://www.recordstore.com/wuname/), Wu Name
Generator (http://www.blazonry.com/scripting/wuname/php) and
the Wu-Hick Name Generator (http://ryan.post891.org/cgi-bin
/wu-hick.cgi/).

Amusements

Newspaper Comic Strips
http://www.kingfeatures.com
http://www.comics.com
The entire works of the Phantom, Mandrake and friends.

The Official Rock-Paper-Scissors Strategy Guide
http://www.worldrps.com
Master such techniques as Speed Play, Rusty and Lowball, then make like Gary Kasparov and play the computer.

The Onion
http://www.theonion.com
Unquestionably the finest news satire on or off the Net, and source of inspiration to: http://www.satirewire.com
http://www.herdofsheep.com
http://www.chaser.com.au
http://www.strewth.org.au

Online Etch-A-Sketch
http://www.hairytongue.com/etchy
Relive your youth and create square animals to your heart's content.

Perpetual Bubblewrap
http://www.urban75.com/Mag/bubble.html/
Seconds of fun for the whole family.

Pet Fish
http://www.petfish.com
Turn your monitor into a virtual fishtank.

Piercing Mildred
http://www.mildred.com
Tattoo, pierce and scar Mildred to your heart's content – no fuss, no pus.

Pocket Internet
http://www.thepocket.com
Gadgets, games, greeting cards, cartoons and more, updated daily.

The Post-Modernism Generator

http://www.elsewhere.org/cgi-bin/postmodern/

Sprinkle your next essay with "postsemanticist dialectical theory" and fool your teacher.

Pranksta's Paradise

http://www.ccil.org/~mika/

All the practical jokes from alt.shenanigans.

Rec.humor.funny

http://www.netfunny.com/rhf/

Archives of the rec.humor.funny newsgroup, updated daily.

The Simulator

http://conceptlab.com/simulator

Put yourself in the shoes of a minimum-wage slave at Mickey D's.

Sissyfight

http://www.sissyfight.com

Scratch, tease and diss your way to playground supremacy.

Soccer Thugs

http://www.bossmonster.com/games/soccerthugs20.swf

Indulge your inner Millwall fan.

Amusements

The Spam Letters
http://www.spamletters.com
Jonathan Land is sick and tired of junk email and isn't going to take it anymore.

The Spark.com
http://www.thespark.com
Most famous for its tests (purity, slut, bastard, etc) which have been taken by some eight million people, plus numerous other ways to laugh at your friends. Find more unreliable information about yourself at Emode (http://www.emode.com).

Star Wars Asciimation
http://www.asciimation.co.nz
The Star Wars saga rendered in vivid ASCII text – George Lucas would be spinning in his grave if he were dead.

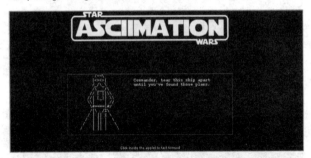

Stick Figure Death Theater
http://www.sfdt.com
Stickcity citizens meet their sticky ends.

Superjam
http://www.super-jam.com
Upload a picture of yourself, paste it on one of the dancing figures and watch yourself do the Smurf.

The Surrealist Compliment Generator
http://www.madsci.org/cgi-bin/cgiwrap/~lynn/jardin/SCG
"In caressing your follicles I am only vaguely reminded of the bitter harvest", and other bon mots.

The Tackiest Place in America Contest
http://www.cdharris.net/tacky/
A building shaped like a bulldozer, the Roadkill Café and Carhenge battle it out for the title of most soulless place in the universe.

Totally Useless Office Skills
http://www.jlc.net/~useless/
If you've exhausted all the Internet options, click here for hundreds of ways to defile office supplies.

The Ultimate Drinking Game Home Page
http://www.geocities.com/TelevisionCity/Set/7200/drinking.htm/
As if you needed more excuses to get drunk.

The Ultimate Suckup Machine
http://www.theschmoozer.com
Junk-mail your quarry with weekly compliments. For something more surreal, try: http://www.geek-boy.com/scg/

UnderGround Online
http://www.ugo.com
Vigilante gang of counterculture sites that's close to the antithesis of AOL.

Universal Translator Assistant Project
http://hometown.aol.com/JPKlingon/uta/
Translate the Bible into Klingon, Vulcan, Romulan – even Esperanto! Of course, you could always just teach yourself Klingon at the Klingon Language Institute (http://www.kli.org).

Web Bugs
http://www.limpfish.com/webbugs
Deface almost any Website with pictures of David Hasselhoff, a polar bear, a fat guy mooning and Osama Bin Laden.

Web Economy Bullshit Generator
http://www.dack.com/web/bullshit.html/
Learn how to "leverage leading-edge mindshare" and "incubate compelling interfaces" at this brilliant site.

Xiaoxiao No. 3
http://www.stileproject.com/kungfu.html/
The Jackie Chan and Bruce Lee of the stick figure world battle to the death.

Antiques and Collectables

Action Figure Collectors
http://www.actionfigurecollectors.com
Looking for that elusive Lando Calrasian toy? Try here first.

Antique Hot Spots
http://www.antiquehotspots.com
No-nonsense and very comprehensive set of links to online antique dealerships.

Antique Quilts
http://www.antiquequilts.com
If you're after that Little-House-on-the-Prairie feel, try this excellent site which sells not only quilts but other bits of Americana like Quimper pottery and Shaker furniture.

Antiques on the Web
http://www.bbc.co.uk/antiques/
The BBC's superb antiques site includes buying advice from Antiques Roadshow experts, feature articles, hints on scoring big at car boot sales, exhibition listings and the latest finds from the Roadshow.

Antiques Trade Gazette
http://www.atg-online.com
The Web home of the *Antiques Trade Gazette* features articles, auction calendars and a page where you can report stolen items.

Antiques UK

http://www.antiques-uk.co.uk
Similar to most antique portals in that it offers links to dealers and salvage warehouses, but it has an excellent want ads feature – allowing you to post a message if you're after a specific item and a dealer can then get in touch with you through the site.

Antiques Web

http://www.antiques-web.co.uk
A comprehensive database of directory information (including the best list of UK antiques fairs on the Net) for the British antiques community.

Cartophilic Society of Great Britain

http://www.csgb.co.uk
Homepage of the organization devoted to card collecting.

Collectics

http://collectics.com/education.html
A variety of essays on collectable antiques covering Clarice Cliff to Lalique.

Reference & Education Topic Index

Collecting Airfix Kits

http://www.djairfix.freeserve.co.uk
A shockingly in-depth site devoted to plastic modelling.

Collecting Comics

http://www.collectingcomics.com

News, reviews, listings, price guides and creator interviews for fans of Marvel and beyond. See also About's comic book collecting page (http://comicbooks.about.com/hobbies/comicbooks/).

Collector Café

http://www.collectorcafe.com

A portal for the collecting community, with channels for just about every collectable from advertising memorabilia to writing instruments. For a UK-based portal, try Antiques Bulletin (http://www.antiquesbulletin.com), Antiques World (http://www.antiquesworld.co.uk) or World Collectors Net (http://www.worldcollectorsnet.com).

Comics International

http://www.comics-international.com

Perhaps the most useful comics site on the Web, this gateway features a near-definitive directory of UK stockists and dealers, an excellent links page, comics reviews and unusually informative FAQs.

Gallery of Antique Costumes and Textiles

http://www.gact.co.uk

Though not much more than sophisticated eye-candy, this sumptuously designed online home of the London gallery includes well-reproduced photos of their featured pieces.

I Collector

http://www.icollector.com

The eBay of the high-end collector's market, this auction site hosts more than 650 auction houses selling everything from Francis Bacon originals to George II armchairs.

I Love Pens

http://www.geocities.com/veggiedemgrrl/main.html

Not a collection of unique pens, just someone who really loves everyday pens. Complete with reviews.

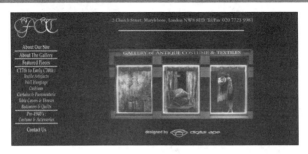

Invaluable

http://www.invaluable.com

If you can't get to the Antiques Roadshow or you're a serious collector, the online branch of *Invaluable* magazine provides an appraisal service, and if you've had an item stolen, it has a tracer service to improve your odds of recovering it. These don't come cheap, but you can try them for free. A similar, less expensive service used to be offered by the American site, Eppraisals, but this has now been integrated into eBay.

Kitsch

http://www.kitsch.co.uk

Great British site for collectors of retro-chic featuring Dukes of Hazzard items, Presleyana, lava lamps, James Bond paraphernalia, etc. As an added bonus, they belong to the Which? Webtrader code of practice, so you know you can buy that Farrah pencil in confidence.

Labelcollector.com

http://www.labelcollector.com

Salute the golden era of fruit crates and jars.

LAPADA

http://www.lapada.co.uk

The homepage of the Association of Art and Antique Dealers features a directory of members, fair and auction listings and advice on buying, selling, taking care and providing security for antiques.

Lunch Box Gallery

Lunchbox Bonanza

http://www.cassidyframes
.com/box/

Lunchbox collecting may be a uniquely American phenomenon, but the rare British box goes for crazy money in the States. Use this site as your guide to digging in the attic.

Modern Moist Towelette Collecting

http://members.aol.com/MoistTwl/index.htm

As opposed to classic moist towelette collecting.

Numismatica

http://www.limunltd.com/numismatica/

With loads of articles, news, listings, FAQs, guides and links, this is the best portal for coin collectors on the Web. For banknote collectors, try Collect Paper Money (http://www.collectpapermoney.com).

Old Bear

http://www.oldbear.co.uk

Don't throw away that beat-up, stinky old teddy bear – it might be worth a few sovereigns. This site will tell you if you can start a trust fund with your Gund or if you're stuck for life with your Steiff.

Philatelic Resources on the Web

http://www.execpc.com/~joeluft/resource.html/

Joseph Luft's listing of some 3800 Websites devoted to stamp collecting.

Sandafayre

http://www.sandafayre.com

Auctions and information from the world's largest stamp dealer.

TV Toys
http://www.tvtoys.com
One of the best sites to explore the ever-expanding world of TV memorabilia with knowledgeable articles about collecting certain shows and links to collectables for sale.

Watchnet
http://www.watchnet.com
Online hub for the fine and vintage wristwatch collecting community.

World War II Collectibles
http://www.wwii-collectibles.com
Lame layout, but beneath the clutter and bad interface lies a treasure-trove of stamps, coins, posters, propaganda material and military ephemera.

Architecture

Online magazines

Architecture http://www.architecturemag.com
The Architectural Review http://www.arplus.com
Architecture Week http://www.ArchitectureWeek.com
Metropolis http://www.metropolismag.com

Adam
http://adam.ac.uk
Designed for university students, this is a search engine of Internet resources for art, architecture and design.

Archibot
http://archibot.com
If you're interested in contemporary architecture and design, this very sexy site is the best portal on the Web. It features news and links that are updated daily (which you can have emailed to you), forums and an excellent metasearch engine to weed out all the building code sites.

Architecture

Architecture.com
http://www.architecture.com
If you're more than a little interested in British architecture, the home page of the Royal Institute of British Architects should be your first port of call. It allows you full access to their database of article abstracts; has a find-an-architect function if you're redesigning your garden shed; and has links to over 1000 sites.

Arcspace
http://www.arcspace.com
Excellent Danish site devoted to contemporary architecture, with copiously illustrated exhibits, feature articles and portfolios.

Building Conservation
http://www.buildingconservation.com
Preserve your palace.

Glass, Steel and Stone
http://glasssteelandstone.home.att.net
A fun site, with browsable galleries (including ones devoted to haunted and odd architecture), forums and news stories that are updated daily.

Great Buildings Online
http://www.greatbuildings.com
An exemplary resource. If you download free Design Lite software you can get three-dimensional models of Stonehenge, Chartres Cathedral, Falling Water and other masterpieces by Alvar Aalto, Le Corbusier and Ludwig Mies van der Rohe. Of course, there are also flat photographs and information on the architects of over 1000 great buildings. The constant pop-up ads are very irritating, though.

National Trust
http://www.nationaltrust.org.uk
The National Trust's homepage includes information on all of their properties, news, a gift shop and accommodation details.

If you're an artist, photograph your work (preferably with a digital camera) and post it online: it's cheap gallery space and your disciples can visit at any time without even leaving home. But don't expect them to stumble across it randomly. You'll need to hand out its address at every opportunity, and don't forget to include news of your exhibitions and contact details. Like in the real world, finding art online is very much a click-and-miss affair (http://www.badart.com), and of course entirely a matter of taste.

If you're looking for online exhibitions, turn to the Museums and Galleries chapter. This chapter is devoted to portals, art education sites, artist resources and places to buy art.

A.A. Art
http://www.1art.com
For budding Constables, this excellent arts education site offers free online painting lessons, video workshops and forums on technique.

Aliens and UFO Art
http://www.wiolawapress.com
Defy the Government by becoming as one with alien sculptures.

AllPosters.com
http://www.allposters.com
http://www.allaboutart.com
Plaster over the cracks in your bedroom walls.

Amico.org
http://www.amico.org
Thumbnails from the top North American galleries.

Art.com
http://www.art.com
With an address like that, you've got to deliver and the site does. With its huge catalogue of reproductions, limited editions, posters, photos, animation and Mona Lisa mugs, this American site (which ships to the UK) is effectively an art shopping mall. If you're just after posters, look no further than Postershop (http://www.postershop.co.uk) or Barewalls (http://www.barewalls.com), but beware of the massive shipping charge on European orders. Of course, if you've got enough money not to need a reproduction, you could always try Christie's (http://www.christies.com) or Sotheby's (http://www.sothebys.com).

Artchive
http://www.artchive.com
Featuring critical biographies, links to images of art works on the Web, excerpts from the art-theory canon and art CD-ROM reviews, this site may be the best jumping-off point for art experts. There are also self-portrait and landscape "tours" for those unfamiliar with art history.

the year in review

Vassily KANDINSKY
In the Blue
Oil on cardboard
80 x 110 cm
Kunstsammlung Nordrhein-Westfalen,
Dusseldorf

From Werner Schmalenbach, "Masterpieces of 20th-Century Art":

"The small-format picture *In the Blue*...uses geometric forms, and here...Kandinsky retains a measure of formal freedom, refusing to

The Art Connection

http://www.art-connection.com

Buy British art.

Art Crimes

http://www.graffiti.org

The first and still the best graffiti site on the Web. Art Crimes features an amazing array of burners, interviews with the most well-known writers, a good FAQ page and an untouchable set of graf links.

Art Deadlines List

http://www.xensei.com/users/adl/

A bulletin board and host page of an email newsletter that alerts artists to competitions, scholarships, grants and employment opportunities.

ArtLex

http://www.artlex.com

This visual arts dictionary is a truly superb resource for students, experts and bluffers alike. Containing extensively cross-referenced definitions of over 3000 terms and examples (reproductions appear either below the definition or are linked to another site hosting one), this is one of the most useful art sites on the Web.

Art Loop

http://www.artloop.com

An excellent resource for the collector, this site allows you to locate works of art for sale by artist or movement and then track the value of your potential investment. Its brief, keyword-heavy artist bios are also useful for budding connoisseurs. Also try Artcult (http://www.artcult.com).

Art Net

http://www.artnet.com

With its frighteningly comprehensive artists' index, excellent exhibition listings and articles both breezy and dense, the homepage of Art Net magazine probably serves as the best art portal on the Web. Other worthwhile portals are Artstar (http://www.artstar.com) and Art Advocate (http://www.artadvocate.com).

Art

Art-Smart
http://www.art-smart.com
If you're interested in buying original art online, this site features links to artists and galleries with lots of search options and different categories to make shopping easier. Also check out d'Art (http://dart.fine-art.com). To buy affordable work from British artists try Art Connection (http://www.art-connection.com), New British Artists (http://www.newbritishartists.co.uk) and Red Dot (http://www.reddot.co.uk).

Arts Council of England
http://www.artscouncil.org.uk
For information on everything from National Lottery funding to online exhibition spaces, this is the first place to check. Also see the Arts Council of Northern Ireland (http://www.artscouncil-ni.org), the Arts Council of Wales (http://www.ccc-acw.org.uk) and the Scottish Arts Council (http://www.sac.org.uk).

Arts Wire
http://www.artswire.org
This site from the New York Foundation for the Arts is geared to the US, but it's probably the best artist resource on the Web, with news, job openings, tutorials, workshops and a database of other arts resources.

Core 77
http://www.core77.com
Get a hand with industrial design.

Elfwood
http://www.elfwood.com
Sketches and tales from a gaggle of junior fantasy and sci-fi buffs.

Fine Art Lease
http://www.artcapitalgroup.com/default.asp
Borrow posh pictures to hang in your snooker room.

Grove Dictionary of Art Online
http://www.groveart.com
Freeload for a day on the definitive work of art reference.

Interactive Collector
http://www.icollector.com
Bid for art and collectables like celebrity cast-offs. Then, of course, there's always eBay (http://www.ebay.co.uk).

Internet Design & Publishing Center
http://www.graphic-design.com
Portal for the graphic design and DTP communities featuring articles, tips, reviews, forums and plenty of goodies to download. Also check out About's excellent graphic design channel (http://graphicdesign.about.com) or Graphic Design Gate (http://www.graphicdesigngate.com) for links.

Raw Vision
http://www.rawvision.com
The online presence of Raw Vision magazine is the best place to start exploring the world of Outsider Art (essentially art made by untrained artists) and Folk Art.

Roadside Art Online
http://www.interestingideas.com/roadside/roadside.htm
Links page to such delights as the world's largest catsup bottle, Route 66 motel signs, art environments and Pancakes Across America.

Soda Connector
http://sodaplay.com/constructor/
Train ingenious spring models that obey the laws of physics and the whims of your idle mind.

Stelarc
http://www.stelarc.va.com.au
No artist has given his body to the Net like Prof. Stelarc. More hanging around at: http://www.suspension.org

3D Artists
http://www.raph.com/3dartists/
Art that looks too real to be real.

Web Museum

http://www.southern.net/wm/

Easily one of the best sites on the Web, the Web Museum hosts a fantasy collection of art – like having the Louvre, the Metropolitan Museum of Art, the Hermitage and the Prado all right around the corner. There is also an extensive glossary of terms, artist biographies and enlightening commentary on each of the works displayed.

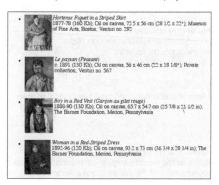

- *Hortense Fiquet in a Striped Skirt*
  1877-78 (160 Kb); Oil on canvas, 72.5 x 56 cm (28 1/2 x 22"); Museum of Fine Arts, Boston; Venturi no. 292

- *Le paysan (Peasant)*
  c. 1891 (130 Kb); Oil on canvas, 56 x 46 cm (22 x 18 1/8"); Private collection, Venturi no. 567

- *Boy in a Red Vest (Garçon au gilet rouge)*
  1888-90 (130 Kb); Oil on canvas, 65.7 x 54.7 cm (25 7/8 x 21 1/2 in); The Barnes Foundation, Merion, Pennsylvania

- *Woman in a Red-Striped Dress*
  1892-96 (120 Kb); Oil on canvas, 93.2 x 73 cm (36 3/4 x 28 3/4 in); The Barnes Foundation, Merion, Pennsylvania

World Wide Arts Resources

http://www.wwar.com

Its URL may lead you to believe that this is a site for military enthusiasts, but this list bank is probably the most comprehensive art search engine, with links to just about everything from art supplies and atelier services to gallery spaces and arts education courses. Also worth a gander are Artcyclopedia (http://www.artcyclopedia.com) and, for a more academic perspective, ADAM (http://adam.ac.uk).

Asian Interest

Click Walla

http://www.clickwalla.com

Certainly the most comprehensive site serving Britain's Asian community, Click Walla is comprised of sections devoted to music, film, news, students, weddings, food, listings, beauty and fashion, health and Asian businesses. Other UK portals include Auntie G (http://www.auntieg.co.uk) and UK Asian (http://www.ukasian.co.uk).

India Abroad
http://www.indiaabroad.com
The focus here is largely on the US and Canada, but this huge site is a model portal in terms of both content and design, with extensive news coverage, a broad array of channels, immigration advice, in-depth interviews and shopping facilities.

Lankaweb
http://www.lankaweb.com
A virtual community for Sri Lankans across the world.

Sada Punjab
http://www.sadapunjab.com
Devoted to keeping Punjabi culture alive. The site's features include a literature archive of folktales, ghazals and poems; a Punjabi jukebox; an archive of Sikh religious texts; language tutorials; and a magazine. See also Punjab Online (www.punjabonline.com) and Punjabi Network (http://www.punjabi.net).

South Asia Network
http://www.southasia.net
This portal features the South Asia search engine and serves as a useful gateway to information on Bangladesh, Bhutan, India, The Maldives, Nepal, Pakistan and Sri Lanka.

Tehelka
http://www.tehelka.com
A very influential Internet newsletter from India which has had a role in exposing corruption in politics and helped to break cricket's match-fixing scandal.

Auctions

You know how auctions work: the sale goes to the highest bidder, as long as it's above the reserve price. Or, in the case of a Dutch auction, the price keeps dropping until a buyer accepts. Well, it's the same online. You simply set a starting bid and then leave an instruction to raise it in preset increments up to a ceiling. If no one outbids you, the deal is struck at your highest offer – which could be your starting bid if it's above the reserve and there weren't any other bidders.

Once the deal's been settled, it's up to the buyer and seller to arrange delivery and payment, though both can be arranged through trusted third parties. There are millions of goods for sale in thousands of categories across hundreds of online auctions. These are but a few of the best auction sites on the Web.

A1 Auctions
http://www.bullnet.co.uk/auctions/
Service allowing you to run auctions from your own Website.

AuctionWatch
http://www.auctionwatch.com
The universal search feature on this site allows to search across hundreds of different auctions as well as fixed price sites, and then you can track your bid with its auction manager feature. Also try BidXS (http://www.biddersedge.com) for similar capabilities.

eBay
http://www.ebay.co.uk
The granddaddy of all auction sites. The pages may be hectic and distracting, but underneath the clutter eBay has millions of items for sale – everything from scuzzy Def Leppard t-shirts to Scottish Masonic kilt pins to the original Robert E. Lee car from *The Dukes of Hazzard*. With features like scorecards on buyers and sellers, round-the-clock customer support, automatic insurance on items up to £120 and chatrooms, eBay is the prototype on which all other auction sites are based. Some of the biggest sites to follow eBay's path are Amazon

(http://www.amazon.co.uk), Bid-Up TV (http://www.bid-up.tv), eBid
(http://www.ebid.co.uk), Freeserve Auctions
(http://669.fairmarket.co.uk), QXL (http://www.qxl.com) and Yahoo
(http://uk.auctions.yahoo.com).

I Collector
http://www.icollector.com
Home to over 650 auction houses, this American site aims to be a high-
end eBay with an emphasis on art and antiques. One for the serious
collector.

Internet Auction List
http://www.internetauctionlist.com
This portal to the online bidding scene is the most comprehensive auction directory on the Web. Another dedicated auction directory is Bidfind
(http://www.bidfind.com).

National Fraud Information Center
http://www.fraud.com
If you're worried about getting swindled by an online auction house or
dealer (in 2000, 78 percent of all Internet fraud occurred on auction
sites), this excellent American site has all the information you need to
protect yourself.

Priceline
http://travel.priceline.co.uk
This travel giant has added a new twist to the auction game by allowing
you to state how much you'd like to pay for airplane tickets, hotels and
car rental, then waiting to see if anyone accepts. Last Minute.com
(http://www.lastminute.com) offers a similar service. Check
www.angelfire.com/nt/priceline before you bid, however.

Sotheby's
http://www.sothebys.com
You won't find that S Club 7 signed photo disc here, but if you've got
money to burn, sites don't come any classier than this online home of the
august auction house. You can bid on live auctions as well as specialist
Internet bidding wars, and there are also chat rooms to make art novices
feel more at home. For similar, if not quite so grand, service, try Bonham's
(http://www.bonhams.com), Christie's (http://www.christies.com) or
Phillips (http://www.phillips-auctions.com).

Auctions

Specialist Auctions

Art
Extra Lot http://www.extralot.com

Books
Dominic Winter http://www.dominic-winter.co.uk

Cars
Birmingham Car Auctions http://www.bca-carauctions.co.uk
Blue Cycle http://www.bluecycle.com
Classic Auctions http://www.classic-auctions.co.uk

Computers
C Net http://www.cnet.com
Computers 4 Sale http://www.computers4sale.co.uk
Morgan Auctions http://www.morgan-auctions.co.uk

Holidays
Holiday Auctions http://www.holiday-auctions.co.uk

Personalized Number Plates
DVLA http://www.dvla-som.co.uk

Railway Memorabillia
http://www.gwra.co.uk

Stamps
Sandafayre http://www.sandafayre.com

Toys
Vectis http://www.vectis.co.uk

What the Heck
http://www.whattheheck.com/ebay/
Your guide to the bizarre stuff people try to unload on eBay. Want to see the legendary listing of the person who auctioned their kidney

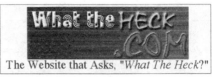

The Website that Asks, *"What The Heck?"*

for $2.5 million? It's here, as are listings for partially used packs of cigarettes, old toilet paper and all sorts of inappropriate ephemera. Also check out Eday (http://eday.shutdown.com) for the day's weirdest item.

Aviation and Aircraft

Aeroflight
http://www.aeroflight.co.uk
One of the best aviation resources on the Web, Aeroflight has comprehensive listings of air shows and museums, a detailed bibliography, photos and a wealth of information on the world's air forces.

Aeroseek
http://www.aeroseek.com
If it takes off and lands, you'll find it on this aviation search engine and portal. Other useful places to start your search are Airliners.net (http://www.airliners.net), About's aviation pages (http://aviation.about.com) and Avitop (http://www.avitop.com).

Airdisaster.com
http://www.airdisaster.com
http://www.aviationnewsweb.com
http://planecrashinfo.com
Way more goes wrong up in the air than you realize. Here's why you should be frightened to fly. For firsthand tales of terror, see:
http://www.pprune.com

Aviation and Aircraft

Airliner Photos
http://www.airlinerphotos.com
Swiss shrine to commercial air travel.

Airport City Codes
http://www.airportcitycodes.com/aaa/index.html
A quirky site that has details (city codes, runway length, etc) on 9000 airports, cheat sheets on the world's commercial aircraft, funny airplane stories and a crucial section on airplane etiquette.

Airport Webcams
http://www.webcamlocator.com/airports/airframe.html
Jumbo-jet heaven.

Airsafe
http://www.airsafe.com
Overcome your fear of plummeting.

Air-Scene UK
http://www.f4aviation.co.uk
All the latest dispatches from the British planespotting scene. See also UK Airshow Review (http://www.uk-airshows.demon.co.uk).

Air Sickness Bag Virtual Museum
http://www.airsicknessbags.com
Bring up some treasured memories.

All Aviation Flightline Online
http://www.aafo.com
This American site covers the entire breadth of the aviation spectrum, but is particularly strong on air racing and old classics like the Spruce Goose.

All the World's Rotorcraft
http://avia.russian.ee
The copter spotter's guide to the universe.

Aviation Forum
http://www.theaviationforum.com
Complain about the awful food on your last flight or help people overcome their fear of flying.

Hot Air Ballooning
http://hotairballooning.com
More than just a load of hot air.

Live Air Traffic Control
http://www.atlascomm.net/faaflyer/live.html
Ambulance-chasers can get a head start at this site, which has live feeds from air traffic centres across the world.

Planes of Fame
http://www.planesoffame.org
The homepage of the Air Museum, dedicated to the preservation of aviation history, has information on the museum's collection of aircraft, which spans the Chanute Hang Glider from 1896 to modern spacecraft.

Sky Corner
http://www.airwar.ru
This impressive Russian site features articles, photos and drawings of over 3000 planes and 1400 weapons used on military aircraft.

Babies and Parenting

ABCs of Parenting
http://www.abcparenting.com
A large, comprehensive directory of parenting Websites organized by category, with each site given star ratings. There are also articles like "Crib Safety Tips" and Q&As with experts.

Aware Parenting Institute
http://www.awareparenting.com
A garish site, but an excellent resource for those interested in child-centred parenting.

Babycare Direct
http://www.babycare-direct.co.uk
Although ordering could be made a lot easier, this is nevertheless one of the better UK sites specializing in nursery goods. The range of their stock is very extensive and they offer some good discounts. Other specialist retailers worthy of attention are Planet Baby (http://www.planetbaby.co.uk) and the Total Baby Shop (http://www.netbabe.co.uk).

BabyCentre
http://www.babycentre.co.uk
Probably the most complete baby site on the Web, with advice on everything from conceiving to lullaby lyrics to sleep routines to coping with your kid bursting into tears on a plane.

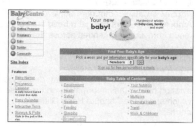

BabyNamer
http://www.babynamer.com
Why not give your babe a cutesy name like Adolph? It apparently means "noble hero". More suggestions to scar it for life at: Baby Names (http://www.babynames.com), Baby Names and Meanings

(http://www.baby-names-meanings.com), Hawaiian Baby Names
(http://www.go.to/babynames/) and Indian Baby Names
(http://www.indiaexpress.com/specials/babynames/). For even more,
consult the Google Baby Name Directory (http://directory.google.com/
Top/Home/Family/Pregnancy/Baby_Names/).

The Baby Registry
http://www.thebabyregistry.co.uk
No, not a who's who of the baby world or a baptism gift-list but an
"advice directory" of helpful organizations and Websites.

Babyworld
http://www.babyworld.co.uk
The homepage of Babyworld magazine offers all the usual chat rooms,
shopping facilities and pregnancy diaries, plus one of the most detailed
health sections around.

Fathers Direct
http://www.fathersdirect.com
A good site aimed at
working dads, with
news on the latest
child development
research, articles on
fatherhood by Red
Or Dead's Wayne
Hemmingway and
Laurence Llewellyn
Bowen, information
on the paternity
leave scheme and
other parental
resources.

Homebirth
http://www.homebirth.org.uk
Lots of advice for parents choosing to give birth at home, including birth
stories and pain relief options as well as recommended books, videos
and articles.

Babies and Parenting

Mothers Who Think
http://www.salon.com/mwt/
As with just about everything else on Salon, this section is funny, informative, engaging and well written, and a perfect antidote to all the sites and publications that treat mums as scarcely more intelligent than their babies.

National Childbirth Trust
http://www.nctpregnancyandbabycare.com
The NCT's official site is a good place to find out about antenatal classes, breast-feeding counsellors, mothers' groups and the NCT's own books on pregnancy and childbirth.

Need a Nanny?
http://www.dfee.gov.uk/nanny/
A guide for parents looking for a nanny. It's not the most exciting site in the world, but it does offer plenty of sensible advice for those seeking childcare. For more general information on childcare options, try the Day Care Trust (http://www.daycaretrust.org.uk) or the National Childminding Association (http://www.ncma.org.uk).

Net Doctor
http://community.netdoktor.com/ccs/uk/pregnancy/index.jsp
http://www.netdoctor.co.uk/children/
Certainly among the best UK health sites, Net Doctor's specialist pages are filled with largely jargon-free information for mother and child. The children's health area is particularly useful as it details the symptoms and treatments of common childhood ailments and illnesses.

Parents.com
http://www.parents.com
Unlike many sites linked to paper publications, the homepage of the American magazine *Parents* doesn't skimp on online content, and because of its ties to a respected publication, the advice and information is authoritative.

Pregnancy Calendar
http://www.pregnancycalendar.com
http://www.parentsoup.com
http://www.parenthoodweb.com
http://www.babycenter.com

Count down the nine months from conception to pregnancy and get prepared to juggle your life around your new family member. If your baby gets sick and you can't get to a doctor, try pediatrician Dr Greene for advice (http://www.drgreene.com).

Pregnancy Today
http://www.pregnancytoday.com
Despite its name, this enormous American site covers everything from pregnancy diaries to dealing with troublesome teenagers. There's a staggering amount of useful stuff here – just avoid the celebrity section featuring Pamela Anderson's pregnancy.

SheilaKitzinger.com
http://www.sheilakitzinger.com
Sheila Kitzinger is one of the gurus of childbirth. With this background, her site may be a bit too campaigning for some, but beneath the occasionally hectoring tone and ill-advised poetry there's a wealth of information on breast-feeding, water births, home births and other childbirth issues.

UK Parents
http://www.ukparents.co.uk
A comprehensive parenting e-zine written in plain and largely unpatronizing language, covering pretty much everything from pre-conception to sending the young 'uns off to school.

Betting and Gambling

It's tempting to say that online betting is for those who like that extra added element of risk, but if you stick to well-known bookmakers who've invested heavily in their security systems and avoid the casinos (which are often pretty dodgy and sometimes require you to buy a CD-ROM or download fifteen megabytes of software) you should be fine. To find a bookmaker, try Bookies Index (http://www.bookiesindex.com). Some of the UK's leading bookmakers are:

Betting and Gambling

BlueSQ http://www.bluesq.com

Coral Eurobet http://www.eurobet.co.uk

Ladbrokes http://www.ladbrokes.com and http://www.bet.co.uk

Littlewoods http://www.bet247.com

Paddy Power http://www.paddypower.com

Sporting Index http://www.sportingindex.com

Tote http://www.totalbet.com

Victor Chandler http://www.victorchandler.com

William Hill http://www.williamhill.co.uk

Fantasy Racing
http://www.fantasy-racing.co.uk
If you're nervous or just like betting for the sport rather than the money, try this risk-free site.

National Lottery
http://www.national-lottery.co.uk
It could be you ... but it probably won't.

Oddschecker
http://www.oddschecker.co.uk
Useful site that allows you to view the odds that all the bookies are offering, linking directly to their sites so you can place a bet.

The Racing Post
http://www.racingpost.co.uk
The online home of the venerable tip sheet.

Settle-a-Bet
http://www.settle-a-bet.co.uk
How to beat the odds.

Sports Betting
http://www.sportsbetting.com
Glossary of betting terms and systems, particularly strong on American sports.

24 Dogs
http://www.24dogs.com
Comprehensive, Wembley-owned greyhound resource and betting service. Also see The Dogs (http://www.thedogs.co.uk).

UK Betting Guide
http://www.ukbettingguide.co.uk
Pretty comprehensive portal that will give you hundreds of ways of parting with your cash online. For even more, try Bet Info (http://www.betinfo.co.uk).

Win 2 Win
http://www.win2win.co.uk
One of the very few free horseracing tipster services on the Web, it also has a section devoted to different betting systems.

World of Gambling
http://www.gamble.co.uk
News, reviews and advice on everything from baccarat to slot machines.

Black Interest

Africa Online
http://www.africaonline.com
This bilingual (French) portal features some of the most comprehensive African news coverage on the Web. Other African portals worth a look are Africa Guide (http://www.africaguide.com), About's African culture pages (http://africancultures.about.com), All Africa (http://allafrica.com) and Africa Homepage (http://www.africahomepage.org).

Africana
http://www.africana.com
This American site is most likely the best black culture portal on the Web. In addition to the expected channels covering lifestyle, the arts, heritage and the homefront, Africana features columns by journalists like Nelson George and Amy Alexander; radio channels playing jazz, blues, Afro-Cuban, Afro-Brazilian, gospel and R&B; and an excellent, searchable encyclopedia of the African diaspora. Also check The Black World Today (http://www.tbwt.com).

Afrisearch
http://www.afrisearch.com
Black culture search engine. Also try Black Search (http://www
.blacksearch.co.uk), the Afrocentric Resource Center
(http://www.jazm.com) and Afro Central (http://www.afrocentral.net).

Black Britain
http://www.blackbritain.co.uk
Although less authoritative than Africana (see above), this site is nevertheless an extensive gateway to black British culture, with a friendly,
inclusive feel. Also try Black Net (http://www.blacknet.co.uk).

Black History Map
http://www.blackhistorymap.com
In essence, this site from Channel 4 is a black history search engine
accessed through a map of Britain or a timeline. But it also includes
features and videos on topics like Black Irish in the Caribbean.

Black Information Link
http://www.blink.org.uk
The 1990 Trust's bulletin board for the UK's black community serves two
functions: it provides news, events listings and links; and serves as a
forum for political advocacy.

Black Presence

http://www.blackpresence.co.uk

A forum and resource for researchers and other people interested in the history of black culture in Britain. Also includes news, features on music and articles on contemporary figures like Chris Ofili.

Windrush

http://www.bbc.co.uk/history/community/multicultural/windrush/

The BBC's celebration of fifty years of Afro-Caribbean culture in Britain, with a heavy slant towards education: timelines, achievements, first-person remembrances, poetry and a literature guide.

Books and Literature

If a squillion Web pages aren't enough to satisfy your lust for the written word, maybe you should use one to order a book. You'll be spoilt for choice, with hundreds of shops offering millions of titles for delivery worldwide. That includes bumper showings from most of the major chains alongside exclusively online book havens such as Amazon and BOL. The superstores typically lay on all the trimmings: user ratings, reviews, recommendations, sample chapters, author interviews, bestseller lists, press clippings, publishing news, secure ordering and gift-wrapping.

Major Chains

Blackwell's http://blackwell.co.uk
Borders http://www.borders.com (now teamed with Amazon)
Hammicks http://www.hammicks.com
Heffers http://www.heffers.co.uk
Ottakar's http://www.ottakars.co.uk
Tesco http://www.tesco.com/books/
Waterstone's http://www.waterstones.co.uk
WHSmith http://www.bookshop.co.uk

Books and Literature

Only on the Web

Alphabet Street http://www.alphabetstreet.com
Amazon http://www.amazon.co.uk
BOL http://www.uk.bol.com
Bookzone http://www.bookzone.co.uk
Buy.com http://www.buy.com
Country Books http://www.countrybookshop.co.uk

Not listed here? Try browsing or subject-searching this directory of booksellers worldwide: http://www.bookweb.org/bookstores/. While Barnes & Noble and Amazon may rightly jostle over the title of "world's most ginormous bookstore", you'll find they all offer a staggering range, usually at substantial discounts. But because books are heavy, any savings could be offset by freight charges. And naturally, the further away you are and the sooner you want it, the more it adds up. So, before you dash to the checkout, make sure you have the best deal:

AddAll http://www.addall.com
BookBrain http://www.bookbrain.co.uk
Kelkoo http://uk.kelkoo.com

Audio Book Collection
http://www.audiobookcollection.com
Thousands of audio book titles for sale. A larger selection can be found at the American sites, Talking Book World (http://www.talkingbooks.com) and Audible.com (http://www.audible.com).

Banned Books Online
http://onlinebooks.library.upenn.edu/banned-books.html
Extracts from books that riled the righteous.

Bartleby
http://www.bartleby.com
Online versions of such classic reference texts as Gray's *Anatomy*,

Strunk & White's *Elements of Style*, the King James Bible and works of fiction and verse by HG Wells, Emily Dickinson and many others.

Bibliofind
http://www.bibliofind.com (now combined with Amazon)
Millions of old, used and rare books from sellers worldwide. If you can't find it here, try Advanced Book Exchange (http://www.abebooks.com), A Book For All Reasons (http://www.abfar.co.uk), Mr Mac (http://www.rmcd.demon.co.uk), Alibris (http://www.alibris.com) or the Central Register of British Internet Bookshops (http://www.clique.co.uk).

Bibliomania
http://www.bibliomania.com
Similar to Project Gutenberg (see p.76) in that it houses the digital versions of some 800 classic literary works. However, Bibliomania also features study aids as well as digital versions of reference books, plus a shopping facility if you'd prefer the real thing.

Bodleian Library
http://www.bodley.ox.ac.uk
The homepage of Oxford's university library houses such digital library projects as the Broadside Ballads Project, the Internet Library of Early Journals, Allegro Catalogues of Japanese and Chinese books, the Toyota City Imaging project plus an array of images from Medieval texts.

Book-A-Minute
http://www.rinkworks.com/bookaminute/
Knock over the classics in a lunch hour.

BookCloseouts
http://www.bookcloseouts.com
Millions of books slightly past their shelf life.

Books and Literature

E-books

As if the Internet wasn't already the ultimate proof of the folly of democratizing publishing, along comes the electronic book. While it's tempting to dismiss e-publishing as the last refuge of desperate authors, the format does have the potential to revolutionize book writing if someone figures out how to take advantage of the possibilities the Internet has to offer. At the moment, though, most e-books are merely regular books but in .pdf format on your desktop, your Palm or a dedicated e-book player such as the Gemstar REB 1200.

Books 24x7 http://www.books24x7.com
Electronic versions of hardware and software manuals for your desktop or palmtop.

eBookstore http://www.gemstar-ebook.com
Thousands of books that can be downloaded, plus magazines and newspapers like *The New York Times*, *Fortune*, *Time* and the *Wall Street Journal*. For bestsellers for your Palm or Pcket PC, try http://www.PeanutPress.com

Bookwire
http://www.bookwire.com
US book trade news, bestseller lists, and author road schedules with content from *Publisher's Weekly* and *Library Journal*. For UK publishing news, see: http://www.thebookseller.com

The British Library
http://portico.bl.uk
At this stage in its development, the British Library's site is of more use to academics and researchers than to most ordinary Joes,

Books and Literature

Electronic Books http://www.electronicbooks.com
A good place to start, giving you all the basics with a grasp of both the potential and the shortcomings of the format, plus samples.

The Electronic Labyrinth http://eserver.org/elab/
An exploration of the implications that the hyperlink has on literature. If only some e-book authors would take them up.

Journal of Electronic Publishing http://www.press.umich.edu/jep/
An academic perspective on e-books.

Planet E-book http://www.planetebook.com
All the latest news, plus an archive of the e-book community since 1996 and all the tools you need to become a publisher.

Riding the Bullet
http://www.simonsays.com/book/book_0743204670.html/
The only real e-book success so far has been Stephen King's thriller. Read review and an excerpt here.

although bookworms will delight in the ability to search the entire catalogue online as well as view select exhibits from the library's collection.

Carol Hurst's Children's Literature Site
http://www.carolhurst.com
Reviews of books for kids, as well as ideas on how to incorporate them into the curriculum.

Classic Novels – In Five Minutes a Day
http://www.classic-novels.com
Get bite-sized chunks of masterworks like *Alice In Wonderland* or *Huckleberry Finn* emailed to you.

CrimeBoss
http://www.crimeboss.com
Shock comic covers from the mid-20th century.

The Electronic Text Center
http://etext.lib.virginia.edu
The University of Virginia's digital archive project is similar to the others but it includes more foreign language texts than any of the competition, so if you're after

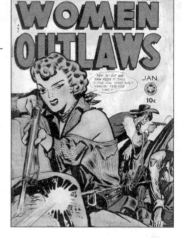

esoterica like Mescalero Apache texts or just Voltaire's *Candide* in the original French, this is the place to look.

Everything Romantic: Romance Novel Central
http://mrsg.lunarpages.com/index.html
Funny and opinionated news and reviews for fans of romance novels. For more broad-chested heroes, check out All About Romance (http://www.likesbooks.com) and The Romance Reader (http://www.theromancereader.com).

E Server
http://www.eserver.org
Over 30,000 online works, including classic novels, academic articles, journals, recipes and plays.

Gallery of "Misused" Quotation Marks
http://www.juvalamu.com/qmarks/
A proofreader's revenge on the world. Not to be confused with the Apostrophe Protection Society (http://www.apostrophe.fsnet.co.uk/).

Books and Literature

Global Books in Print
http://www.globalbooksinprint.com/GlobalBooksInPrint/
The bible of the publishing industry online: the most comprehensive database of English books anywhere. It'll set you back a few bob to use it though.

The Internet Public Library
http://www.ipl.org
Browse online books, magazines, journals and newspapers.

January Magazine
http://www.januarymagazine.com
Dissecting books and authors.

Journal Storage
http://www.jstor.org
Organization devoted to digitally archiving scholarly journals.

JournalismNet
http://www.journalismnet.com
Tips and tools for tapping into the big cheat sheet. More facts for hacks: http://www.facsnet.org and http://www.usus.org

Literary Criticism on the Web
http://start.at/literarycriticism/
Links to literary criticism organized both by author and subject, as well as a list of general sites.

Literary Marketplace
http://www.literarymarketplace.com
Find publishers and literary agents to pester with your manuscript.

London Review of Books
http://www.lrb.co.uk
Everything you'd expect from the paper version of this literary institution, including a good – if not complete – archive of articles from writers like Christopher Hitchens, Iain Sinclair, Edward Said and Marjorie Garber. See also *The New York Review of Books* (http://www.nybooks.com).

Books and Literature

MysteryNet
http://www.mysterynet.com
Hmm, now what could this be?

Open Letters
http://www.openletters.net
The Internet may be all about the future, but this site is all about the largely lost, age-old art of letter writing. Epistles from writers both famous and unknown recount little details from everyday life in a strangely intimate, and very readable, style.

Poetry.com
http://www.poetry.com
Your complete poetry resource: advice on rhyming and technique, online poetry slams, the 100 greatest poems and love poems, and, if you're good enough, they'll even publish your own.

Poetry Society
http://www.poetrysociety.org.uk/ (UK)
http://www.poets.org (US)
Halfway-houses for budding poets and their victims. You have to start somewhere: Worst Verse (http://www.nylon.net/poetry/).

Powerpoint Hamlet
http://www.myrtle.co.uk/art/hamletppt1.pps
The Bard's greatest work remade as a Powerpoint presentation.

Project Gutenberg
http://www.gutenberg.net
Copyrights don't live forever; they eventually expire. In the US, that's seventy-five years after first publication. In Europe, it's some seventy years after the author's death. With this in mind, Project Gutenberg is gradually bringing thousands of old texts online, along with some more recent donations. Sounds great but you might prefer the convenience of hard copy. See also: http://digital.library.upenn.edu/books/

Pure Fiction (US, UK)
http://www.purefiction.com
For pulp worms and writers alike. Not a word of it is true.

Random Access Memory
http://randomaccessmemory.org
A truly wonderful concept: this vast repository of memories (of anything at all) is the embodiment of what the Web is meant to be all about. Simple, compelling, about real people and real lives, with no corporate intrusion.

Religious and Sacred Texts
http://davidwiley.com/religion.html
Links to online versions of the holy books of many of the world's major religions – everything from the Bhagavad Ghita to the Zand-i Vohuman Yasht.

Science Fiction Weekly
http://www.scifi.com/sfw/
The first portal of call for both Isaac Asimov and Gene Rodenberry fans.

Shakespeare
http://the-tech.mit.edu/Shakespeare/
The Bard unbarred online.

The Slot: A Spot For Copy Editors
http://www.theslot.com
Soothing words of outrage for grammatical pedants.

Tech Classics Archive
http://classics.mit.edu
Hundreds of translated Greek and Roman classics. For more ancient and Medieval literature, see: http://argos.evansville.edu and Online Medieval and Classical Library http://sunsite.berkeley.edu/OMACL/

Books and Literature

Text files
http://www.textfiles.com
Chunks of the junk that orbited the pre-Web Internet. For a slightly more modern slant, see: http://www.etext.org

Urban Legends
http://www.urbanlegends.com
http://www.snopes.com
Separate the amazing-but-true from the popular myths.

Vatican Library
http://www.ibiblio.org/expo/vatican.exhibit/exhibit/a-vatican_lib/Vatican_lib.html
The Library of Congress's online exhibit of artefacts from the Pope's library.

Village Voice Literary Supplement
http://www.villagevoice.com/vls/
The online version of *The Village Voice*'s literary supplement is the complete printed version for non-New York residents and includes writing from major new voices and insightful reviews.

Web Del Sol
http://webdelsol.com
A portal for small literary reviews and journals, hosting such prestigious American names as Kenyon Review, Mudlark, Sulfur and Prairie Schooner.

The Western Canon
http://horus.ucr.edu/hist-topics/intelcan.html
Links to digital versions of the "great books" that shaped European civilization.

The Word Detective
http://www.word-detective.com
http://www.quinion.com/words/
Words never escape him.

The Yarn
http://www.theyarn.com
A story that offers you the choice of two paths at the end of each chapter. If one leads you to a dead end, you're asked to contribute.

Business

These homepages of prominent business magazines offer much of the same content as their paper versions, but often at a cost:

Advertising Age http://www.adage.com

Adweek http://www.adweek.com

Barrons http://www.barrons.com

Campaign http://www.campaignlive.com

Fast Company http://www.fastcompany.com

Financial Times http://www.ft.com

Forbes http://www.forbes.com

Upside http://www.upside.com

Wall Street Journal http://www.wsj.com

See also News, Newspapers and Magazines (p.239) and Finance (p.131).

AccountingWeb
http://www
.accountingweb.co.uk
Safe playpen for British
beancounters.

Adbusters
http://www.adbusters.org
Headquarters of the
world's culture jammers,
dedicated to declaring
independence from the
ever-encroaching corpo-
rate state. More culture

jamming to be found at ®TMArk (http://www.rtmark.com) and Blow the
Dot Out Your Ass (http://www.blowthedotoutyourass.com).

Setting Up Shop Online

Ad Critic

http://www.adcritic.com
http://www.superbowl-ads.com
Make a cuppa while you wait for this year's best US TV ads. For the best of the past twenty, see http://www.usatvads.com. For Australian ads going back to the 50s: http://www.tvc.com.au. For "Badvertising", go to http://www.bad-ad.org

Ad Forum

http://www.adforum.com
http://www.sourcetv.com
http://www.portfolios.com
Gateway to thousands of agencies, their ads and the humble creatives behind them.

Annual Report Gallery
http://www.reportgallery.com
View the annual reports of over 2000 publicly traded companies for free.

The Biz
http://www.thebiz.co.uk
A business-to-business portal for British companies.

Bizymoms
http://www.bizymoms.com
Crafty ways to cash up without missing the afternoon soaps.

Business.com
http://www.business.com
Attempting to become the Yahoo of business sites.

Business Advice Online
http://www.businessadviceonline.org.uk
Information and advice on taxes, regulations, e-commerce and consultations from the Small Business Service. For more resources see
http://home3.americanexpress.com/smallbusiness/tool/interactive_tools
.asp and http://www.businesslink.org

Business Ethics
http://www.business-ethics.com
Apparently it's not an oxymoron.

BVCA
http://www.bvca.co.uk
Homepage of the British Venture Capital Association, offering basic advice for businesses seeking funding.

City Wire
http://www.citywire.co.uk
Probably the best place to come for UK financial news. City Wire also contains research reports on what the directors are up to.

Clickz
http://www.clickz.com
The Web as seen by the marketing biz.

Business

Cluetrain Manifesto
http://www.cluetrain.org
Modern-day translation of the "customer is always right". Read it or perish. Alternatively, if you'd prefer an update on "never give a sucker an even break" consult the Ferengi Rules of Acquisition:
http://www.psiphi.org/DS9/rules.html/

CommerceNet
http://www.commerce.net
It may be US-heavy, but this is the main source for e-commerce news and an essential bookmark for any company doing business online.

Confederation of British Industry
http://www.cbi.org.uk/home.html
Tomorrow's public policy today.

Customers Suck!
http://www.customerssuck.com
Grumbling dispatches from the retail front.

www.customerssuck.com

Delphion Intellectual Property Network
http://www.delphion.com
Sift through a few decades of international patents plus a gallery of obscurities. Ask the right questions and you might stumble across tomorrow's technology long before the media. For UK patents see:
http://www.patent.gov.uk

DTI
http://www.dti.gov.uk
The homepage of the Department for Trade and Industry offers policy news and resources that affect every UK business.

Entrepreneur.com
http://www.entrepreneur.com
Get rich now, ask us how.

Flame Broiled
http://www.geocities.com/capitolhill/lobby/2645/
The disgruntled ex-Burger King employee homepage. If only every company had one.

Flounder's Mission Statement Generator
http://www.giantflounderpenis.com/mission.html/
It is this site's "business to holistically re-engineer economically sound resources to exceed customer expectations".

The Foundation Center
http://fdncenter.org
Companies who might happily spare you a fiver.

Fucked Company
http://fuckedcompany.com
Join the rush to gloat over startup shutdowns.

Garage.com
http://www.garage.com
Matchmaking agency for entrepreneurs and investors founded by Apple's Guy Kawasaki. For more help milking funds to feed your online white elephant, see: http://www.moneyhunter.com

Guerilla Marketing
http://www.gmarketing.com
Get ahead by metaphorically butchering your competitors' families and poisoning your customers' water supply.

Inc
http://www.inc.com
Online presence of American magazine for entrepreneurs and small businesses; includes advice and services like assistance with creating business and marketing plans, health insurance quotes and financing.

InfoUSA
http://www.infousa.com
Find likely Americans to bug with your presentation.

Disgruntled Customer Sites

The Web may be the most important business tool ever invented, but it just may be the most important consumer tool ever invented as well. This is what happens when companies don't follow the customer is always right rule.

BTopenwoe
http://www.btopenwoe.co.uk
Chronicling incompetence along the information superhighway.
See also **http://www.nthell.co.uk**

Ford Really Sucks
http://www.fordreallysucks.com
A cautionary tale for businesses that try to prevent anyone from buying domain names even remotely connected to them. See also **http://www.verizonreallysucks.com**

Fuck Microsoft
http://www.fuckmicrosoft.org
Yes, someone actually hates Bill Gates more than you.

IOU Sport
http://www.IOU-Sport.co.uk
What happens when you piss off football fans.

International Trademark Association
http://inta.org
Protect your brand identity.

Killer Internet Tactics
http://www.killertactics.com
How to murder brain-dead Web surfers with HTML.

Mondaq
http://www.mondaq.com
Regulatory information and financial commentary on over 80 world economies.

Patent Café
http://www.patentcafe.com
Protect your crackpot schemes and see them through to fruition.

Planet Feedback
http://www.planetfeedback.com
Let US companies know what you think of their service.

The Prince's Trust
http://www.princes-trust.org.uk
Learn new skills thanks to Charlie.

Statistical Data Locators
http://www.ntu.edu.sg/library/stat/statdata.htm
Links to economic and demographic data of just about every world economy.

Super Marketing: Ads from the Comic Books
http://www.steveconley.com/supermarketing.htm
The ads that kept you lying awake at night wishing you had more money.

Cars and Bikes

The Wonderful Wankometer
http://www.cynicalbastards.com/wankometer/
Measure corporate hyperbole. Couple with:
http://www.dack.com/web/bullshit.html/

Cars and Bikes

Buying a Car

Before you're sharked into signing for a new or used vehicle, go
online and check out a few road tests and price guides. You can
complete the entire exercise while you're there, but it mightn't
hurt to drive one first. Start here:

Autobytel http://www.autobytel.com
Autohit http://www.autohit.co.uk
Autolocate http://www.autolocate.co.uk
Autotrader http://www.autotrader.co.uk
BBC Top Gear http://www.topgear.beeb.com
Car Importing http://www.carimporting.co.uk
Car Shop http://www.carshop.co.uk
Carseekers http://www.carseekers.co.uk
DealerNet http://www.dealernet.com
Exchange & Mart http://www.exchangeandmart.co.uk/index.htm
4 Car http://www.4car.co.uk
Kelly Blue Book http://www.kbb.com
Oneswoop http://www.oneswoop.com
Upgrade Your Car http://www.upgradeyourcar.com/index.xsp
What Car? http://www.whatcar.com

Automobile Association
http://www.theaa.com
Not merely an online rest stop trying to hawk you memberships, the
AA's site has useful free features like a cheap petrol finder and route
planner. See also The RAC (http://www.rac.co.uk) and National
Breakdown (http://www.internationalbreakdown.com).

Breath Testing
http://www.copsonline.com/breath_test.htm
Slurring your swearwords, wobbling all over the road, mounting gutters
and knocking kids off bikes? Pull over and blow into this site.

Car Net
http://www.carnet.co.uk
Massive automotive portal, including advice and information on collecting, research facilities, trivia, forums, links, classifieds, want ads, rallying
news and more.

Circuit Driver
http://www.circuitdriver.com
This e-zine for speed junkies includes
racing information (with online booking
facilities), car and gear reviews, rallying
and drag racing advice, car databases,
photos and driving technique guides.

Classic Car Directory
http://www.classic-car-directory.com
Good resource for classic car enthusiasts, with price guides, dealer directories, events listings, classifieds and links.

Full Pull
http://www.fullpull.com
All the latest from the American tractor-pulling scene.

The Highway Code
http://www.roads.dtlr.gov.uk/roadsafety/hc/
Fail your driving theory test online first.

Layover
http://www.layover.com
Long, wide loads of truckin' stuff for prime movers and shakers.

License Plates of the World
http://server.oit.gatech.edu/~mk5/index.html
Ring in sick, cancel your date, unplug the phone and don't even think
about sleep until you've seen EVERY LICENSE PLATE IN THE WORLD.

Cars and Bikes

Lowrider.com
http://www.lowrider.com
Online community for vatos locos and other connoisseurs of barely-street-legal motor vehicles with the lowest clearance known to man.

MOT
http://www.ukmot.com
Let Malcolm the mechanic help you make sure your car is road worthy.

Mudpuppy's CB Radio Page
http://www.angelfire.com/wi/citizensband/
That's a 10-4 good buddy, this here's the Rubber Duck and I'm about to put the hammer down.

Parkers Online
http://www.parkers.co.uk
Car price and specs database going back twenty years. For new models and insurance quotes, try New Car Net (http://www.new-car-net.co.uk).

Speedtrap.com
http://www.speedtrap.com
A great resource for drivers who want to know, umm, where traffic flashpoints might occur. See also UK Speed Traps (http://www.ukspeedtraps.co.uk).

Street Trucks Magazine
http://www.streettrucksmag.com
Custom trucking bible for fans of bags, grilles, rims, souped-up air intake manifolds and other things they could only dream up in the States.

Woman Motorist
http://www.womanmotorist.com
The demographic group that motor vehicle insurers prefer.

World Parts
http://www.world-parts.com
If you're seeking a hubcap or an entire engine, tell this site the car's make and model and the country in which you live, and it will tell you who stocks your part. Also try Find a Part (http://www.find-a-part.com).

Bikes

Bicyclenet

http://www.bicyclenet.co.uk

They claim to be the UK's number-one online cycle shop and it's hard to disagree. Their stock ranges from bikes for kids to high performance road bikes for pros, and they also have a wide range of accessories. Most of their merchandise is available within four working days. Other good shopping sites: Bicycle Apparel (http://www.bicycleapparel.com), Bromley Bike (http://www.bromleybike.com) and Cycle Centre (http://www.cyclestore.co.uk).

Bike Park

http://www.bikepark.co.uk

Not only a pretty good shop, but advice for beginners and weather reports for two-wheeled enthusiasts.

Bike Trader

http://www.biketrader.co.uk

Part of the Autotrader group, this site offers the same services as its parent site: good search tool, advice on buying and selling motor bikes and links to insurance and finance companies.

Cyclesource

http://www.cyclesource.co.uk

Portal for British cycling enthusiasts.

Motorcycle News

http://www.motorcyclenews.com

Everything on two wheels ... plus the obligatory bikini babes. More at Bikersweb (http://www.bikersweb.co.uk), while a slightly more measured approach can be found at Motorcycle Action Group (http://www.mag-uk.org).

Classifieds

MTB Britain
http://www.mtbbritain.co.uk
Pretty much everything a mountain biker of any skill level could want from a site: movies, news, training tips, articles and product reviews.

Classifieds

Online classifieds need no explanation. They're like the paper version, but easier to search and possibly more up to date. In fact, most papers are moving their classifieds to the Net, though you might have to pay to see the latest listings. Here's a small selection:

Ad-Mart http://www.ad-mart.co.uk
Ad Trader http://www.adtrader.co.uk
Bidworth http://www.Bidworth.com
Economist Classifieds Market Place http://www.classified
.economist.com/globalExecutive/Toolkit/Classifieds.cfm
eDeluxe http://deluxe.trader.com
Exchange And Mart http://www.exchangeandmart.co.uk
Excite Classifieds http://classifieds.excite.com
Friday-Ad http://www.friday-ad.co.uk
Its Bazaar http://www.itsbazaar.com
Local Bounty http://www.localbounty.com
London Classifieds http://www.mercurie.co.uk/londonclassified/
Loot http://www.loot.com
Net Trader http://www.nettrader.co.uk
Photo Ads http://www.photoads.co.uk
Preloved http://www.preloved.co.uk
Reel Exchange http://www.reelexchange.co.uk
Sell It Net http://www.sellitnet.com

Computing and Tech News

Every decent PC brand has a site where you can download the latest drivers, get support and find out what's new. It won't be hard to find. Usually it's the company name or initials between a www and a com.

So you'll find Dell at: http://www.dell.com, Compaq at: http://www.compaq.com, Gateway at: http://www.gateway.com, and so forth. Most of the big names also have international branches, which will be linked from the main site. Consult Yahoo if that fails. If you're in the market for new computer bits, check out the best price across online vendors:

AnandTech http://www.anandtech.com/guides.html/

FindComp http://www.findcomp.com/uk/

Price Watch http://www.pricewatch.com

StreetPrices.com http://Europe.StreetPrices.com

Popular package software vendors include:

Buy.com http://www.buy.com

Chumbo.com http://www.chumbo.com

Jungle.com http://www.jungle.com

Bear in mind that if you buy from US sites, imports might be taxed upon arrival.

Apple
http://www.apple.com
Essential drop-in to update your Mac, pick up QuickTime and be hard-sold the latest hardware. To top up with news, software, and brand affirmations, see: http://www.macaddict.com
http://www.appleinsider.com
http://www.tidbits.com
http://www.macintouch.com
http://www.macnn.com
http://www.macslash.com

Computing and Tech News

For the latest applications, hints and news on the Macintosh's new operating system, seek out Mac OS X Apps (http://www.macosxapps.com), and Mac OS X Hints (http://www.macosxhints.com). If you're still desperately clinging on to your old Quadra or Performa, Low End Mac (http://www.lowendmac.com) will help you from reaching absolute zero on the depreciation curve. Diagnose your ailing Mac at MacFix-it (http://www.macfixit.com).

Bastard Operator from Hell
http://bofh.ntk.net
http://www.theregister.co.uk
If you work in a big office, you know this man.

Chankstore FreeFont Archive
http://www.chank.com/freefonts.htm/
Download a wacky Chank Diesel display font free each week. If there's still space in your font sack, arrive hat in hand at:
http://www.printerideas.com/fontfairy/
http://www.pizzadude.dk/fonts.html
http://www.fontface.com
http://www.flashkit.com/fonts/

Clip Art
http://webclipart.about.com
Bottomless cesspit of the soulless dross used to inject life into documents.

CNET
http://www.cnet.com
Daily technology news and features plus reviews, shopping, games, and downloads, along with schedules, transcripts and related stories from CNET's broadcasting network.

Desktop Publishing
http://desktoppub.about.com
http://desktoppublishing.com
Get off the ground in print.

Dingbat Pages
http://www.dingbatpages.com
For when you just can't get enough symbol fonts.

Easter egg archive

http://www.eeggs.com

A racing game in Excel 2000, a basketball game in Windows 95 and a raygun-wielding alien in Quark Xpress? They're in there all right, but you'll never find them on your own. Here's how to unlock secrets in scores of programs.

Electronic Privacy Information Center

http://www.epic.org

Since 1994, EPIC has been at the vanguard of the campaign to protect privacy over the Internet. For a withering attack on the UK's Regulation of Investigatory Powers Act, go to the Regulation of Investigatory Powers Information Centre (http://www.fipr.org/rip/). For coverage of free speech issues on the Net, go to the Electronic Frontier Foundation (http://www.eff.org).

Forward Garden

http://www.forwardgarden.com

The resting place of every piece of junk email you've ever received. True masochists should also tune their browser into Spamradio (http://www.spamradio.org).

FreeDrive

http://www.freedrive.com
http://www.myspace.com
http://www.xdrive.com
http://www.anuvio.com
http://www.kturn.com
http://itools.mac.com

Storage space on the Net that's perfect for backups and file transfers, but iDisk from Macintosh's iTools and K Turn are the only ones that are still free. For more, check out the directory at

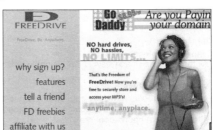

http://www.freewebsiteproviders.com/virtual-disk-drives.htm. If you want the files stored on your virtual disk drive burned on a CD-ROM and sent to you, try XBurn (http://www.XBurn.com).

Ghost Sites: The Museum of E-Failure
http://www.disobey.com/ghostsites/
A chronicle of the rise and fall of the cyber empire.

Gibson Research Corporation
http://grc.com
If you're at all interested in computer security or are a raving paranoiac, you owe it to yourself to check out this site.

The GNU Project
http://www.gnu.org
The homepage of Richard Stallman's efforts to create a free operating system. You might know it better as Linux, named after Linus Torvald's kernel. For more on GNU/Linux, try Linux Online (http://www.linux.org).

Guide to Flaming
http://www.advicemeant.com/flame/index.shtml
Learn how to win friends and influence people on newsgroups, forums and chat rooms.

Hackers' Homepage
http://www.hackershomepage.com
Everything you shouldn't do to your computer or someone else's. More at Attrition (http://www.attrition.org), Cult of the Dead Cow (http://www.cultdeadcow.com) and 2600.com (http://www.2600.com) – just make sure you run every antivirus utility you've got after stopping by.

InfoAnarchy
http://www.infoanarchy.org
All the latest news and views from the battle to keep information free.

Internet Speed Test
http://computingcentral.msn.com/internet/speedtest.asp
Wallow in the grim truth that you don't have broadband access. More at http://www.dslreports.com/stest

ISP Review
http://www.ispreview.co.uk
Compare your Internet Service Provider with the rest and get the latest broadband news. Also try Net4Nowt (http://www.net4nowt.com) and UK Broadband Help (http://www.broadband-help.com/home.asp).

IT Reviews
http://www.itreviews.co.uk
Independent, jargon-free reviews of hardware, software, games, etc. For more reviews, try About's Computer Reviews (http://compreviews.about.com/compute/compreview/) and Review Finder (http://www.reviewfinder.com).

Microsoft
http://www.microsoft.com
If you're running any Microsoft product (and the chance of that seems to be approaching 100 percent), drop by this disorganized scrapheap regularly for upgrades, news, support and patches. That includes the latest free tweaks to Windows, Office and all that falls under the Internet Explorer regime.

Modem Help
http://www.modemhelp.org
http://www.56k.com
Solve your dial-up dramas for modems of all persuasions including cable, ISDN and DSL. And be sure to check your modem maker's page for driver and firmware upgrades, especially if it's X2 or K56flex.

The Museum of Counter Art
http://www.counterart.com
"THE showcase for over 500 sets of counter digit artwork".

Need to Know
http://www.ntk.net
Weekly high-tech wrap-up with a sarcastic bite.

Newslinx
http://www.newslinx.com
Have the top Net technology stories, aggregated from around 50 sources, delivered to your mailbox daily.

Computing and Tech News

Old Computers
http://www.old-computers.com
Relive the days when your Sinclair ZX81 or Commodore Vic 20 could barely play solitaire. More at HCM (http://www.homecomputer.de).

Old English Computer Glossary
http://www.u.arizona.edu/~ctb/wordhord.html
All your favourite computer terms translated into Arthurian dialect.

Palmgear
http://www.palmgear.com
Know your palm like the back of your hand. For the PocketPC, see:
http://www.pocketmatrix.com

PC Mechanic
http://www.pcmech.com/byopc/
http://www.tweak3d.net
http://arstechnica.com/tweak/hardware.html/
How to build or upgrade your own computer.

PC Tweaking
http://www.anandtech.com
http://www.arstechnica.com
http://www.pcextremist.com
http://www.pureperformance.com

http://www.sharkyextreme.com
http://www.shacknews.com
http://www.tweaktown.com
http://www.ugeek.com
http://www.mvps.org/serenitymacros/

How to overclock your processor into the next millennium, tweak your bios and upgrade your storage capacity to attract members of the opposite sex.

PC Tyrant

http://www.pctyrant.com

A useful corrective to the relentless optimism and gung-ho futurism of most online computer zines.

PCWebopedia

http://www.pcwebopedia.com

Superb illustrated encyclopedia of computer technology.

Peer to Peer Central

http://www.peertopeercentral.com/

News on peer-to-peer systems like Napster and Gnutella.

The Register

http://www.theregister.co.uk

Punchy tech news that spins to its own tune.

SafeWeb

http://www.safeweb.com

Originally designed for surfers in countries with repressive regimes, SafeWeb is a service that encrypts all data sent from and received by your computer while surfing the Net so that all of your downloads are safe from prying eyes. For more anonymous surfing, try The Anonymizer (http://www.anonymizer.com).

Scantips

http://www.scantips.com

Become a scan-do type of dude.

Slashdot.org

http://slashdot.org

News for those who've entirely given up on the human race.

Computing and Tech News

PC Help

The best place to find an answer to your computer problems is usually on Usenet. Chances are it's already been answered, so before you rush in and post, search the archives through Google Groups.

Google Groups http://groups.google.com

That's not to say you won't find an answer on the Web. You probably will, so follow up with a Web search. You'll find a choice of engines at the very bottom of the results page. If you click on Google, for example, it will perform the same search in the Web database. Apart from Usenet, there are several very active computing forums on the Web, such as:

Computing.net http://www.computing.net

Tek Tips http://www.tek-tips.com

And there are hundreds of troubleshooting and Windows news sites, such as:

ActiveWin http://www.activewin.com
Annoyances http://www.annoyances.org
Common Problems http://www.users.qwest.net/~careyh/fixes.htm
Virtual Dr http://virtualdr.com
WinOScentral http://www.winoscentral.com

Don't forget to keep your hardware installation drivers up to date. You'll find the latest files for download direct from the manufacturer's Website, or at driver guides such as these:

Driver Forum http://www.driverforum.com
Driver Guide http://www.driverguide.com
Drivers HQ http://www.drivershq.com
Windrivers http://www.windrivers.com

Tech Dirt

http://www.techdirt.com
Keeping tabs on the dark under-
belly of the Internet economy.

Techtales

http://www.techtales.com
Customers – they might always be
right but they sure do ask the
darndest things.

TechTales
The funniest tech support stories on the Internet

They come at all hours of the day and night.
From places near and far,
often beyond belief.

Tom's Hardware Guide

http://www.tomshardware.com
One of the most important sites on the Net, at least for the hardware
industry. Tom and his reporters are credited with the delayed release of
Pentium's 1GHz Pentium III processor because the site gave it a
thumbs down. This is the best source for bug reports and benchmark
tests.

WebReference

http://www.webreference.com
If you don't know your HTML from your XML or DHTML, try this reference and tutorials site. For more tips and tricks, try Webmonkey
(http://hotwired.lycos.com/webmonkey/), and for streaming video tutorials, try Virtual Dr (http://www.virtualdr.com).

Windrivers

http://www.windrivers.com
http://www.driverforum.com
http://www.drivershq.com
http://www.driverguide.com
Driver file updates and hardware reviews compiled by a Windows fanat-
ic of such maniacal proportions he even named his son "Gates".

Wired News

http://www.wired.com
The Net's best source of breaking technology news plus archives of
Wired magazine. For more, try Geek.com (http://www.geek.com).

Computing and Tech News

Woody's Office Portal
http://www.wopr.com
Beat some sense out of Microsoft Office. For Outlook, see:
http://www.slipstick.com/outlook

Yahoo Computing
http://www.yahoo.com/Computers/
The grandpappy of all computing directories.

ZDNet
http://www.zdnet.com
Computing info powerhouse from Ziff Davis, publisher of *PC Magazine*, *MacUser*, *Computer Gaming World* and scores of other IT titles. Each magazine donates content such as news, product reviews and lab test results; plus there's a ton of prime Net-exclusive techno-chow. The best place to start researching anything even vaguely computer-related.

Play it safe

Unless you're 100 percent certain that a download or attachment is safe, even if it's been sent by your best friend, DON'T OPEN IT! Instead, save it to your Desktop or a quarantine folder and examine it carefully before proceeding. That should include running it past an up-to-date antivirus scanner such as AVG (http://www.grisoft.com). You'll find everything you need to know about viruses at:

About.com http://antivirus.about.com
Alt.comp.virus FAQs http://www.faqs.org/faqs/computer-virus/
AVG Anti-Virus http://www.grisoft.com
Computer Associates http://www3.ca.com/virus/
Symantec http://www.symantec.com/avcenter/

Crafts

About Hobbies

http://www.about.com/hobbies/

Your first portal of call for any crafts search should be About's impressive hobbies page which contains links to their basketry, beadwork, candle-making and woodworking sites as well as twenty other crafts sites that they host.

Allan's Wood Miser's Workshop

http://members.aol.com/woodmiser1/

Great site full of tips and advice for the thrifty woodworker. For more carpentry tips, try About's woodworking site (http://woodworking.about.com) and Woodweb (http://www.woodweb .com) if you're a pro.

Classic Stitches

http://www.classicstitches.com

The homepage of *Classic Stitches* magazine includes some 150 downloadable charts to set your needles working.

Crafts Council

http://www.craftscouncil.org.uk

News on and listings of craft shows, events, exhibitions, seminars and workshops. The Crafts Council also provides a regional list of shops selling contemporary crafts as well as buying guides.

Crafts Unlimited

http://www.crafts-unlimited.co.uk

Over 1100 cross-stitch patterns to buy, plus downloadable beginner's and advanced guides to cross-stitch technique. Also check out Cross-Stitch Design (http://www.maurer-stroh.com).

Home Sewing Association

http://www.sewing.org

An essential bookmark for budding Gallianos and hopeless bachelors alike. The site is packed with sewing lessons for absolute beginners and tips and trends and advanced techniques for more experienced seamstresses.

Education

Internet Craft Fair

http://www.craft-fair.co.uk
Put a stitch in time at this massive online community for the UK's crafts scene.

Planet Patchwork

http://www.planetpatchwork.com
Blocks and vectors of information devoted to the mystique of quilting.

Gallery

The *Planet Patchwork Gallery* is dedicated to presenting the best in virtual quilt shows on the web.

Popular Crafts

http://www
.popularcrafts.com
The digital home of *Popular Crafts* magazine includes event listings, book reviews, forums, news and online crafts projects with step-by-step instructions on decorating flower pots and making birthday party cards.

Wool Works

http://www.woolworks.org
Containing an archive of more than 250 patterns, an extensive hints and tips section on making socks and knitting for dolls and a comprehensive links page – this is a darn good knitting site.

Education

This chapter is perhaps a bit of a misnomer as the entire Internet is potentially the greatest single educational resource that's ever been invented: the latter-day equivalent of the library at Alexandria. Here you'll find educational resources (for students, teachers and parents), general homework sites, information on distance learning and admissions guides. For other study tools, try the Reference chapter or other subject headings (Art, Politics, History, etc).

Education

About Education
http://education.about.com
They may be geared towards the US, but, as usual, About's education pages are an excellent source of information and news. Having trouble with times tables or conjugating Latin verbs? Try About Homework (http://homework.about.com).

Academic Info
http://www.academicinfo.net
Research directory for students and teachers.

A-levels
http://www.a-levels.co.uk
Links to sites that will help in A-level revision. For GCSE help, try Project GCSE (http://www.projectgcse.co.uk); Scottish Highers students should log on to the Scottish Qualification Authority (http://www.sqa.org.uk).

Ask an Expert
http://www.cln.org/int_expert.html/
Links to hundreds of experts who will happily answer your homework question or offer you careers advice. There are also teaching experts awaiting questions from harried pedagogues.

Babelfish Translator
http://babelfish.altavista.com
If you're reading T.S. Eliot and you come across a passage that's all Greek to you, type the text in here and it will translate it into English or virtually any language you want.

Best Websites for Students
http://www.unn.ac.uk/~iniw2/bestsite.htm
Links to help you write your next essay.

Channel 4: Homework High
http://www.homeworkhigh.co.uk
Channel 4's homework site allows you to ask experts questions and browse the archive of responses. Much better than the BBC's similar site because it's not linked to the station's programmes.

Click Teaching
http://www.clickteaching.com
A site for primary school teachers largely written by primary school teachers.

Evil House of Cheat
http://www.cheathouse.com
Thousands of college essays, termpapers and reports. But beware, teachers can check http://www.turnitin.com for traces of plagiarism.

Good Schools Guide
http://www.good-schoolsguide.co.uk
Unfortunately, in order to gain full access to this very useful site, you need to buy the paper version of the popular book, which then lets you get to the weekly updates and the school reviews written by parents for parents.

Guide to Grammar and Style
http://andromeda.rutgers.edu/~jlynch/Writing/
Handy online guide to English language usage. It won't replace Strunk & White or the *Chicago Manual of Style*, but if you're in a pinch, could be

worth a try. For more basic grammar instruction, try Pop-Up Grammar (http://www.brownlee.org/durk/grammar/) – but just make sure JavaScript is enabled on your browser.

International Centre for Distance Learning
http://www-icdl.open.ac.uk
The Open University's distance learning resource centre contains a huge database on courses and organizations as well as abstracts of journal articles and research papers pertaining to distance education. Also check out its related site, The Learning Network (http://www.netlearn.co.uk) and the International Distance Learning Course Finder (http://www.dlcoursefinder.com).

Internet Public Library
http://www.ipl.org
Browse the catalogue of some 16,000 online texts, utilize the original resources and ask homework questions – all without a horn-rimmed librarian telling you to down your Discman.

ISIS
http://www.isis.org.uk
The homepage of the Independent Schools Information Service allows parents and teachers to search their database for information on prospective schools and employers.

Learn.co.uk
http://www.learn.co.uk
A huge resource for both students and teachers, with dowloadable sample SATs, lesson plans, an online community for teachers, revision advice and information on the national curriculum.

Learning Alive
http://www.learningalive.co.uk
It claims to be the largest educational resource on the Net, but to access its Living Library (where most of these resources are stored), you have to subscribe – at £49 a year.

Maths Help
http://www.maths-help.co.uk
Send this site's boffins a question and they'll email back an answer. For more help with numbers, try Maths Net (http://www.mathsnet.net).

Education

National Curriculum Online
http://www.nc.uk.net
The government's definitive national curriculum site for teachers, with outlines, goals and FAQs. For the Scottish curriculum, go to the Scottish CCC Homepage (http://www.sccc.ac.uk/).

National Grid for Learning
http://www.ngfl.gov.uk
This site is the centrepiece of the Government's plans to harness the Net as the future of education. As you might guess, it's a bit of a sprawling mess, but there are sections devoted to just about every educational issue you can think of, as well as tons of links, a virtual teacher centre and so on.

National Union of Students
http://www.nus.org.uk
How to buy a pint if your grant runs out.

SearchEdu
http://www.searchedu.com
Search millions of university and education pages.

Sova (Sleep)
http://sova.lulea.org
Pictures of your tuition fees hard at work.

Study Abroad
http://www.studyabroad.com
Hop grass that's greener.

StudyWeb
http://www.studyweb.com
An absolutely enormous education portal, with links to some 160,000 resources, all organized by grade level (some translation from American required).

The Teacher Network
http://www.theteachernet.co.uk
Resources, links, job search for teachers.

Topmarks Education
http://www.topmarks.co.uk
This excellent and very easy-to-use site searches the Web for educational sites pertaining to your subject and appropriate age-level, so if you're searching for sites to help you with GCSE revision it will weed out all the sites aimed at Key Stage 1 students. See also Schoolzone (http://www.schoolzone.co.uk).

UCAS
http://www.ucas.co.uk
Information on university courses, including admissions requirements and general facts and figures, from the University and Colleges Admissions Service.

Unofficial Guides
http://www.unofficial-guides.com
Get the real dope on the unis from the students themselves, not the marketing boards.

Up My Street
http://www.upmystreet.com
Type in your postcode and get quick access to the performance tables of local schools.

Web66: International School Web Site Directory
http://web66.coled.umn.edu/schools.html/
Add your school's Web page if it's not already listed.

Word Central
http://www.wordcentral.com
A site designed to broaden kids' vocabulary by introducing them to the joys of wordplay. There's also a section for teachers with lesson plans and a history of the English language.

Employment

If you're looking to move on up, beware that if you post your CV online your boss could find it – embarrassing at the very least. The same situation could also arise if you leave it online once you're hired. Most job agencies have sites these days, and the better ones update at least daily, so there are far too many to attempt to list here. What's best for you will depend on what field you're in and where you want to work. Bigger isn't always better, as you'll find yourself competing with more applicants. On the other hand, your prospective employer isn't likely to restrict their job search to a site that isn't well known. Whether you're looking for a job or to fill a vacancy, try:

Fish4Jobs http://www.fish4jobs.co.uk

Go Job Site http://www.jobsite.co.uk

Gradunet http://www.gradunet.co.uk

Guardian Jobs Unlimited http://jobs.guardian.co.uk

Job Search http://www.jobsearch.co.uk

Jobsin http://www.jobsin.co.uk

Monster http://www.monster.co.uk

Overseas Jobs http://www.overseasjobs.com

People Bank http://www.peoplebank.com

Personnel Net http://www.personnelnet.com

Reed http://www.reed.co.uk

Stepstone http://www.stepstone.com

Total Jobs http://totaljobs.com

Work Thing http://www.workthing.com

All Jobs UK
http://alljobsuk.com
This recruitment portal claims to give access to every job vacancy on the Internet – all two million of 'em.

A–Z Guide to British Employment Law
http://www.emplaw.co.uk
Get the upper hand on your boss.

The Best Resumes on the Net
http://tbrnet.com
Helpful advice on building the perfect CV, featuring a software program – the Resume Creator 3.1 – for the lazy.

Brilliant Careers
http://www.channel4.com/brilliantcareers
Channel 4's employment site is a no-nonsense guide to the job market, with advice, support, vacancies and personality tests.

Buzzword Bingo
http://www.progress.demon.co.uk/Fun/Buzzword-Bingo.html/
When your boss says something like, "proactive" or "quality management system", check it off on your card – you're a winner if you complete a row.

Cool Works
http://www.coolworks.com
Seasonal jobs in US resorts, national parks, camps, ranches and cruise lines.

Despair Inc.
http://www.demotivators.com
Take the mickey out of your boss and colleagues with a range of bitter and twisted calendars and mugs.

Expat Network
http://www.expatnetwork.co.uk
Subscription placement and settling service for working globetrotters.

FT Career Point
http://career.ft.com/careers
Advice from the suits at the *Financial Times*.

Employment

Hungry and Homeless
http://www.hungryandhomeless.co.uk
No, not another site mocking yesterday's dotcom millionaires, but one that houses pictures and histories of homeless people looking for work.

Integrity Based Interviewing
http://www.interviewing.net
Ex-federal agents show you how to get to the truth without drawing any blood.

Internet Career Guide
http://www.careerguide.net
This directory functions as a portal for both jobseekers and employers. Included are links to headhunters, CV writing services, recruitment and outplacement services.

I-resign.com
http://www.i-resign.com
Quit now while you're ahead.

Mindless Jobs of America
http://www.geocities.com/Area51/Vault/9932/mja.html
Think your job sucks?

The Riley Guide
http://www.rileyguide.com
Messy but massive directory of job-hunting resources.

Salary Info
http://www.salary.com
http://jobsmart.org/tools/salary/
See what you're worth, and then how much you'd need in another town: http://www.homefair.com/homefair/calc/salcalc.html

Temp 24-7
http://jobsearch.about.com/cs/tempjobs/
Share the pain of temporary work at this online community for temps.

UK Jobs Sites
http://www.transdata-inter.co.uk/jobs-agencies/

An excellent resource for the jobseeker, this directory lists and ranks all the major British online headhunters and ranks them by number of vacancies, services, regions and industries they serve.

Washington Alliance of Technology Workers
http://www.washtech.org
This American homepage of the first dotcom union is an excellent source of news, rumours and advice for the largely unorganized technology sector.

Working Wounded
http://www.workingwounded.com
Get back at your boss and your co-workers without getting fired.

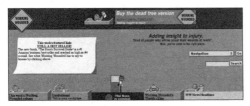

Yahoo Careers
http://careers.yahoo.com
As ever, Yahoo is in on the act, and as ever, does it superbly. This arm, however, handles only US placements. But key "employment" as a search term or click on "international" and you'll be awash with options spanning the globe.

Environment

Earth Systems Virtual Library
http://www.earthsystems.org/virtuallibrary/vlhome.html
Probably the most complete set of environmental links on the Net.

eNature.com
http://www.enature.com
Vibrant field guides to North American flora and fauna.

Envirolink Network

http://envirolink.netforchange.com
Online community for the environmentally aware, containing links to articles on sustainable energy sources and pesticides, daily news updates, a green marketplace and forums on topics like genetic engineering. See also EcoNet (http://www.igc.org/igc/gateway/enindex.html/).

Environmental Organization Directory

http://www.eco-portal.com
Find primary production and green-minded sites.

ForestWorld

http://www.forestworld.com
http://forests.org
Timber tales from both sides of the bulldozer.

Friends of the Earth

http://www.foe.co.uk
The homepage of the environmental pressure group features information on local, national and international campaigns, and information on the issues involved.

Greenpeace

http://www.greenpeace.org
In addition to the charity's campaigns, the Greenpeace homepage covers genetic engineering, ocean preservation, toxic waste and the transport of nuclear materials.

Lycos Environment News

http://www.ens-news.com/index.html
The Web's best source for unbiased environmental news.

Museum of Dirt
http://www.planet.com/dirtweb
Don't just walk on by.

Rainforest Information Portal
http://www.rainforestweb.org
News from the frontline against deforestation. For more Amazonia try
the Rainforest Alliance (http://www.rainforest-alliance.org) and the
Tropical Rainforest Coalition (http://www.rainforest.org).

Subsea Explorer
http://www.subseaexplorer.com
This site for scuba divers may force you to subscribe, but if you do you
could win a diving expedition to the Titanic – plus there are excellent
educational resources for kids, articles on the subaquatic environment,
underwater Webcams and cheap diving equipment from the shop. To
explore the sky as well as the sea try the equally excellent Sky and Sea
(http://www.seasky.org).

UK National Air Quality Information Archive
http://www.aeat.co.uk/netcen/airqual/
Worried about foot-and-mouth pyres or diesel emissions? Check the air
quality for your area here. To feel guilty about the amount of carbon
dioxide you are responsible for, check out the Carbon Calculator
(http://www.carboncalculator.org).

Events and Entertainment

Aloud
http://www.aloud.com
Book music, festival and event tickets online from this member of the
Which? Code of Practice. See also Ticketmaster (http://www
.ticketmaster.co.uk).

Ananova - Going Out
http://www.ananova.com/whatson/
Comprehensive and nationwide general entertainment listings which you
can have sent to your WAP phone.

Events and Entertainment

British Arts Festivals
http://www.artsfestivals.co.uk
Keep tabs on the UK's highbrow festivals from Brighton to Edinburgh on this comprehensive site.

eFestivals
http://www.efestivals.co.uk
If you can't get enough of playing your bongos in the mud, point your virtual caravan to this site which contains ticket information, line-ups, rumours and reviews of festivals like Homelands, T in the Park, Glastonbury, Creamfields and the Essential Festival.

London Theatre Guide
http://www.londontheatre.co.uk
This venerable site boasts not only excellent theatre listings but regularly updated cast news and seating plans. See also What's On Stage (http://www.whatsonstage.com) for regional as well as London listings.

Nightclubbin UK
http://www.nightclubbinuk.com
Listings and links for a large majority of Britain's clubs.

Planit4Kids
http://www.planit4kids.co.uk
Listings and events information organized by region for the most demanding audience of them all.

Scene One
http://www.sceneone.co.uk
UK-wide entertainment guide covering music, film, theatre and comedy with an excellent search facility.

This Is London
http://www.thisislondon.co.uk:80/dynamic/
The *Evening Standard*'s Website includes, film, theatre, comedy and clubbing listings for the capital as well as a visitor's guide and reviews of pubs and restaurants.

Events and Entertainment

Time Out

http://www.timeout.com

Definitive London listings from the venerable magazine, as well as global city guides if you're planning to venture abroad.

Regional Listings

Most UK events sites can seem like a Big Smoke screen with all the emphasis on London. Here are a few that attempt to redress the balance:

Bournemouth	http://www.bournemouth.co.uk
Brighton	http://www.whatsonguide.co.uk
Cardiff	http://www.metroplex.co.uk/WhatsOn/cardiff/
Chester	http://www.chestercc.gov.uk/asp/events/
Coventry	http://www.cwn.org.uk/whatson
Edinburgh	http://www.edinburghguide.com/index.htm
Glasgow	http://www.glasgow.gov.uk/html /whatson/windex.htm
Hampshire	http://www.hants.gov.uk/whatson/
Manchester	http://www.manchesteronline.co.uk
Newcastle	http://www.tyne-online.com/whatson.asp
Sheffield	http://www.sheffnet.co.uk/events/events.asp

Webflyers
http://www.webflyers.co.uk
Guide to clubbing in Edinburgh and Glasgow.

Yack
http://www.yack.com
Perhaps the best guide to online events, Yack lists the Webcasts, chats, film, animation and other events occurring on the Internet everyday.

Fashion and Beauty

Unless it entirely erodes your reading time, the Net isn't likely to cut your guilty expenditure on glossy mags. While there's a spree of fledgling style zines and something from nearly all the big rack names, nothing compares to getting it in print. Nonetheless it will certainly supplement your vice. What you will find the Net better for is researching products, checking out brands and saving money on consumables like cosmetics at stores such as:

http://www.drugstore.com
http://www.gloss.com
http://www.ibeauty.com
http://www.perfumania.com
http://www.reflect.com
http://www.sephora.com
http://www.theperfumeshop.com
http://www.hqhair.com
http://www.thinknatural.com

Buying clothes online is tough but popular nonetheless. They're out there, if you know what you're doing, but you'll soon see why Boo.com failed. Label sites are sometimes interesting for new season looks, stockists and direct ordering.

Afro Hair and Beauty
http://www.afrohairandbeauty.co.uk
Links to, and resource pages for, black haircare and beauty products.

Bad Fads Museum
http://www.badfads.com
Revisit your past fashion mistakes.

BK Enterprises
http://www.b-k-enterprises.com
The only place to get that authentic '70s Elvis jump suit. Prices range from $900 to $5000. Also has links to boot dealers, glasses shops and the place to get show scarves to complete the look.

Cosmetic.org
http://www.cosmetic.org
http://www.ienhance.com
Adjust your imperfection without pills or creams.

Debenhams
http://www.debenhams.com
Do some etail therapy at the site of everyone's favourite department store.

Enoki World
http://www.enokiworld.com
All the accessories you need for that vintage lifestyle: Pucci dresses, jadeite juicers, Pierre Cardin pink tweed skirts, 1960s Gucci handbags.

FashionBot
http://www.fashionbot.com
Search several UK high-street retailers' catalogues.

Fashion Icon
http://www.fashion-icon.com
Irreverent New York fashion zine.

Fashion Information
http://www.fashioninformation.com
Pay for trend-forecasting reports.

Fashion Net
http://www.fashion.net
Handy shortcut to the highest-profile shopping, designer, magazine,

modelling and fashion industry sites, with enough editorial to warrant an extended stopover.

Fashion Live
http://www.fashionlive.fr
Splashy, sexy Parisian e-zine covering both *haute couture* and more achievable fashion trends. They've taken over the Place de Mode shopping site, allowing you quick access to the looks you see on its pages.

Fashionmall.com
http://www.fashionmall.com
http://www.brandsforless.com
http://www.bluefly.com
Mail-order familiar, and mostly American, labels.

Fashion UK
http://www.fuk.co.uk
Minimal but fresh vanity monthly from London.

Figleaves.com
http://www.figleaves.com
Online underwear superstore for both men and women.

Firstview
http://www.firstview.com
See what's trotting the catwalks – sometimes at a price. For more previews, seek out Virtual Runway (http://www.virtualrunway.com).

Fragrance Direct
http://www.fragrancedirect.co.uk
It may look like a site for kids, but this etailer offers tremendous bargains on a good range of perfumes, cosmetics and skincare products.

The Lipstick Page

http://www.thelipstickpage.com

Cosmetic appliances for fun and profit.

Moda Italia

http://www.modaitalia.net

Patch through to the Italian rag traders.

Net-à-Porter

http://www.net-a-porter.com

Can't get to Harvey Nick's? Try here for posh frocks and accessories: Bottega Veneta, Clements Ribeiro, Missoni, Fake London and Paul & Joe are some of the cult labels this site stocks. Plus there's no snooty attitude. For Marc Jacobs, Fendi and Louis Vuitton, try eLuxury (http://www.eluxury.com) or Yoox (http://www.yoox.com).

Organization for the Advancement of Facial Hair

http://www.ragadio.com/oafh/

Includes an archive of classic beard styles and a library of grooming tips. For more advice on beard trimmers and how to keep your hulihee at its best (or just to see pics of guys who look like '70s country singers), try these other hirsute sites: Bad Burns (http://www.badburns .com), Beard Guy (http://members.aol

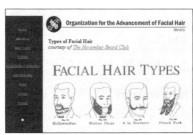

.com/beardguy/) and Men Who Look Like Kenny Rogers (http://www.menwholooklikekennyrogers.com).

osMoz

http://www.osmoz.com

They haven't invented scratch 'n' sniff technology for the Web yet, but this French site (in English) is the next best thing. A fragrance test will tell you whether floral or hesperide scents suit you best, and if you register they will send you free samples.

Fashion and Beauty

Salonweb
http://www.salonweb.com
Frizzy, fly-away, mousy, permed hair? Try this haircare portal for all the tips and advice you'll ever need.

Solemates: The Century in Shoes
http://www.centuryinshoes.com
Stepping out in the 20th century.

Studs And Spikes
http://www.studsandspikes.com
Trick out your leather jacket.

Style.com
http://www.style.com
With an impressive archive of images from all the major catwalk shows of the past two years, the online home of American *Vogue* is one of the best resources for fashionistas. If you're after a more standard magazine approach, try the British equivalent (http://www.vogue.co.uk).

Style Maven
http://www.stylemaven.com
Your guide to hip boutiques in London, New York, LA and San Francisco.

Textile Dictionary
http://www.ntgi.net/ICCF&D/textile.htm
Don't know your buckram from your qiviut? Check here.

Victoria's Secret
http://www.victoriassecret.com
Order online or request the catalogue preferred by nine out of ten teenage boys.

Wellbeing.com
http://www.wellbeing.com
Boots' revamped site has everything you'd expect from the high-street pharmacy.

Mullets

The Kentucky Waterfall, the Soccer Rocker, the Missouri Compromise, Business Up Front/Party In The Back, Neck Blanket, Ape Drape, the Tennessee Top Hat – whatever you want to call it, no hairstyle in the history of the civilized world has generated so much scorn, derision or passion as the mullet. Here are a few sites where you can mull over "the hairstyle of the gods":

Dan's Mullet Haven
http://www.fortunecity.co.uk/southbank/pottery/3/
Wrestlers, musicians and footballers.

Football Mullets
http://www.mullets.co.uk
Site of the Mullet World Cup.

Mullet Gods
http://www.mulletgods.com
Your complete mullet resource.

Mullet Junky
http://www.mulletjunky.com
Homepage of the mullet hunters.

Mullet Lovers
http://www.mulletlovers.com
Galleries, galleries, galleries.

Mullet Madness
http://www.mulletmadness.com
The official haircut of the Salt Lake City Winter Olympics.

Mullets Galore
http://www.mulletsgalore.com
The most comprehensive mullet site.

Rate My Mullet
http://www.ratemymullet.com
Heap even more scorn at the poor sods.

Film

Zoom
http://www.zoom.co.uk
Portal for the Arcadia group shops (Dorothy Perkins, Top Shop, Principles, Burton Menswear, etc), allowing you to recreate your high-street experience on the information superhighway.

When it comes to movies, one site clearly rules:
The Internet Movie Database http://www.imdb.com

To say that it's impressive is an understatement. You'll be hard-pressed to find any work on or off the Net as comprehensive as this exceptional relational database of screen trivia from over 100,000 movies and a million actors. It's all tied together remarkably well – for example, within two clicks of finding your favourite movie you can get full filmographies of anyone from the cast or crew and then see what's in the cooker. Still, it's not perfect, or without competition. You'll find a similar service with superior biographies and synopses at the colossal:
All Movie Guide http://www.allmovie.com

Or for more Chan, Li and Fat:
Hong Kong Movie Database http://www.hkmdb.com

For cinema listings:
Cinemas Online http://www.cinemas-online.co.uk
Cineworld http://www.cineworld.co.uk
Odeon http://www.odeon.co.uk
Teletext-Cinema http://www.teletext.co.uk/bigscreen/
UCI Cinemas http://www.uci-cinemas.co.uk
Virgin Net http://www.virgin.net/movies/
Warner Village http://www.warnervillage.co.uk

Ain't It Cool News

http://www.aintitcool.com

The movie news and gossip site that has Hollywood execs quaking in their boots. Founder Harry Knowles has been blamed several times when movies have tanked at the box office, and *Premiere* magazine has ranked him as one of Hollywood's most powerful people. Receive the wisdom of Harry here, along with whispers of what's in production and interviews. More production gossip can be overheard at CHUD (http://www.chud.com), Coming Attractions (http://www.corona.bc.ca/films/), Dark Horizons (http://www.darkhorizons.com) and IMDB (http://www.imdb.com/Sections/Inproduction/).

asSeenonScreen

http://www.asseenonscreen.com

Buy stuff you've seen on TV or in movies. For more, try MovieProp (http://www.movieprop.com) and The Prop Store (http://www.propstore.co.uk).

The Astounding B Monster

http://www.bmonster.com

Excellent resource for fans of Mamie Van Doren, Rondo Hatton and other cult '50s and '60s drive-in/late-show fodder. For fans of more modern fare like *Cannibal Women in the Avocado Jungle of Death*,

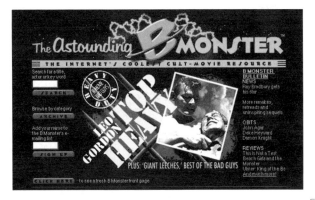

there's Bad Movie Planet (http://www.badmovieplanet.com), The Bad Movie Report (http://www.stomptokyo.com/badmoviereport/), The Bad Movie Review (http://www.badmovies.org), Oh The Humanity (http://www.ohthehumanity.com) and Shock Cinema (http://members.aol.com/shockcin/). If your critical faculties are so deadened that you might actually like to own one of these celluloid atrocities, try Science Fiction Continuum (http://www.sfcontinuum.com) – just make sure you've got a NTSC-compatible VCR.

Atom Films
http://www.atomfilms.com
Watch entertaining short films. For sixteen-colour silliness see:
http://www.pixelfest.com

Bad Movie Night
http://www.hit-n-run.com
Invite a couple of mates over to your house, get in a few beers, rent an aggressively mediocre movie and hurl invective at the screen. More snide remarks available at Filthy Critic (http://bigempire.com/filthy/), Mr Cranky (http://www.mrcranky.com), The Stinkers (http://www.thestinkers.com). But to really unveil box office evil, try: Childcare Action Project (http://www.capalert.com) and Screen It! (http://www.screenit.com).

Black Star
http://www.blackstar.co.uk
Based in Northern Ireland, this is perhaps the best British DVD and video shop on the Net: good selection, excellent search facility and great prices. Other video and DVD etailers worth checking out are DVD World (http://www.dvdworld.co.uk), Mr Benson's World of Home Entertainment (http://www.bensonsworld.co.uk) and The Video Shop (http://www.videoshop.co.uk). To compare prices: DVD Price Search (http://www.dvdpricesearch.com) or For Movies (http://www.formovies.com).

Blaxploitation.com
http://www.blaxploitation.com
Superfly guys and gals stickin' it to the man. More Afros and dashikis at BadAzz Mofo (http://www.badazzmofo.com).

Blooper Files

http://www.blooperfiles.com

Archive of screw-ups and inconsistencies from Hollywood's finest. More continuity errors at Movie Mistakes (http://www.movie-mistakes.co.uk) and The Nitpickers Site (http://www.nitpickers.com).

Bollywood World

http://www.bollywoodworld.com

Massive portal for the Indian film industry, with everything from production news to ringtones for your mobile.

Brutesquad Movies

http://www.brutesquad.com/MOS/movie_body.htm/

Preview movies like *Schindler's List II* (starring Arnold Schwarzenegger) and *Titanic: Horror of the Deep* (Jeff Goldblum saving the world against a pack of marauding blue whales).

Carfax-Abbey Horror Film Database

http://www.carfax-abbey.com

Splatter-flick Central, with loads of info on gore masters like Dario Argento and Wes Craven. More zombies and fake blood at Arrow in the

Head (http://www.joblo.com/arrow/), Dr Geoff's Horror House (http://www.dune12.demon.co.uk), Sex Gore Mutants (http://www.sexgoremutants.co.uk) and Zombie Girls (http://www.zombiegirls.net), while fans of Christopher Lee and Peter Cushing should grab some garlic and head to Ghoul Britannia (http://www.edhouse.clara.net/ghoul.html/).

Dogme95
http://www.dogme95.dk
Homepage of the Danish film movement led by Lars Von Trier, including the manifesto, a how-to page and the latest news from the film vanguard.

Drew's Script-O-Rama
http://www.script-o-rama.com
http://www.scriptshack.com
Hundreds of entire film and TV scripts. Need help writing or selling your own? Try: http://www.scriptfly.com

DVD Debate
http://www.dvddebate.com
All the latest UK DVD release news and reviews, plus a mighty useful section on the codes that enable you to change the regional setting on your DVD player. For more on DVD hardware and software:
http://www.dvdfile.com
http://www.dvdtimes.co.uk
http://www.dvdweb.co.uk

E! Online
http://www.eonline.com
Daily film and TV gossip, news and reviews.

Empire Magazine
http://www.empireonline.co.uk
Reviews of every film showing in the UK.

555-LIST
http://home.earthlink.net/~mthyen/
Catalogue of fake telephone numbers used in TV and film.

Gil*galad's Martian Theaethyr
http://www.televar.com/~gnostran/
Applying AstroTarotry to old movies makes them so much clearer.

Golden Raspberry Award Foundation
http://www.razzies.com
The Oscars in an alternate universe.

Hollywood Reporter
http://www.hollywoodreporter.com
Tinseltown tattle, previews and reviews daily, plus a flick biz directory.

In-Movies
http://www.in-movies.com
If you've got broadband access you can watch trailers and short films. For shorts from closer to home, try Brit Shorts (http://www.britshorts.com). For more trailers, pull up to The Trailer Park (http://www.movie-trailers.com). For specially commissioned full-length features, point your ADSL hookup to SightSound (http://www.sightsound.com).

Melon Farmer's Video Hits
http://www.dtaylor.demon.co.uk
Challenges British screen censorship.

Movie Cliches
http://www.moviecliches.com
Nothing unfamiliar.

MovieFlix
http://www.movieflix.com
Download hundreds of movies, some free but most require a monthly subscription of $4.95.

MovieLens
http://movielens.umn.edu
Become a member of this site and it will give you movie recommendations based on your tastes. It may be a bit of a behavioural research exercise, but it's still a pretty neat way of avoiding video shop malaise. Another site plays it safe: Greatest Films (http://www.filmsite.org).

Film

Moviemags.com
http://www.moviemags.com
Directory of film print and e-zines.

Movie Review Query Engine
http://www.mrqe.com
This specialist search engine dedicated to finding film reviews on the Web has a database of more than 25,000 titles and does an excellent job of finding info on obscure titles. But perhaps you'd prefer a summary: Rotten Tomatoes (http://www.rottentomatoes.com). For British reviews, try Filmreview (http://www.filmreview.co.uk) and Film Unlimited (http://www.filmunlimited.co.uk).

Movies.com
http://www.movies.com
http://www.universalstudios.com
http://www.film.com
Preview box office features and trailers direct from the major studios.

The Movie Shelf of Apartment 304
http://www.compusmart.ab.ca/kroyea/movie.htm
Cool martial arts and Yakuza flick site, with good features on Sonny Chiba and cover art.

Mr Kiss Kiss Bang Bang
http://www.ianfleming.org
An outrageously complete and obsessive guide to the shaken, not stirred universe of James Bond, with daily news and rumour updates.

My Movies
http://www.mymovies.net
Huge film site with production news, gossip, reviews, competitions, shopping, trailers and, if you've got broadband, movies on demand.

SciFi.com
http://www.scifi.com
http://scifi.ign.com
http://www.cinescape.com
Science fiction news, reviews and short films.

Share Reactor
http://www.sharereactor.com
God (and film industry lawyers) only knows how long this site will be around, but if you've got broadband and want to download the latest films (while they're still in cinematic release) check this site.

Showbizwire
http://www.showbizwire.com
Entertainment newsbreaks from about 50 major sources.

The Silents Majority
http://www.silentsmajority.com
This great online journal devoted to silent film is certainly one of the best film sites on the Web, even if you don't know Fatty Arbuckle from ZaSu Pitts.

Smoking List Movie Reviews
http://SmokingSides.com/asfs/m/
A history of smoking on the silver screen. Non-smokers might want to try Soup at the Movies (http://www.soupsong.com/imovies.html).

Variety
http://www.variety.com
Screen news fresh off the PR gatling gun.

Lo-tech Film Recreations

Who needs a £20 million special effects and pyrotechnics budget when you've got a couple of Lego sets?

Being Puffy
http://www.urbanentertainment.com/2
Being John Malkovich becoming P. Diddy.

The Fountainhead – A Parody
http://www.jeffcomp.com/faq/parody/
Ayn Rand's capitalist parable starring Skull Force.

Kevin's Custom Star Wars Minifigs
http://members.aol.com/jmacroy/update/legos/customs.html
But it's so lifelike.

Lego Star Wars Trilogy
http://www.tanukikoji.or.jp/yes/lsw/
Thankfully, there's no Jar Jar Binks.

Monty Python & the Holy Grail
http://www.lego.com/eng/studios/screening/movie
.asp?title=montypython
Even funnier than the real thing.

Shark Attack
http://www.exposure.co.uk/eejit/3act/sharkattack.html
Jaws in Lego vision.

Silent But Deadly
http://atomfilms.shockwave.com/af/content/silent_deadly
George Lucas sends some Stormtroopers to prevent fans from revealing the end of *Star Wars Episode 2*.

Star Wars ASCIImation
http://www.asciimation.co.nz
The ultimate hi-tech flick rendered in glorious letter art.

Titanic Legos At Sea
http://www.prtc.net/~kisspr/index2.htm
At least there's no Celine Dion soundtrack.

VCR Repair Instructions
http://www.fixer.com
How to take a VCR apart and then get all the little bits back in so it fits easier into the bin.

Warning6
http://www.cinepad.com/warning6.htm/
If you don't want to know the twists at the end of *The Usual Suspects* or *The Crying Game*, don't you dare visit this site.

Westerns.com
http://www.westerns.com
A great site for fans of classic oaters. They've got streaming videos of some obscure low budget shoot-'em-ups like *Fury* and *Can Be Done ... Amigo*, plus MP3s of Roy Rogers and Gabby Hayes, bios and filmographies of your favourite cowboys and cowgirls, and, of course, a tradin' post.

Finance

If your bank's on the ball it should offer an online facility to check your balances, pay your bills, transfer funds and export your transaction records into a bean-counting program such as Quicken or Money. If that sounds appealing and your bank isn't already on the case, start looking for a replacement. Go for one you can access via the Internet rather than by dialling direct. That way you can manage your cash through a Web browser whether you're at home, work or in the cybercafé on top of Pik Kommunisma. For help finding a true online bank:

Online Banking Report http://www.netbanker.com

Qualisteam http://www.qualisteam.com

If you can resist the urge to daytrade away your inheritance, the Net should give you greater control over your financial future. You can research firms, plot trends, check live quotes, join tip lists and stock forums, track your portfolio live, trade shares and access news. By all means investigate a subscription service or two – at least for the free trial period – but unless you need split-second data feeds or "expert" timing advice you should be able to get by without paying. Start here:

Yahoo UK http://quote.yahoo.co.uk

Apart from housing the Net's most exhaustive finance directory, Yahoo pillages data from a bunch of the top finance sources and presents it all in a seamless, friendly format. Enter a stock code, for example, and you'll get all the beef from the latest ticker price to a summary of insider trades. In some markets stocks have their own forums, which, let's face it, are only there to spread rumours. In other words, be very sceptical of anything you read or that's sent to you in unsolicited email.

Yahoo is by no means complete nor necessarily the best in every area, so try a few of these as well:

Bloomberg http://www.bloomberg.co.uk
CBS MarketWatch http://cbs.marketwatch.com
Digital Look http://www.digitallook.com
Free Real Time Quotes http://www.freerealtime.com
Gay Financial Network http://www.gfn.com
Hemscott http://www.hemscott.net
Interactive Investor http://www.iii.co.uk
Microsoft MoneyCentral http://moneycentral.msn.com
Money Extra http://www.moneyextra.com
Raging Bull http://www.ragingbull.com
Sharepages http://www.sharepages.com
Thomson FN http://www.thomsonfn.com
Wall Street City http://www.wallstreetcity.com
Wall Street Research Net http://www.wsrn.com

You'll no doubt be after a broker next. As with banking, any broker or fund manager who's not setting up online probably doesn't deserve your business. In fact, many traders are dumping traditional brokers in favour of the exclusively online houses. E★Trade (http://www.etrade.co.uk), for example, offers discount brokerage in at least nine countries (click on "International" to find your local branch). But traditional brokers are catching on. Many have cut their commissions, and offer online services in line with the Internet competition, so it pays to shop around. You might find you prefer to research online and trade by phone. To compare brokers: **Gomez.com** http://uk.gomez.com

For a British e-trading portal, try E-Trader UK (http://www.e-traderuk.com).

A word of warning, though: some online brokers have experienced outages where they were unable to trade. So if the market crashes in a big way, it mightn't hurt to play safe and use the phone instead.

Advice Online
http://www.adviceonline.co.uk
Contact an independent financial advisor for help on everything from mortgages to PEP transfers.

Bank of England
http://www.bankofengland.co.uk
Keep tabs on financial policy decisions.

BigCharts
http://bigcharts
.marketwatch.com
http://stockcharts.com
Whip up family-sized
graphs of US stocks,
mutual funds and market
indices. Or if you'd prefer
them streaming at you
live, proceed to:
http://www.livecharts
.com
For UK charts, try
Advanced Financial Network (http://www.advfn.com) and City
Comment (http://www.citycomment.co.uk).

Finance

BillPay
http://www.billpayment.co.uk
Pay your electricity, gas and water bills over the Net with this new service from Girobank.

Blay's Guides
http://www.blays.co.uk
Tracks and ranks finance rates across every UK market. Also links to hundreds of banking sites and investment products. For more rates, try Buy.co.uk (http://www.buy.co.uk), Moneygator (http://www.moneygator.com), MoneyNet (http://www.moneynet.co.uk) and Money Supermarket (http://www.moneysupermarket.com).

Bonehead Finance
http://ourworld.compuserve.com/homepages/Bonehead_Finance/
No-nonsense financial basics for dummies.

British Bankers' Association
http://www.bankfacts.org.uk
Review the Banking Code, find a cash machine, convert currency and consult a glossary of banking terms.

Clearstation
http://clearstation.etrade.com/
Run your stock picks through a succession of gruelling obstacle courses to weed out the weaklings or simply copy someone else's portfolio.

Debt Advice
http://www.debtadvicecentre.co.uk
Get yourself out from the hole.

The Desktop Accountant
http://www.thedesktopaccountant.com
Advice and tips to help small businesses and freelancers navigate their way around the tax code.

Earnings Whispers
http://www.earningswhispers.com
When a stock price falls upon the release of higher-than-expected earnings, chances are that the expectations being "whispered" amongst

traders prior to opening were higher than those circulated publicly.
Here's where to find out what's being said behind your back.

Financial Planning Horizons
http://www.financial-planning.uk.com
Good, unbiased information on the full range of financial products available in the UK.

Financial Times
http://www.ft.com
Business news, commentary, delayed quotes and closing prices from London. It's free until you hit the archives.

Find
http://www.find.co.uk
The Financial Information Net Directory houses some 6000 links to UK financial Websites, organized into categories like investment, insurance, information services, advice and dealing, bankings and savings, mortgages and loans, business services and life and pensions.

Foreign Exchange Rates
http://quote.yahoo.com/m3?u
http://www.xe.net/ucc/
Round-the-clock rates, conversion calculators and intraday charts on pretty close to the full set of currencies. To chart further back, see:
http://pacific.commerce.ubc.ca/xr/plot.html/

Frugal Corner
http://www.frugalcorner.com
Learn how to be thrifty from the experts.

FTSE
http://www.ftse.com
All the data and indices you could ever want.

HedgeWorld
http://www.hedgeworld.com
Allowing the average Joe a peek inside the secretive world of hedge funds.

Finance

Hoovers
http://www.hoovers.com
Research US, UK and European companies.

iCreditReport
http://www.icreditreport.com
Dig up any US citizen's credit ratings.

Inland Revenue
http://www.inlandrevenue.gov.uk
Tax information straight from the horse's mouth. To find a qualified advisor, try the Chartered Institute of Taxation (http://www.tax.org.uk). For a rough estimate of how much you'll have to pay, try the UK Wage/Tax Calculator (http://listen.to/taxman/).

Investment FAQ
http://www.invest-faq.com
Learn the ropes from old hands.

InvestorWords
http://www.investorwords.com
Can't tell your hedge rate from your asking price? Brush up on your finance-speak here.

Island
http://www.island.com
See US equity orders queued up on dealers' screens.

MAXfunds
http://www.maxfunds.com
Great site that allows you to track the performance of mutual funds. You have to register, but it's free. For more on managed funds and unit trusts, try Standard & Poor's Find Services (http://www.funds-sp.com) and TrustNet (http://www.trustnet.com).

Missing Money
http://www.missingmoney.com
http://www.findcash.com
Reclaim those US dollars you're owed.

MoneyChimp
http://www.moneychimp.com
Plain English primer in the mechanics of financial maths.

Money Origami
http://www.umva.com/~clay/money/
It's much more fun when you can make something out of it.

Motley Fool
http://www.fool.co.uk
Forums, tips, quotes and sound advice. More people telling you what to do with your money at City Pigeon (http://www.citypigeon.co.uk), Citywire (http://www.citywire.co.uk), Mrs Cohen (http://www.mrscohen.com) and This Is Money (http://www.thisismoney.com).

Paypal
http://www.paypal.com
Arrange online payments through a third party.

Pension Sorter
http://www.pensionsorter.com
Protect yourself against the scandals of the '80s with this site's impartial advice. Also check out the Pension Advisory Service at http://www.opas.org.uk. For the Government's angle, try Pension Guide (http://www.pensionguide.gov.uk) or the DSS's site (http://www.dss.gov.uk/lifeevent/penret/).

Screentrade
http://www.screentrade.co.uk
General insurance site, offering quotes from a range of insurers. Try also 1st Quote (http://www.1stquote.co.uk) and InsuranceWide (http://www.insurancewide.co.uk).

Tax & Accounting Sites Directory
http://www.taxsites.com
Links to everything you need to know about doling out your annual pound of flesh.

Technical Analysis Tutorials
http://www.e-analytics.com/techdir.htm
Beginner's guide to fortune-telling the markets using charts and indicators.

UK Insurance Guide
http://www.ukinsuranceguide.co.uk
Star ratings of nearly all of the UK's insurers.

Wall Street Journal Interactive
http://www.wsj.com
Not only is this online edition equal to the print one, its charts and data archives give it an edge. That's why you shouldn't complain that it's not free. After all, if it's your type of paper, you should be able to afford it, bigshot.

Where's George?
http://www.wheresgeorge.com
Put a tail on your greenback.

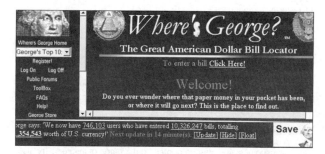

Flowers

About Flowers
http://www.aboutflowers.com
The meanings of flowers and the right ones for various occasions. See also All Occasion Flowers (http://www.all-occasion-flowers.com).

Clare Florist
http://www.clareflorist.co.uk
A Which? Webtrader offering a good range of bouquets, from classic to funky.

Daisys2Roses
http://www.daisys2roses.com
Despite a slight design flaw, this site allows you to create your own bouquet, a service which almost no other online florist offers. On top of that, this site has a special offer of half-a-dozen roses for £10 plus delivery.

First Flowers Direct
http://www.firstflowers.com
The flowers from this site come straight from the Covent Garden Flower Market and because of that they offer a better, less old-fashioned, range of bouquets. They also belong to the Which? Webtrader Code of Practice.

Flowers2Send
http://www.flowers2send.com
"The UK's first virtual florist" offers an impressively wide range of bouquets, although you can't create your own.

Interflora
http://www.interflora.co.uk
Interflora may be the biggest name in flowers, but their site is pretty run-of-the-mill. Aside from reliability and name recognition, its main feature is a personal organizer that will remind you of anniversaries and birthdays.

Teleflorist
http://www.teleflorist.co.uk
Like most of the big players, Teleflorist's site seems to offer a fairly limited range of bouquets and arrangements. It does, however, feature Internet exclusives and a percentage of certain orders are donated to charity.

Food and Drink

About French Cuisine
http://frenchfood.about.com
Everything you need to become the next Escoffier. To become the next Fanny Craddock, go to the Great British Kitchen (http://www.greatbritishkitchen.co.uk/gbk/).

African Studies Cookbook
http://www.sas.upenn.edu/African_Studies/Cookbook/
A frighteningly comprehensive database of African recipes.

Al Mashriq
http://almashriq.hiof.no/general/600/640/641/recipes/misc.html
No-nonsense list of Middle Eastern recipes.

The Alternative to Food and Drink UK
http://www.alternative-food-and-drink.co.uk
Bachelors' paradise: ratings of supermarket booze, a guide to "dehydrated things in pots" and other essential aspects of single life.

BBC Food
http://www.bbc.co.uk/food/
A very branded site (there are lots of familiar faces) but with a good database of solid recipes that you can be sure will have been tested properly.

Beershots
http://micro.magnet.fsu.edu/beershots/
Beers of the world put under a microscope.

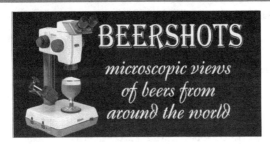

Berry Brothers & Rudd
http://www.bbr.co.uk
Although the site looks a little intimidating, don't be put off: this is one of the country's best wine ordering services and you can pick up wines for around £6, although at the other end the sky's the limit. Try also Oddbins (http://www.oddbins.co.uk) and Virgin Wines (http://www.virginwines.com).

Bevnet
http://www.bevnet.com
Know your new-age beverages.

Breworld
http://www.ge98.dial.pipex.com/
None of the usual beer yarns like waking up in a strange room stark-naked with a throbbing head and a hazy recollection of pranging your car. Here beer is treated with the same dewy-eyed respect usually reserved for wine and trains. Like to send your chum a virtual beer? Stumble over to: http://www.pubworld.co.uk

Cheese
http://www.cheese.com
Excellent cheese information site with an exhaustive list of cheeses and detailed info on composition.

Cheeseburger in Paradise
http://www.fdu.com/cburger.htm
Stranded in Alabama or Helsinki and jonesing for a cheeseburger? Check here for your nearest vendor.

Food and Drink

Chile-Heads
http://www.exit109.com/~mstevens/chileheads.html
http://www.ringoffire.net
Get 'em while they're hot.

Chocolate Lover's Page
http://chocolocate.com
The good gear: where to find recipes and dealers.

Chopstix
http://www.chopstix.co.uk
Good site for Chinese recipes (from the likes of Ken Hom) and information on ingredients too. For more recipes and contextual information, head to Chinatown Online (http://www.chinatown-online.co.uk /pages/food/index.html).

Cigar Aficionado
http://www.cigaraficionado.com
Archives, shopping guides, and tasting forums from the US glossy that sets the benchmark in cigar ratings. Modelled on: http://www .crackaficionado.com

Cocina Mexicana
http://cocinamexicana.com.mx/ingles/menu/frame.html
A great site devoted to authentic Mexican cuisine ... unfortunately, it's in Spanish.

Cocktail Time
http://www.cocktailtime.com
http://cocktails.about.com
http://www.webtender.com
http://www.barmeister.com
http://www.drinkboy.com
Guzzle your way to a happier home. Yes, do buy the book.

Cook's Thesaurus
http://www.foodsubs.com
Find substitutes for fatty, expensive or hard-to-find ethnic ingredients.

Specialist Shopping Sites

Club Chef Direct http://www.clubchefdirect.co.uk
Suppliers of restaurant-quality meat, fish and produce.

Cyber Candy http://www.cybercandy.com
Brilliant site for exploring candy from all over the world – great for US and Japanese expats looking for a sugary flavour of home.

Fifth Sense http://www.fifthsense.co.uk
An excellent site if you want to experiment a bit with spices or sauces from around the globe – mostly dry or bottled goods, though.

Fortnum & Mason http://www.fortnumandmason.co.uk
Excellent luxury food shopping site sensibly separated into goods that can be sent in the UK only and those worldwide.

Marchents http://www.marchents.com
A good site that offers food delivery on everything from meat to veg, plus there's kitchen kit to buy too.

Real Meat http://www.realmeat.co.uk
A decent site that sells very good products - the firm behind the site is well known in foodie circles for producing top-notch flesh.

Thornton's http://www.thorntons.co.uk
Yummy chocolates and the site ain't bad either: easy to shop, with lots of gift ideas.

Cooseman's Specialty Produce Guide
http://www.1webblvd.com/coosemans/guide.htm
An excellent guide to all the weird and wonderful things at your green-grocers.

Cucina Direct
http://www.cucinadirect.co.uk
Excellent online kitchen equipment site with a solid bricks-and-mortar business behind it.

Food and Drink

Curryhouse
http://www.curryhouse.co.uk
Make the perfect vindaloo or look up your nearest balti house if you're
too lazy. For more masala matters, try Death By Curry
(http://rubymurray.com).

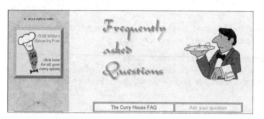

Delia Online
http://www.deliaonline.com
A double-header of a site: lots of good recipes and useful tips plus the
alarming Delia diary for true fans who really want to know about her life.
Go to MarthaStewart.com (http://www.marthastewart.com) to see
where all the site's ideas came from or to JamieOliver.net
(http://www.jamieoliver.net) for more of the most overexposed man in
European media.

Dolce Vita
http://www.dolcevita.com/cuisine
Life is sweet at this Italian cookery site.

The Empty Bowl
http://www.emptybowl.com
"The definitive source for all your cereal needs."

Epicurious
http://www.epicurious.com
The best food Website there is. Online marriage of Condé Nast's
Gourmet, *Bon Appetit*, and *Traveler* magazines, crammed with recipes,
culinary forums and advice on dining out worldwide.

The Espresso Index

http://www.espresso.com
http://www.espressotop50.com
Kickstart your morning with the FAQs on coffee.

Famers' Markets

http://www.farmersmarkets.net
Excellent site that helps you track down your nearest farmers' market.

Final Meal Requests

http://www.tdcj.state.tx.us/stat/finalmeals.htm
The prospect's enough to spoil your appetite.

Food Allergy and Anaphylaxis Network

http://www.foodallergy.org
All the news and developments from the peanut intolerance frontline.

Foodlink

http://www.foodlink.org.uk
Your complete guide to food safety. See also http://www.foodpres.com,
but if you can't remember anything about food safety unless it's set to
music go to http://foodsafe.ucdavis.edu/music.html

FoodnDrink

http://www.foodndrink.co.uk
A useful site with an online version of Harden's restaurant guide (created
by people rather than food critics) and a restaurant booking facility
(through http://www.5pm.co.uk) plus links to shopping sites, gourmet
bookshop and a good cookery school directory.

Fruitarian Site

http://www.fruitarian.com
The joys of chomping on raw fruit and the chance to make new fruitari-
an friends.

Generic Mac and Cheese Gallery

http://www.geocities.com/macandcheesebox/
Gawp in wonder at the diet of the American student.

Food and Drink

Good Pub Guide
http://www.goodguides.com
Offers a good pub locator for the UK, as if you needed help.

Internet Chef
http://www.ichef.com
Over 30,000 recipes, cooking hints ("Ground Beef Meals"), kitchen talk and more links than you can jab a fork in.

Lakeland
http://www.lakelandlimited.co.uk
Everything you could and couldn't possibly need in the kitchen.

Leaping Salmon
http://www.leapingsalmon.com
Quality prepared food that you simply assemble according to instructions – barely a chopping board required, and excellent food to boot. If you get the munchies in the middle of the night and need food cooked to order delivered to your door, try Room Service (http://www.roomservice.co.uk).

Meals For You
http://www.mealsforyou.com
A decent American recipe search engine – each recipe listing includes the details of the fat and cholesterol present in each recipe.

Moonshine
http://moonshine.co.nz
Get blind (possibly literally) on homemade spirits.

Moulage Cookbook
http://www.patrol.org/instructor/oec/moulage/moucock.htm
Moulage is the art of injury simulation, so come here to learn how to make fake blood and vomit for next Halloween.

New York Seafood
http://www.nyseafood.org
Great site for loads of piscine information. For cod and haddock delivered to your door, try The Fish Society (http://www.thefishsociety.co.uk).

Eating Out

The AA http://www.theaa.co.uk
Decent search engine for nationwide restaurants and pubs.

Grabameal http://www.grabameal.co.uk
A database of over 23,000 restaurants and take-aways in the UK.

Square Meal http://www.squaremeal.co.uk
One of the better restaurant finders, plus news and views from the dining world.

This Is London http://www.thisislondon.co.uk
The *Evening Standard* site is the best site for searching for bars and pubs and restaurants in London: comprehensive and with good-length reviews so you get an idea of exactly what you'll be getting.

Time Out http://www.timeout.com/london/rest.xml
Frequently updated rundown of London eateries, searchable by area or cuisine.

Toptable http://www.toptable.co.uk
No-nonsense site that covers London and some surrounding areas.

Zagats http://www.zagats.com
Excellent search engine for restaurant reviews the world over plus restaurant news.

An Ode to Olives
http://www.emeraldworld.net/olive.html
You'll never look at an olive ambivalently again.

Oreo Stuff
http://www.jeffmajor.com/oreos/index.html
Someone with way too much time on his hands.

Our Food
http://www.ourfood.com
An excellent collection of scientific articles pertaining to food science and food safety.

Food and Drink

Porkrind.com
http://www.porkrind.com
Everything you wanted to know about deep-fried pork fat and more.

Ray's List of Weird and Disgusting Foods
http://www.andreas.com/food.html
How many have you tried?

Recipe Link
http://www.recipelink.com
Points to more than 10,000 galleries of gluttony.

Recipe Search
http://www.birdseye.com/search.html/
Cast your line into the Fish Finger king's own recipe database or trawl through hundreds of other Net collections. See also:
http://www.lycos.com/search/recipedia.html/
http://recipes.alastra.com
http://www.mealsforyou.com

Restaurant Row
http://www.restaurantrow.com
Key in your dining preferences and find the perfect match from hundreds of thousands of food barns worldwide.

Scope GM Food
http://scope.educ.washington.edu/gmfood
Forums, FAQs, email lists and reference library concerning mutant seeds.

ScotchWhisky.com
http://www.scotchwhisky.com
Excellent site with loads of info on whisky plus a shopping facility.

Spice Advice
http://www.spiceadvice.com
Encyclopedia of spices covering their origins, purposes, recipes and tips on what goes best with what.

Switcheroo

http://www.switcheroo.com

Seriously clever and useful site that offers you both an encyclopedia of ingredients and help if you're missing an ingredient when cooking. For example, if you're making a cake but there's no fat in the house, substitute mashed banana. Yes, really.

Tasty Insect Recipes

http://www.ent.iastate.edu/misc/insectsasfood.html
http://www.eatbug.com

Dig in to such delights as Bug Blox, Banana Worm Bread, Rootworm Beetle Dip and Chocolate Chirpie Chip Cookies (with crickets).

Tea & Sympathy

http://www.enteract.com/~robchr/tea/

Home of the Rec.Food.Tea FAQ. For more, try the Tea Council (http://www.teacouncil.co.uk). To buy tea, try Whittard's (http://www.whittard.com).

Thai Recipes

http://www.importfood.com/recipes.html

Just click if you don't have an ingredient.

Tokyo Food Page

http://www.bento.com

Where and what to eat in Tokyo, plus recipes. More help packing sushi at http://www.thesushibar.com and http://www.sushilinks.com

Top Secret Recipes

http://www.topsecretrecipes.com
http://www.copykat.com

At least one commercial recipe, such as KFC coleslaw, revealed each week. Many are surprisingly basic.

Tudocs

http://www.tudocs.com

Rates cooking links across the web. Search under "fruit", for instance, and get linked to such ever-useful sites as 104 Things to Do With a Banana.

Food and Drink

Buying Groceries Online

Your chances of being able to order home-delivered groceries online will be much higher if you live in a big city, but expect to pay a premium for the convenience. Although most of the following have physical stores, they mightn't offer their full range online.

Simply Organic http://www.simplyorganic.net
Excellent organic shopping site with a full range of 1900 products to choose from, easy to use and well-organized deliveries too. For more of Mother Nature's bounty, try Organics Direct (http://www.organicsdirect.co.uk).

Tesco http://www.tesco.co.uk
Perhaps the best of the Internet shopping sites. The system takes a while for you to set up, but once it's up and running fans say it's a real doddle even if they sometimes get five kilos of tomatoes instead of five tomatoes.

Waitrose http://www.waitrose.com
One of the best supermarket shopping sites. It's not currently offering regular grocery delivery nationwide (although it is being tested in certain areas of the UK as this book goes to press), but this site offers organic box delivery plus wine, flowers and chocs. The site also has a link to Waitrose *Food Illustrated* magazine with access to articles and restaurant reviews.

Other sites include:
Asda http://www.asda.co.uk
Iceland http://www.iceland.co.uk
Safeway http://www.safeway.co.uk
Sainsbury's http://www.sainsburys.co.uk
Somerfield http://www.somerfield.co.uk

The Ultimate Cookbook
http://www.ucook.com
Pinch recipes from hundreds of popular cookbooks. More food porn
unplugged at: http://www.cook-books.com

Vegetarian Society of the UK
http://www.vegsoc.org
Support for veggies.

Wine Spectator
http://www.winespectator.com
Research your hangover.

Zack's Bug Eating Page
http://eat.bees.net
You better get used to it, because it'll be your diet soon.

Furniture and Interiors

BBC Good Homes
http://www.beeb.com/goodhomes
The BBC's interior magazine has all the features you've come to expect,
offering advice on everything from Moroccan living rooms to the good
flooring guide.

Design Gap
http://www.design-gap.co.uk
Directory of work by 300 contemporary British designers and furniture
makers that includes everything from tchotchkes to chests-of-drawers.

Design-Online
http://www.design-online.co.uk
A database of British interior designers, feng shui consultants, building
services, soft furnishing companies and other providers of interiors
essentials.

Furniture and Interiors

Furniture Guide
http://www.furnitureguide.com
Very impressive site covering all aspects of furniture, with glossaries, buying guides, shop locator, articles, style guide, etc.

Furniture Wizard
http://www.furniturewizard.com
Loads of tips on how to restore your Louis XIV chair after your cat pees on it.

Geomancy.Net – The Centre for Applied Feng Shui Research
http://www.geomancy.net
Harmonize Qi and recreate the ambience of a Chinese restuarant. For more wizard assistance, try Qi Whiz (http://www.qi-whiz.com) and Feng Shui Fanzine (http://www.fengshui-fanzine.co.uk).

History of Furniture Timeline
http://maltwood.finearts.uvic.ca/hoft/
Detailed history of furniture, with glossary and links.

Illustrated History of Furniture
http://www.cwru.edu/UL/preserve/stack/Furniture.html
Complete text of an 1893 historical study of furniture in PDF format.

Interstyle
http://www.interstyle.net
Homepage of a Florida shop that sells classics of 20th-century design by Alvar Aalto, Ludwig Mies Van Der Rohe, Le Corbusier and Charles Eames.

Let's Go Retro
http://www.letsgoretro.com
Relive your youth and get a Space Invaders machine for your living room.

Furniture and Interiors

Nubold.com
http://www.nubold.com
Home of lighting, glass, ceramics and tableware from contemporary designers like Bodo Sperlein and Nic Wood. They even offer a wedding list service for couples with impeccable taste.

Ocean
http://www.oceanuk.com/index_live.htm
Stylish, contemporary furniture and accessories.

On-Line Furniture Style Guide
http://www.connectedlines.com/styleguide
Detailed guide to styles from Jacobean to Scandinavian contemporary.

Sotheby's Collecting Guides
http://www.sothebys.com/connoisseur/guides
The venerable auction house's guides to collecting ceramics, furniture, prints, rugs, clocks and silver.

StyleSource Design
http://www.stylesource.co.uk/design/
The peach colour-scheme and the face of Laurence Llewelyn-Bowen might suggest otherwise, but this site is a good source of information and advice on everything from frosted mirrors to colour trends and period design.

Tribu-Design
http://www.tribu-design.com/en/
A fascinating database of 20th-century furniture and design.

Games

20th Century Design Collection
http://www.deanclough.com/arts/20thcentury1.html/
Some beautiful, well-researched pages devoted to postwar British design, including examples of furniture by Robin Day, Basil Spence and Terence Conran.

Wallpaper Online
http://www.wallpaperonline.co.uk
Apparently wallpaper hasn't been this trendy since the '70s, so stock up at this easy-to-use site, featuring a database of 20,000 papers, borders and fabrics.

The Work of Charles and Ray Eames
http://lcweb.loc.gov/exhibits/eames/
The Library of Congress's online exhibition of the work of the most influential designers of the 20th century.

Games

Most multiplayer games can be played across the Net. There are also thousands of simple table, word, arcade and music games as diverse as Chess, Blackjack, Connect 4, and Frogger that can be played on the Web courtesy of Java and Shockwave. In some cases you can even contest online opponents for prizes. Peruse the selection on offer at:

Coffee Break Arcade http://www.coffeebreakarcade.com
Flash Kit http://www.flashkit.com
Flazoom http://www.flazoom.com
Flipside http://www.flipside.com
FreeArcade.com http://www.freearcade.com
Gamesville http://www.gamesville.com
Playsite http://www.playsite.com
Pogo.com http://www.pogo.com
Shockwave.com http://www.shockwave.com
The Station http://www.station.sony.com

Yahoo Games http://games.yahoo.com
Web Games http://www.happypuppy.com/web/

Al Menconi Ministries
http://www.gospelcom.net/menconi/topics/games/
Videogame reviews from a Christian perspective.

The Atari Time Machine
http://homepage.eircom.net/~morrikar/
Museum and homage to the videogame console that just about started
it all. For fans of its chief rival, there's Intellivision Lives
(http://www.intellivisionlives.com).

Blues News
http://www.bluesnews.com
Keep up with what's Quakin'.

Cheat Station
http://www.cheatstation.com
Get Sonic to do what you want him to do. For more devious tricks, try
The Codebook (http://www.codebook.pp.se/).

Games

ContestGuide
http://www.contestguide.com
http://www.contestlistings.com
http://home.iwon.com/index_gen.html
http://www.loquax.co.uk
http://www.uggs-n-rugs.com.au/contests/
Get junk-mailed for life by entering loads of competitions.

Croft Times
http://www.cubeit.com/ctimes/
More news about the Tomb Raider bombshell than you could ever want.
For the truly smitten, you can download a customized version of
Internet Explorer featuring Lara's likeness everywhere.

Freeloader
http://www.freeloader.com
Download free games (like *Grand Theft Auto* and *Hidden & Dangerous*)
for your PC. The catch: you have to look at ads ... lots of ads.

Game Downloads
http://www.fileplanet.com
Stock up on even more gaming software.

GameFAQs
http://www.gamefaqs.com
Stuck on a level or just want to know more?

Game Girlz
http://www.gamegirlz.com
Team up with other game grrls and prepare to kick dweeb-boy butt
right across their own turf. More reinforcement at
http://www.womengamers.com.

Gameplay
http://www.gameplay.com
Fifteen years old and still going strong, this is certainly the best British
gaming portal, with an excellent magazine, shop and loads of online
gaming options. Check out UK Games (http://www.ukgames.com) for
cheats, lotsa links and lower prices.

Games

For reviews, news, demos, hints, patches, cheats, downloads, and other PC game necessities try:

Adrenaline Vault http://www.avault.com
Gamers.com http://www.gamers.com
Games Domain http://www.gamesdomain.co.uk
Gamespot http://www.gamespot.com
GameSpy http://www.gamespy.com
Happy Puppy http://www.happypuppy.com
Mac Gamer http://www.macgamer.com
Old Man Murray http://www.oldmanmurray.com
Total Games http://www.totalgames.net

Console Games

Absolute Playstation
http://www.absolute-playstation.com/index.php

Console Domain http://www.gamesdomain.co.uk
Console Nation http://www.consolenation.com
Hotgames.com http://www.hotgames.com
Psx Extreme http://www.psxextreme.com
Total Games http://www.totalgames.net
Videogame Strategies http://vgstrategies.about.com
XBox http://xbox.ign.com

Gaming Age
http://www.gaming-age.com
All the latest news from the gaming frontline, plus interviews with designers and previews of big games before they hit the shops.

Kasporov Chess
http://www.kasparovchess.com
http://chess.about.com
Take tips from the Russian master and then find an opponent.

Games

Multi-Player Online Gaming
http://www.mpog.com
Everything you need to know to start playing Quake III and Counter-Strike online, plus patches, demos, betas, cheats and other gaming essentials.

The Odyssey Resource
http://www.run.to/odyssey
Relive those halcyon days when Pong seemed like the greatest thing since striped toothpaste.

PC Game Finder
http://www.pcgame.com
Search the leading game lairs.

Pointless Games
http://pointlessgames.com
Believe it or not, a selection of games that are actually worse than Pong.

Popex
http://www.popex.com
Similar to Fantasy Football or Fantasy Shares, but with pop bands.

RPG Vault
http://rpgvault.ign.com
Role Playing Gamers' heaven.

Vintage Gaming
http://www.vg-network.com
http://www.emuunlim.com
http://www.download.net
Revive old school arcade games like Xevious on your home PC. More '80s fun at Smilie Games (http://www.smiliegames.com) and Retrospec (http://www.retrospec.org).

Zany Video Game Quotes
http://zanyvg.overclocked.org
Chronicling the contribution to the English language made by video games.

Gardening

About gardening
http://gardening.about.com
About's home gardening guide.

The Botanical Dermatology Database
http://bodd.cf.ac.uk
Why you should wear gardening gloves.

British Trees
http://www.british-trees.com
Dedicated to the preservation of British woodland, including an excellent
guide to native trees.

The Carnivorous Plant FAQ
http://www.sarracenia.com/faq.html
Novel solutions for garden pests.

Gardening

Crocus
http://www.crocus.co.uk
The main draw of this online garden centre is that plants are delivered by trained gardeners who will help bolster your borders. There are also sections devoted to plant finding, jargon busting and news and advice on organic gardening.

Dig It
http://www.dig-it.co.uk
Comprehensive gardening site, including a shopping service where everything is allegedly sourced from environmentally friendly companies, a good magazine section and a facility to email the site's experts. For more, see Gone Gardening (http://www.gonegardening.co.uk) and Just Gardeners (http://www.justgardeners.com).

E-Garden
http://www.e-garden.co.uk
Initially this large site appears to be heavy on the hard sell, but lurking beneath the commerce are a well-organized magazine section, a Latin translator and very useful problemsolvers on subjects like diseases, climbers and herbaceous perennials.

English Country Gardening
http://www.suite101.com/welcome.cfm/english_country_gardening/
Jane Hollis's site devoted to the grand old art of English country gardening includes discussion groups, articles, virtual tours and flower show and garden reports.

Expert Gardener
http://www.expertgardener.com
Has the usual features, with the added extra of Charlie Dimmock calendars available for purchase.

Garden Forum
http://www.gardenforum.co.uk
All the latest news, views, advice, job postings and gossip from the gardening community.

Garden Guides
http://www.gardenguides.com
Has most of the features you should expect from the better general gar-

dening sites (plant guides, discussion forums, advice), but this site sets itself apart with its lengthy book extracts on topics like choosing bulbs and designing herb gardens.

Garden Visit
http://www.gardenvisit.com
Maps of gardens open to the public around the world and a history of garden design.

Garden Web
http://www.gardenweb.com
One of the best horticultural resources on the Web, this site hosts a multitude of regional and specialist forums (roses, wild flowers, kitchen gardens), plus a glossary, plant database, calendar of events, plant and seed exchange, plenty of articles and shopping areas.

Gothic Gardening
http://www.gothic.net/~malice/
Grow a little greenhouse of horrors.

GOTHIC GARDENING — Welcome to the Garden that mAlice built...

Growing Lifestyle
http://growinglifestyle.com
A dedicated home-and-garden search engine.

Internet Garden
http://www.internetgarden.co.uk
Quirky but useful links, divided by subjects like tropical, hothouse and containers.

Kitchen Gardener
http://www.taunton.com/finegardening/pages/fg_feat_kitchgard.asp
Online presence of *Kitchen Gardener* magazine, dedicated to foodies who grow their own produce. Also check out
http://www.thevegetablepatch.com for a more organic perspective.

Open Directory Gardens
http://dmoz.org/Home/Gardens/
The Open Directory Project's comprehensive set of links.

Postcode Plant Database
http://www.nhm.ac.uk/science/projects/fff/
This excellent resource from the Natural History Museum allows you to find the right native trees, shrubs and flowers for your area.

Royal Botanic Gardens
http://www.rbgkew.org.uk
Featuring access to its enormous academic database, the homepage of Kew Gardens is one for the real horticulturalist.

Royal Horticultural Society
http://www.rhs.org.uk
The online presence of the RHS includes plant databases, seasonal advice and a garden finder.

The Vine Weevil Advice Centre
http://www.vine.weevil.org.uk
Dedicated to combating Britain's number-one garden pest.

Gay and Lesbian

AEGIS
http://www.aegis.com
Claiming to be the largest HIV/AIDS related site on the Web, AEGIS is an amazing resource filled with the latest news from the treatment front, bulletin boards, a law library of judicial cases and an archive of publications from organizations like Gay Men's Health Crisis, Act Up and the Government. For more news, advice and dispatches from the activist front, try Gay Men's Health Crisis (http://www.gmhc.org) and Act Up New York (http://www.actupny.org).

The AIDS Memorial Quilt
http://www.aidsquilt.org
View the quilt online, find out how to become involved with the project and contribute to the memory book.

Gay.com UK
http://uk.gay.com
The British version of the enormous American portal has a huge array of channels for everyone from scene queens to those not yet out of the closet. Other portals of call are Planet Out (http://www.planetout.com), Queer Theory (http://www.queertheory.com) and Queery (http://www.queery.com).

Gay Britain Network
http://www.gaybritain.co.uk
Homepage of the network that hosts sites like UK Gay Shopping, UK Gay Guide and Gay Video Shop.

Gay & Lesbian Alliance against Defamation
http://www.glaad.org
Stand up against media stereotyping and discrimination of those deviating from the heterosexual norm.

Gay and Lesbian

Gayscape
http://www.gayscape.com/gayscape/
Probably the best gay search engine on the Web. See also the Queer
Resource Directory (http://www.qrd.org). For more Brit-specific links,
try The Gay Index (http://www.gayindex.co.uk) and for less mainstream
links, try Larry-bob's Queer Hotlist
(http://www.io.com/~larrybob/hotlist.html/).

Gay to Z
http://www.gaytoz.com
Directory of gay-friendly hotels, bars, clubs, builders, plumbers, electri-
cians and erotica in London, Manchester and Brighton. Give them your
email address and they'll send you more complete guides on the above
cities plus Paris. For more hotels in the UK and abroad, try UK Gay
Hotel Guide (http://www.gayhotel.co.uk).

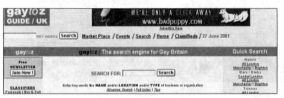

Gay Travel Guide
http://www.gaytravel.co.uk
This excellent site has detailed guides to destinations such as Mykonos,
Benidorm, Ibiza, New York and Amsterdam, plus a good search facility
for gay-friendly hotels in more exotic locales.

Holy Titclamps
http://www.holytitclamps.com
Homepage of San Francisco's fab queer zine which features fiction by the
likes of Sarah Schulmann and Steve Abbot plus comics, poetry, rants and
humour from some of the best writers and artists on the scene.

Lesbian UK
http://www.lesbianuk.co.uk
A database of resources, both on- and offline, for Britain's lesbian community.

The Old Dyke
http://www.rowfant.demon.co.uk
Essays devoted to lesbian and women's history.

OutRage!
http://outrage.nabumedia.com/
Peter Tatchell's organization fighting for equal rights and fighting against assimilation into straight society.

Pink Passport
http://www.pinkpassport.com
A site with all the usual features, but it does have one of the best gay venue selectors on the Web covering the entire world.

Rainbow Network
http://www.rainbownetwork.co.uk
As its name suggests, this site covers pretty much the entire spectrum of gay and lesbian life, from the Eurovision Song Contest to rallying the pink vote in the General Election.

Stonewall
http://www.stonewall.org.uk
The homepage of the lesbian and gay rights organization may strike some as dull and worthy, but it's a good source of information on British activism and issues like the age of consent.

Techno Dyke
http://www.technodyke.com
Part of the Indie Gurl Network (http://www.indiegurl.com) of zines, this fun e-zine has galleries of drag kings, astrology, articles on sex and relationships and a "Biosphere" section. For an e-zine with a British perspective, try Dyke Universe (http://dykeuniverse.com).

UK Gay Guide
http://www.gayguide.co.uk
The design is slightly irritating, but this site features excellent guides to gay-friendly services throughout the UK plus advice and personals.

Genealogy

Don't expect to enter your name and produce an instant family tree, but you might be able to fill in a few gaps.

Ancient Faces
http://www.ancientfaces.com
Picture your ancestors.

Chineseroots.com
http://www.chineseroots.com
An amazing resource for people of Chinese ancestry. The site has made an agreement with the Shanghai Library allowing access to its archive of ancestral documents dating back to the 10th century.

Cyndi's List
http://www.cyndislist.com
Twenty million users can't be wrong. With just about 100,000 links, the genealogy resource you're after is undoubtedly here. For Brit-specific links, try Suzy's Genealogy Page
(http://www.geocities.com/heartland/3934/britain.htm).

Ellis Island Records
http://www.ellisislandrecords.org
If you're family had a stopover in the US in the past 150 years or so, their records will be here.

Family History
http://www.familyhistory.com
This site, a section of the massive Ancestry.com umbrella, hosts some 130,000 message boards organized by surname or location. You can also set up your own family Website here for free.

FamilySearch
http://www.familysearch.org
If you're going to be doing family research on the Web you'll come here at one stage or another. This site (also known as the LDS Resource) is run by the Mormons, who believe it is their duty to record the ancestry of every living soul. The religious aspect is played down in favour of sheer information, and what they have collated is nothing short of astonishing: some 450 million family names.

Freebies for Genealogists
http://www.jodenoy.clara.net/dealers/freebies.htm
Links to free, downloadable programs of use to the genealogist.

Genuki
http://www.genuki.org.uk
This should be your first stop on your search for your family roots. They have an excellent section for beginners, offering advice on how to search and how to use the Internet's resources. More beginner's advice can be found at Starting English Research
(http://www.xmission.com/~nelsonb/starte.htm/).

Historical Text Archive
http://historicaltextarchive.com
A very useful resource for people with Caribbean and African ancestry, including a Caribbean ancestry newsletter and a database of slave names. Also check Christine's Genealogy Website (http://ccharity.com).

JaysKids
http://www.jayskids.com
Find out if the prodigious '50s rock 'n' roller Screamin' Jay Hawkins put a spell on your mama.

Public Record Office
http://www.pro.gov.uk
Not a great resource in itself, but if you need to approach the Public Record Office or National Archive for materials this site gives you the lowdown on how to go about it. More information can be found on the Government's new site, Family Records
(http://www.familyrecords.gov.uk).

Gossip

RootsWeb
http://www.rootsweb.com
The oldest, largest and probably the best free genealogy site on the Net. It features a very good search engine, links to resources and lots of humour preventing things from getting too dull. More gene gardening can be done at Ancestry.com (http://www.ancestry.com), the Family Tree Maker (http://www.familytreemaker.com), Genealogy Homepage (http://www.genhomepage.com), Genealogy Today (http://www.genealogytoday.com).

Surname Listings
http://www.surnameweb.org
Dig up dirt on your family name.

Gossip

Every celebrity has at least one obsessive fan site (http://www.ggower.com/fans/) in their honour, but finding them can sometimes be tricky. If they're not listed in Yahoo, try:
http://www.celebhoo.com
http://www.celebrityweb.com
http://www.webring.org
http://www.csotd.com

Search engines tend to find porn scuttlers who've loaded their HTML metatags with celebrity names. Easy bait, when you consider that most fans would love a glimpse of their idol in various states of undress (http://www.cndb.com). If they succeed in catching your attention, at least have the sense not to pull out your credit card. Adding **–naughty –naked –nude** to your search term, or enabling an adult filter such as Google's SafeSearch (under **Preferences**), might help weed them out.

ABC News Entertainment
http://abcnews.go.com:80/sections/entertainment/
Rumours and legit showbiz news from one of America's big three TV networks.

Beat Box Betty
http://www.beatboxbetty.com/showbiznews/crowreport.htm/
Gossip and industry news "with a twist of blonde".

Bizcotti
http://bizcotti.com
Attempting to be *The Onion* of the gossip world.

Celebrity Babies
http://celebritybabies.webjump.com
What would the offspring of your favourite celebrity couple look like?

Celebstatus
http://www.celebstatus.com
One of the Web's greatest games, this is fantasy football for celeb spotters with a cast of A, B and C list "stars" accumulating points for tabloid appearances.

Chic Happens
http://www.hintmag.com/chichappens/chichappens.php
Horacio Silva and Ben Widdicombe's superb gossip page.

Cinescape
http://www.cinescape.com
The latest insider industry news. Not as good as *The Hollywood Reporter*, but you don't have to subscribe.

Gossip

Coat Hangers of the Rich and Famous
http://www.geocities.com/hangmycoat/
A revealing look inside the closet of some
of the world's biggest stars. For those who
prefer to give their object of desire some
TLC, there's Stars auf Krücken
(http://www.fortunecity.de/spielberg
/quincy/28/) – stars on crutches.

Donna's Long and Short of It
http://www.metal-
sludge.com/LongShort.htm
The skinny (or the chubby) on the members of the heavy metal fraternity.

Drudge Report
http://www.drudgereport.com
Rumours from inside the Washington
Beltway with a right-wing slant from the
online columnist who almost brought down
a president.

E! Online
http://www.eonline.com
The latest from the States courtesy of the homepage of the American
cable TV channel.

Famous Birthdays
http://www.famousbirthdays.com
http://us.imdb.com/OnThisDay/
See who shares your birthday.

Famous Name Changes
http://www.famousnamechanges.com
The truth behind celebs trying to give themselves some personality.

Fanzine
http://www.fanzine.co.uk
The official addresses of stars and pop groups. For more direct access,
try Chip's Celebrity Home E-mail Addresses

(http://www.addresses.site2go.com). Reach out to more stars at Celebrity Addresses (http://www.writetoaceleb.com) and CelebrityEmail.com (http://www.celebrityemail.com).

Filth2Go
http://www.filth2go.com
Outrageous, scandalous, rude gay gossip zine. Unfortunately, you have to subscribe.

Find a Grave
http://www.findagrave.com
See where celebrities are buried.

Gene Simmons' Celebrity Bedroom
http://www.kissdominion.com/BEDROOM.HTM
See how your fave celeb looks in the bedroom of the Kiss bassist who has dated Cher, Diana Ross and Shannon Tweed.

The Gossip Lowdown
http://www.mindspring.com/%7Ealexfan/lowdown.html/
Click here to subscribe to Simone Sentral's crucial newsletter.

Groupie Central
http://www.groupiecentral.com
For adults only, this site doesn't pull any punches, but along with Popbitch it's the best gossip site on the Web.

Hello!
http://www.hello-magazine.co.uk
All the jet trash and desperate celebs you expect from the glossy, only with lower production values. For an American version of the same without the minor royalty, try People (http://people.aol.com).

Hollywood Gossip
http://www.jtj.net/jtj/gossip.shtml
Is Keanu Reeves gay? Fading stars and other matters of international import.

Gossip

National Enquirer

http://www.nationalenquirer.com
All the news that's not fit to print elsewhere. Even less believable "news" can be found at Weekly World News (http://www.weeklyworldnews.com).

New York Post

http://www.nypostonline.com/gossip/gossip.htm/
The latest dish from the columnists of the Big Apple's most notorious tabloid. For even more tittle-tattle, try their sister site, Page Six (http://www.pagesix.com). For more from their crosstown rivals, try Daily Dish (http://www.mostnewyork.com/today/News_and_Views/Daily_Dish/).

PeopleNews

http://www.peoplenews.com
Who did what, where and when, updated twenty times a day. As recommended by Tara Palmer-Tomkinson.

Popbitch

http://www.popbitch.com
Scurrilous, rude, fun and yes, downright bitchy, this is without question the best British pop gossip site. Their weekly mailing lists have brought

down careers and halt work all over the capital every Thursday.

Pop Justice

http://www.popjustice.com
Fabulously bitchy site taking aim at the teen pop hordes.

RumorsRumorsRumors

http://www.rumorsrumorsrumors.com
Goss headlines, rumours, conspiracy theories and urban myths culled from around the Net.

Showbiz Wire

http://www.showbizwire.com
Entertainment newswire service, featuring stories gathered from just about every entertainment site.

The Smoking Gun
http://www.thesmokinggun.com
Tom Cruise's petition for divorce, Linda Fiorentino's nudity rider and other documents of celebrity misbehaviour. More at:
http://www.apbnews.com/media/gfiles/

TeenHollywood.com
http://www.teenhollywood.com
All the latest dirt and news on Tinsletown's pretty young things.

Variety
http://www.variety.com
Screen news fresh off the PR gatling gun.

Who would you kill?
http://www.whowouldyoukill.com
So who would you toss into Dawson's Creek?

Greetings Cards

http://www.freegreetingcards.org
http://www.postcard-heaven.com
http://www.postcards.com
http://www.cardlady.com

If stretching the bounds of good taste doesn't bother you, you'll find thousands of sites that will gladly speckle your message with multimedia tutti-frutti. Rather than forward your "card" directly, your victim will generally receive an invitation to drop by and collect it from the site. And of course being masked by a third party makes it perfect for harassing valentines and sending ransom notes. The above directories list hundreds of virtual card dispensers, but check out the most popular ones first:

Blue Mountain http://www.bluemountain.com
eGreetings http://www.egreetings.com
Hallmark http://www.hallmark.com

Greetings Cards

Pulp Cards http://www.pulpcards.com
Regards.com http://www.regards.com
Tackymail http://www.tackymail.com
Virtual Insults http://www.virtualinsults.com
Yahoo Greetings http://greetings.yahoo.com

Banner Greetings
http://www.bannergreetings.com
Create your own personalized greetings by uploading your photo and choosing from their music or art library.

Brides and Grooms
http://BridesandGrooms.com/cards/
Propose to your loved one with an intimate virtual proposal card.

Card Corp
http://www.cardcorp.co.uk
Need some business cards or invitations fast? Design them online for snappy delivery via email or on the paper of your choice. Naturally, the latter option costs.

Digital Voodoo
http://www.pinstruck.com
Curse thy neighbour.

Hotpaper.com
http://www.hotpaper.com
Fill in the blanks to create handy everyday documents like greetings cards, references, eviction notices and credit card disputes.

Invites
http://invites.yahoo.com
http://www.regards.com
http://www.egreetings.com
Throwing a slide night? Here's an easy way to create an instant email invitation and manage the thousands of RSVPs. For help planning:
http://www.theplunge.com

Kiss My Ass
http://www.kissmyass.com
If a Hallmark card doesn't have quite the right sentiment you're after, tell someone to kiss your ass in style here.

ManCards
http://www.queerzone.com/mancards
Come out of the closet with a ManCard.

Matoox
http://www.matoox.com
Tell your boss he's a male chauvinist pig, tell your neighbour he's got bad breath, tell that fox in History lectures your true intentions – but all under the cover of anonymity.

Postcardland
http://postcardland.com
Confuse your parole officer by sending them a postcard from the other side of the world.

Virtual Beer Server
http://beer.trash.net
Say it with a brew.

Virtual Presents
http://www.virtualpresents.com
http://www.it3c.co.uk
Why waste money on real gifts when, after all, isn't it the thought that counts?

Web Greeting Cards
http://www.web-greeting-cards.com
If you're after something classier than the average e-card, this site offers high-quality images that can be extensively customized.

Health

While the Net's certainly an unrivalled medical library, it's also an unrivalled promulgator of the 21st-century equivalent of old wives' tales. So by all means research your ailment and pick up fitness tips online, but like the pill bottles say, check with your doctor before putting them to work. And while you're with your GP, ask if they use the Net for research and if so, which sites they recommend.

Don't expect to go online for first-aid advice. If it's an emergency, you won't have time. The Net is better for in-depth research and anecdotal advice, none of which comes quickly. But once you've spent a few sessions online studying your complaint, you'll be fully prepared to state your case. To find a doctor, dentist or specialist, try: http://www.netdoctor.co.uk.

WorldClinic (http://www.worldclinic.com) provides phone, fax or email response that could save your life on the road.

It's hard to say where to start your research. Perhaps a directory: Yahoo et al have seriously stacked medical sections, or you could try one of the specialist health portals:

Achoo http://www.achoo.com
Hospitalweb UK http://www.hospitalweb.co.uk
MedExplorer http://www.medexplorer.com
Patient UK http://www.patient.co.uk
SearchBug http://www.searchbug.com/health/

Or a government gateway:
Health on the Net http://www.hon.ch

NHS Direct (UK) http://www.nhsdirect.nhs.uk
US National Library of Medicine http://www.nlm.nih.gov
World Health Organization http://www.who.int/home-page

You'll find tons of excellent self-help megasites, though the presence of sponsors may raise ethical questions. Their features vary, but medical encyclopedias, personal health tests and Q&A services are fairly standard fare. Starting with the former US Surgeon General's site, try:

Dr Koop http://www.drkoop.com
HealthAtoZ.com http://www.healthatoz.com
HealthCentral http://www.healthcentral.com
HealthWorld http://www.healthy.net
Intelihealth http://www.intelihealth.com
Mayo Clinic http://www.mayoclinic.com
Netdoctor.co.uk http://www.netdoctor.co.uk
Surgery Door http://www.surgerydoor.co.uk
24Dr.com http://www.24dr.com
WebMD http://www.webmd.com
WebMD (Lycos) http://webmd.lycos.com
Yahoo Health http://health.yahoo.com

But for serious research go straight to Medline, the US National Library of Medicine's database. It archives, references and abstracts thousands of medical journals and periodicals going back to 1966. You can get it free at PubMed, but the subscription services may have access to more material. These are aimed more at health pros and students:

BioMedNet http://www.bmn.com
Medline Plus http://www.nlm.nih.gov/medlineplus/
Medscape http://www.medscape.com
Ovid http://www.ovid.com
PubMed http://www.ncbi.nlm.nih.gov/PubMed/

Despite first appearances, Martindale's maintains an outstanding directory of medical science links:

Martindale's Health Science guide
http://www-sci.lib.uci.edu/HSG/HSGuide.html

If you know what you have and you want to contact other sufferers, use a search engine (http://www.google.com) or directory (http://dmoz.org) to find organizations and personal home pages. They should direct you to useful mailing lists and discussion groups. If not, try Google Groups (http://groups.google.com) to find the right newsgroups, and PAML (http://www.paml.org) for mailing lists.

Acne Regimen
http://www.acne.org
Out, out damn spot.

Acupuncture.com
http://acupuncture.com
Probably the best and certainly the most comprehensive site dealing with Chinese medicine. As well as acupuncture, it covers Chinese herbal remedies, Qi Gong and Tui Na (massage) for patients, students and practitioners alike. For more information, try Oriental Medicine (http://www.orientalmedicine.com).

Alex Chiu's Eternal Life Device
http://www.alexchiu.com
Live forever or come back for your money.

All Nurses
http://www.allnurses.com
Springboard to chat groups, research data, professional bodies, jobs and other nursing resources.

Alexander YC Chiu

Eternal Life Device
Physical Immortality

alexchiu.com

Alternative Medicine

http://altmedicine.about.com
http://www.alternativemedicine.com
http://www.wholehealthmd.com
http://www.alternativedr.com
http://dmoz.org/Health/Alternative/

Part of the Net's ongoing research function is the ability to contact people who've road-tested alternative remedies and can report on their efficacy. Start here and work your way to an answer. See also the entry for Quackwatch.

Aromatherapy

http://www.aromaweb.com

Psuedoscience it might be (http://skepdic.com/aroma.html), but you'll be on the way to smelling better. And surely that can't be a bad thing.

Ask Dr Weil

http://www.drweil.com

Popdoctor Andrew Weil's eagerness to prescribe from a range of bewildering and often conflicting alternative therapies has seen him called a quack in some quarters, but not by Warner. *Time* put him on the front cover and gave him a job peddling advice beside vitamin ads. Whether or not you believe in food cures, his daily Q&As are always a good read.

Biopharm Leeches

http://www.biopharm-leeches.com

Cure your ailments the old-fashioned way.

The Biting Edge of Science

The leech was indispensable in 19th Century medicine for bloodletting, a practice believed to be a cure for anything from headaches to gout. Leeching was largely abandoned as medical science advanced, only occasionally being called upon to treat bruising and black eyes. However, the medicinal leech is making a comeback in modern medicine thanks in part to the work of Dr. Roy Sawyer, an American scientist who established the world's first leech farm. Based at Hendy near Swansea, South Wales, Biopharm is home to over 50,000 leeches which are supplied to hospitals and research laboratories around the world.

Health

Calorie Counter
http://www.caloriecounter.co.uk
Diet sensibly. For more dieting advice, check out the Open Directory's
Weight Loss pages (http://dmoz.org/Health/Weight_Loss/). To lose
"weight and hair through stress and poor nutrition", try The Hackers'
Diet (http://www.fourmilab.to/hackdiet/www/hackdietf.html/).

CancerHelp UK
http://www.cancerhelp.org.uk
Jargon-free guide to living with the disease, plus information on treatments, ongoing studies and trials.

Chirohelp.com
http://www.chirohelp.com
Don't get bent out of shape: this is a good introduction to chiropractic
health care.

Color Vision Test
http://www.umist.ac.uk/UMIST_OVS/UES/COLOUR0.HTM/
Do you dress in the dark or are you merely colour-blind?

ConsumerLab
http://www.consumerlab.com
An independent testing authority which publishes its studies online. It
tests herbal remedies, vitamins, supplements, sports products and
functional foods for effectiveness, purity, potency, consistency and
bioavailability (ie whether the body can deal with the product properly).

Dr Squat
http://www.drsquat.com
http://www.weightsnet.com
Avoid getting sand kicked in your face through deep full squats.

Drugs
http://www.erowid.org
http://www.lycaeum.org
http://www.trashed.co.uk
http://www.perkel.com/politics/issues/pot.htm
http://www.neuropharmacology.com
http://www.druglibrary.org

Everything you ever wanted to know about the pleasure, pain and politics of psychoactive drugs and the cultures built around them. Even more at Drugs, Solvents and Intoxicants (http://area51.upsu.plym.ac.uk/~harl/).

Embarrassing Problems
http://www.embarrassingproblems.com
Help with everything from anal itching to wind.

GYN101
http://www.gyn101.com
Swot up for your next gynaecological exam. But if you're after honours go straight to: http://www.obgyn.net

Gyro's Excellent Hernia Adventure
http://www.cryogenius.com/mesh
Holiday snaps from under the knife.

HandHeldMed
http://www.handheldmed.com
http://www.medicalpocketpc.com
http://www.pdamd.com
Arm your pocket computer with medical software and references.

Health Fitness Tips
http://www.health-fitness-tips.com
Ironically, the site itself is somewhat flabby, but hopefully the exercise tips, low-fat recipes and motivational quotes will help you shed the inches. For more instruction, try Netsweat (http://www.sickbay.com/netsweat/).

Internet Health Library
http://www.internethealthlibrary.com
Information on complementary therapy from the University of Essex.

Lab Tests
http://www.labtestsonline.org
Get inside your sample.

Health

Medicinal Herb Faq
http://ibiblio.org/herbmed/faqs/medi-cont.html
If it's in your garden and it doesn't kill you, it can only make you stronger. More leafy cures and love drugs at:
http://www.algy.com/herb/
http://www.botanical.com
http://www.herbal-ahp.org

Mental Health
http://www.mentalhealth.com
It's guaranteed that you'll come out of this site convinced there's something wrong with you. Worry your way along to
http://www.anxietynetwork.com

Museum of Questionable Medical Devices
http://www.mtn.org/quack
Gallery of health-enhancing products where even breaks weren't bundled free.

National Institute of Ayurvedic Medicine
http://niam.com/corp-web/
A good, low BS guide to balancing your life energies with the ancient Indian practice.

Violet Ray Generators

NOTICES OF JUD-GEMENT

3450. Misbranding of violet ray device, S. v. 2 Cases * * * (F. D.C. No. 30801. Sample no. 3838-L.):

LIBEL FILED: Between March 2 and April 24, 1951, District of Maryland.

ALLEGED

The device we are most often asked about is the Violet Ray Generator, sometimes called an "ultra violet device." Tens of thousands of these devices were sold for home use between about 1915 and 1950 under brand names such as Masters, Elco and Renulife. Literature accompanying the devices claimed to cure just about everything including heart disease, paralysis, wry neck and writers cramp!

19th Century Medical Curios
http://www.zoraskingdom.freeserve.co.uk
The Elephant Man, bearded women and other strange Victoriana.

Nutritional Supplements
http://www.nutritionalsupplements.com
First-hand experiences with vitamins, bodybuilding supplements, and other dubious health-shop fodder. For the real deal, go to the British Nutrition Foundation (http://www.nutrition.org.uk).

Quackwatch

http://www.quackwatch.com
http://www.ncahf.org
http://www.hcrc.org
http://nccam.nih.gov

Separating the docs from the ducks. Don't buy into any alternative remedies until you've read these pages.

Reuters Health

http://www.reutershealth.com

Medical newswires, reviews, opinion and reference.

RxList

http://www.rxlist.com
http://www.virtualdrugstore.com

Look up your medication to ensure you're not being poisoned.

Spas Directory

http://www.thespasdirectory.com

Locate a British spa or health resort.

Talk Surgery

http://www.talksurgery.com

Discuss your operation with people who appear interested.

ThinkNatural

http://www.thinknatural.com

Order homeopathic, herbal, Ayurvedic and Chinese remedies for next-day delivery, plus advice on how to use them properly.

Travel Health

http://www.travelhealth.co.uk

Come back in one piece.

The Virtual Hospital

http://www.vh.org

Patient care and distance learning via online multimedia tools such as illustrated surgical walkthroughs.

Virtual Periodontology
http://www.odont.lu.se/depts/par/virtual.html/
Click here if you don't want to end up in *The Simpsons'* "Big Book of British Smiles".

The Visible Human Project
http://www.nlm.nih.gov/research/visible/
Whet your appetite by skimming through scans of a thinly filleted serial killer, and then top it off with a fly-through virtual colonoscopy. For higher production values, see the Virtual Body:
http://www.medtropolis.com

What Have I Got?
http://www.whathaveigot.net
Worry yourself sick through self-diagnosis.

Wing Hop Fung
http://www.winghopfung.com
Chinese cures by mail order.

Womens' Health
http://www.bbc.co.uk/health/womens
A refreshingly relatively unbranded site from the Beeb.

World Sexual Records
http://www.sexualrecords.com
Go for gold in slap and tickle.

World Wide Online Meditation Center
http://www.meditationcenter.com
Connect with your essence.

The Yoga Site
http://www.yogasite.com
A good, general site on the various asanas and vinyasas so you can stretch yourself back into shape. For even better karma, try the Yoga Homepage (http://www.holisticonline.com/Yoga/hol_yoga_home.htm), Yoga Nation (http://www.yoganation.com) and Yoga Studio (http://www.timages.com/yoga.htm/).

History

ArchNet
http://archnet.asu.edu
Digital directory to online archeology sites with a leaning towards the academic. See also the Archaeological Resource Guide to Europe (http://odur.let.rug.nl/arge/), or for general history links, try History Links on the Internet (http://www.nyu.edu/gsas/dept/history/internet/).

BBC Online – History
http://www.bbc.co.uk/history/
As you'd expect, the Beeb's history pages are well designed and informative – if a bit too traditional and not as complete as you'd like.

Britannia
http://britannia.com/history/
Easily the best British history site on the Web, with biographies of the "bravest knights of the fourteenth Century", virtual tours of Sussex churches, a history of Welsh royalty and an electronic version of the *Anglo-Saxon Chronicle*.

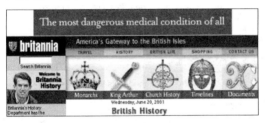

Dead Media Project
http://www.deadmedia.org
Documenting the roadkill on the information superhighway.

History Buff
http://www.historybuff.com
A collection of press clippings through the ages.

History Channel
http://www.historychannel.com
This Web home of the American cable TV channel has perhaps too much of an American slant for most British users, but it does have some great features like an amazing archive of great speeches, both as text and as RealAudio documents.

History House
http://www.historyhouse.com
Dedicated to rescuing history from the historians, this excellent American site tells the stories of real people with very real human foibles who have had an impact on the world's major and not so major events. A necessary corrective to the "great man of history" myths.

History Ring
http://members.tripod.com/~PHILKON/ring.html/
Homepage of the history ring, linking you to hundreds and hundreds of non-commercial history sites.

Internet History Sourcebooks Project
http://www.fordham.edu/halsall/
Professor Paul Halsall's site is a fantastic resource for students of history, especially the marginalized variety. His directory of Internet articles has links to thousands of articles on women's history, Jewish history, Islamic history, African history, lesbian and gay history, medieval studies and the more standard ancient and modern cultures.

Journal for Multimedia History
http://www.albany.edu/jmmh
Academic history journal with hyperlinked bells and whistles.

1940s Sound Library
http://freespace.virgin.net/ian.bayley/sounds/sounds.htm/
Ian Bayley's amazing sound archive of the 1940s, including Lord Haw Haw's broadcasts.

Regia Anglorum
http://www.regia.org
Relive the age of the vikings.

Hobbies

All Magic Guide
http://www.allmagicguide.com
Your passport to the world of illusion.

Antler Art
http://www.wic.net/antler/
Only in America number 2,346: "Enjoy antler art in a variety of settings"
including a table and chairs, bed stand, chandelier, hall table and mirror.

The Art & Science of Dumpster Diving
http://www.geocities.com/CollegePark/Union/7807/
Reconnect with your ancestral roots as a hunter-gatherer.

Balloon HQ
http://www.balloonhq.com
Become a part of pop culture.

The Contortion Home Page
http://www.contortionhomepage.com
Hey, Stretch, how do you do that?

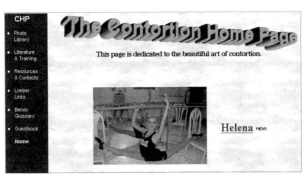

Hobbies

Experimental Aircraft
http://exp-aircraft.com
Online resource for lunatics interested in building their own planes.

Firewalking.com
http://www.firewalking.com
The official Website of Tolly Burkan, the father of the firewalking movement.

International String Figure Association
http://www.isfa.org
Perfect your cat's cradle technique.

Joseph Wu's Origami Page
http://www.origami.vancouver.bc.ca
Gateway to the wide world of paper folding, including diagrams, galleries and links. To make your folds fly see
http://www.paperairplanes.co.uk

Juggling Information Service
http://www.juggling.org
If you can't keep your balls up, this site has just about everything any sane human could ever want to know about juggling. There's a collection of juggling software so you can see how the pros do it, a history of juggling and other arcane stuff. For the "best beanbag kit on the market" try Juggling Store (http://www.jugglingstore.com).

Kitez
http://www.kitez.com
Go fly a kite at this dedicated search engine for kitesurfers.

Knots on the Web
http://www.earlham.edu/~peters/knotlink.htm/
Why knot?

Model Mart
http://www.modelmart.co.uk
Model online community for modellers. There's more putty filler at Scale
Models Central (http://www.geocities.com/Athens/Crete/1111/) and
Modelmasters Online (http://www.modelmasters-online.com).

NMRA Directory of World Wide Rail Sites
http://www.ribbonrail.com/nmra/
The National Model Railroad Association's vast site of model railway
links across the world.

Potato Cannon Fun Page
http://www.geocities.com/Yosemite/Rapids/1489/
Charm and delight your parents for years to come.

The Puppetry Homepage
http://www.sagecraft.com/puppetry/
The ups and downs of puppetry, from Animatronics to ventriloquism.

Reenactors World
http://www.reenactorsworldplus.com
A Web directory of sites devoted to historical re-enactment and living
history.

Rocketry.org
http://www.rocketry.org
Send your worst enemy to the Moon. To buy a "really big, potentially
dangerous aircraft loaded with large amounts of propellant", try
Suborbital (http://www.suborbital.com).

TreasureNet
http://www.treasurenet.com
Exchange tall tales and learn about metal detection.

Home Improvement

Ask the Builder
http://www.askthebuilder.com
An excellent site from American DIY columnist Tim Carter offering tons of advice from his archived columns and e-zines with a very good search engine.

Ask the Master Plumber
http://www.clickit.com/bizwiz/homepage/plumber.htm/
Save a small fortune by unblocking your own toilet.

B&Q
http://www.diy.com
They may dominate the British DIY market, but B&Q's Website is ugly (it looks like a circular inserted in a Sunday paper), clumsy and too expensive. Homebase (http://www.homebase.co.uk) is only slightly better.

BarPlans
http://www.barplans.com
Move the Queen Vic into your basement.

Buy.co.uk
http://www.buy.co.uk/Personal/
Clinch the best deal on UK utilities and loans.

Cooksons
http://www.cooksons.com
The best place for power tools on the Net, with loads of special offers and free delivery if you spend more than £45.

Coping With Winter
http://www.ag.ndsu.nodak.edu/coping/
Building a ski house in the Alps or moving to Irkutsk? Follow these building and DIY tips from North Dakota State University.

DIY Fix It
http://www.diyfixit.co.uk
Since most of the best DIY sites are American, this decent UK home
improvement encyclopedia is very useful for information regarding Brit-
specific problems.

Fine Homebuilding
http://www.taunton.com/fh/
American magazine for real DIY enthusiasts, with loads of information
on frame construction, garage doors, tools and safety.

HomeCentral
http://homecentral.sierrahome.com
Standard DIY site, but with a range of calculators and estimators that
will tell you the exact amount of paint and wallpaper you need for your
job or how much leaving the outside light on all night will cost.

Home Improvement Encyclopedia
http://www.bhglive.com/homeimp/
Lots of step-by-step guides and illustrated how-tos from the American
Better Homes and Gardens magazine. Again the information is designed
for Yanks, but the language is simple, the illustrations clear and the ani-
mated guides are a very clever idea.

Home Repair Stuff
http://www.factsfacts.com/MyHomeRepair/
Design-free site answering questions like "Which caulk?" and "Squirrel
in your belfry?", plus beginner's guides and basic tool kits.

Home Sewing Association
http://www.sewing.org
Pick up hints from a bunch of sew and sews.

Home Tips
http://www.hometips.com
http://www.homestore.com
http://www.doityourself.com
http://www.naturalhandyman.com
Load your toolbox, roll up your sleeves and prepare to go in.

Home Improvement

How to Clean Anything
http://www.howtocleananything.com
Just add elbow grease.

Improveline
http://www.improveline.com
http://www.homepro.com
Peruse the latest design ideas and find someone to do the job. You can
even screen your local builders against public records and find the one
least likely to quaff all your home brew and sell your nude holiday snaps
to the *National Enquirer*.

ImproveNet
http://improvenet.com
Yankee DIY giant with more advice, calculators, shopping facilities and
so on than any sane person can handle. It even includes archives from
Popular Mechanics and *Today's Homeowner* as well as energy conservation articles, project guides and personal project managers.

MFI
http://www.mfi.co.uk
Redo your kitchen with some modular cabinets. For more chi-chi
options, try Kensington Kitchens (http://www.kensington-kitchens
.co.uk), Magnet (http://www.magnet.co.uk) and PS4 Kitchens
(http://www.ps4kitchens.co.uk).

The Old House Web
http://www.oldhouseweb.net
An excellent resource for those restoring the old money-pit. Again, the site is American so the product info may not be entirely appropriate, but there are good articles on choosing the right primer, selecting synthetic slates and quick fixes for wallpaper repair problems.

ThePlumber.com
http://www.theplumber.com
Includes tips and online repair handbooks plus the history of plumbing from Babylonia through the inventions of Thomas Crapper to water-works in the White House. For more plumbing sites, try The PlumbingWeb (http://www.PlumbingWeb.com).

Skills Register
http://www.skills-register.com
Thinking of hiring a plumber or handyman? Try this great service: a directory of British tradespeople who have passed site owner Will Stevens' stringent quality assurance tests. For a bigger database, try Improveline (http://www.improveline.com).

This to That
http://www.thistothat.com
So what would you like to glue today?

Wacky Uses
http://www.wackyuses.com
Using Coca-Cola to clean corrosion from batteries, pantyhose to polish furniture and other wacky household hints from Joey Green.

Horoscopes and Fortune-telling

American Federation of Astrologers
http://www.astrologers.com
Impress your hairdresser by becoming a fully accredited seer by correspondence course.

Astro Advice
http://www.astroadvice.com
Aside from its treasure-trove of arcane astrological systems (like Nine Star Ki) and slightly dodgy advice pages (astrological financial forecasts, for example), this site's best feature is its free, in-depth astrological charts.

Astrology.com
http://www.astrology.com
This sprawling site contains advice and predictions from just about every soothsaying system under the sun. There are horoscopes both free and charged, past-life reports, celebrity horoscopes, self-empowerment guides, karmic profiles, crystal balls, Chinese astrological readings and plenty more.

Astrology – Atlas and Time Zone Database
http://www.astro.com/cgi-bin/atlw3/aq.cgi?lang=e
Know exactly what was happening upstairs the second of your birth. Or if you prefer your cold readings
(http://www.skepdic.com/coldread.html) with a touch less pseudoscientific mumbo-jumbo, try http://astrology.about.com or
http://www.astrocenter.com. Then see what old sensible shoes has to say: http://www.skepdic.com/astrolgy.html/

Biorhythm Generator
http://www.facade.com/attraction/biorhythm/
Generate a cyclical report that can double as a sick note.

Dreamstop
http://www.dreamstop.com
Analyse your night visions and jot them into a journal to share with your friends.

Ask the Eight Ball

There must be a hundred sites on the Web based on the old Magic Eight Ball toy. Here are some of the most novel twists on the theme.

Archie McPhee's Ask the Sarcastic Ball
http://www.archiemcphee.com/goodies/sarcastic.html/
Yeah, right.

Ask Bubba
http://www.arkansas-web.com/rednecksonly/askbubba/
Redneck agony uncle.

Ask Frank's Magic Hi-Ball
http://www.snarkbite.com/askfrank.htm/
Pearls of wisdom from Ol' Blue Eyes.

Ask a Klingon
http://www.ai.mit.edu/people/paulfitz/plank/advice.html/
Highly illogical advice.

The Magic Mr T Head
http://www.uidaho.edu/~bokm9606/magic/magict.htm/
Pity the fool who doesn't listen to him.

Mystical Smoking Head of Bob
http://www.resort.com/~banshee/Misc/8ball/
Articles of faith from the head of the Church of the Subgenius.

800 Predict
http://www.800predict.com
Put your hands on your mouse for free psychic readings, love compatibility charts, daily lottery numbers, love casts and star gossip.

Horoscopes and Fortune-telling

Free Will Astrology
http://www.freewillastrology.com
The homepage of guerrilla oracle and the funniest astrologer around, Rob Brezsny.

Metalog
http://www.astrologer.com
The home of the Astrological Association of Great Britain and the Centre for Psychological Astrology, this site "is devoted to promoting serious quality astrology; hopefully a place where many people will discover the richness of their own unique chart and learn that they are more than 'just' their sun-sign."

Mood Ring
http://www.ajcockrell.com/ajcockrell/moodring.htm/
Put your hands on your mouse and this site will tell you how you're really feeling.

◄ Back to ajcockrell.com

Welcome to the Mood Ring Page!

Click here to
tell a friend!

Slateblue is the color of love and joy. Talk about peace and inner harmony! You are supremely happy with yourself, with everyone and everything around you. Here it's good to have the Blues.

Oracle of Changes
http://www.iching.com
This excellent site enables you to virtually consult the I Ching, the ancient Chinese book of divination and soothsaying. The user casts coins into a pool six times which creates a hexagram that the oracle interprets according to the laws of ancient wisdom. See also:
http://www.facade.com/Occult/iching/

Panchang
http://www.panchang.com
Get a personalized time-planner based on this ancient Indian astrological system.

Past Life Regression
http://www.pastlives.cc
All the information you need to send your worst enemy back to the Stone Age.

Psyche Tests
http://www.psychtests.com
http://www.keirsey.com
http://www.queendom.com/tests.html/
http://www.emode.com
http://buster.cs.yale.edu/implicit/
So, what breed of dog are you? Smug sceptics (http://www.skepdic.com/myersb.html/) say you'll get closer to the truth here: http://www.learner.org/exhibits/personality/

RealAge
http://www.realage.com
Compare your biological and chronological ages. Here's how long you can expect to live: http://www.msnbc.com/modules/quizzes/lifex.asp/

Russell Grant Astrology
http://www.live-astro.com/horoscopes
Chirpy, cheerful advice from the chubby prognosticator, thankfully without having to look at his collection of garish sweaters.

Sarena's Tarot Page
http://www.talisman.net/tarot/
Look no further if you need help with your chandelier, fan or 7 triplet spreads. Also, for the expert only, a section on tarot spells. Also consult Tarot Magic (http://www.tarot.com).

Spirit Network

http://spiritnetwork.com

Portal for horoscopes, psychic readings, biorhythms, I Ching readings, paranormal activity and other New Age pursuits.

Stichomancy

http://www.facade.com/stichomancy/

Type in your question and the computer will choose a book and a passage at random that miraculously will apply to your query. See also Bibliomancy (http://www.facade.com/bibliomancy/), which chooses Bible passages at random to aid you in your quest for the answers.

The Voice of the Woods

http://www.pixelations.com/ogham

Seek guidance from the Ogham, an ancient Celtic divination method.

What's in your name?

http://www.kabalarians.com/gkh/your.htm/

The Kabalarians claim names can be boiled down to a numerical stew and served back up as a character analysis. Look yourself up in here and see what a duff choice your parents made. Then blame them for everything that's gone wrong since.

Kids and Teens

It's your choice whether to let them at it headlong or bridle their experience through rose-coloured filters. But if you need guidance or pointers towards the most kidtastic chowder, set sail into these realms:

American Libraries Assoc http://www.ala.org/parentspage/greatsites/

Cybersmart Kids http://www.cybersmartkids.com.au
Internet Detectives http://www.madison.k12.wi.us/tnl/detectives
Kids Click http://www.worldsofsearching.org
Kids Domain http://www.kidsdomain.com
NetMom http://www.netmom.com
Open Directory: Kids http://dmoz.org/Kids_and_Teens/
Scholastic International http://www.scholastic.com
Surfing the Net with Kids http://www.surfnetkids.com
Yahooligans (Yahoo for kids) http://www.yahooligans.com

The search engines Google and Altavista can also be set to filter out adult content. For encyclopedias and dictionaries, see p.274.

Barbie
http://www.barbie.com
It's a huge, Flash-intensive, slow-loading site, but there's a massive amount of stuff here to keep any girl entertained for hours – so just give in to the inevitable.

Beakman & Jax
http://www.bonus.com
Answers to typical kid questions from the likes of "why poo is brown" and "why farts smell" to "why your voice sounds different on a tape recorder" and "why the TV goes crazy while the mixer is on".

The Belch Page
http://www.goobo.com/belch/
Gross out your parents and your little sister.

Bigchalk
http://www.bigchalk.com
Study collections for all grades through to college.

Bizarre Things You Can Make In Your Kitchen
http://freeweb.pdq.net/headstrong/
Rainy-day science projects and general mischief such as volcanoes, stink bombs, cosmic ray detectors, fake blood and hurricane machines.

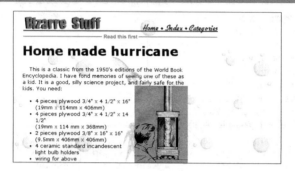

Home • Index • Categories

Bizarre Stuff
— Read this first —

Home made hurricane

This is a classic from the 1950's editions of the World Book Encyclopedia. I have fond memories of seeing one of these as a kid. It is a good, silly science project, and fairly safe for the kids. You need:

- 4 pieces plywood 3/4" x 4 1/2" x 16" (19mm x 114mm x 406mm)
- 4 pieces plywood 3/4" x 4 1/2" x 14 1/2" (19mm x 114 mm x 368mm)
- 2 pieces plywood 3/8" x 16" x 16" (9.5mm x 406mm x 406mm)
- 4 ceramic standard incandescent light bulb holders
- wiring for above

Bob the Builder
http://www.bobthebuilder.org
Yes, he can.

Bullying Online
http://www.bullying.co.uk
Advice and support channels for bullied children and their parents. Perhaps a few sessions of self-defence might be a good place to start: http://www.blackbeltmag.com/bbkids/

The Bug Club
http://www.ex.ac.uk/bugclub/
Creepy-crawly fan club with e-pal page, newsletters and pet care sheets on how to keep your newly bottled tarantulas, cockroaches and stick insects alive.

Children's Literature Web Guide
http://www.ucalgary.ca/~dkbrown/
Critical roundup of recent kids' books and links to texts.

Club Girl Tech
http://www.girltech.com
Encourages smart girls to get interested in technology without coming across all geeky.

Cyberteens
http://www.cyberteens.com
Submit your music, art or writing to a public gallery. You might even win a prize.

Decoding Nazi Secrets
http://www.pbs.org/wgbh/nova/decoding/
http://www.thunk.com
Use World War II weaponry to exchange secret messages with your clued-in pals.

Disney.com
http://www.disney.com
Guided catalogue of Disney's real-world movies, books, theme parks, records, interactive CD-ROMs and such, plus a squeaky-clean Net directory. For an unofficial Disney chaperone, see:
http://laughingplace.com

eHobbies
http://www.ehobbies.com
Separating junior hobbyists from their pocket money.

Funbrain
http://www.funbrain.com
Tons of mind-building quizzes, games and puzzles for all ages.

Funschool
http://www.funschool.com
Educational games for preschoolers.

Goofyface
http://www.goofyface.com
Gurning from the pros.

what's new at goofyface.com

Goofyface.com continues its journalistic tradition with this month's **Goofy Gazette**. At the **Goofy Gazette**, we provide formal documentation of our illustrious gooficolonial achievements. The **Goofy Gazette** takes a unique and hard (and slightly twisted) nosed look at the events that make up our Goofy world. As the photograph attests, even world leaders are never too far away from a good goof.

Goosebumps
http://www.tcfhe.com:80/goosebumps/thrillold.html/
Scary stories for your next sleepover.

The History Net
http://www.thehistorynet.com
http://www.historybuff.com
Bites of world history with an emphasis on the tough guys going in with guns.

Horse-Country.com
http://www.horse-country.com
A great site for horse-crazy kids, with a seemingly endless array of games and quizzes designed to teach children about horses and how to care for them.

The Idea Box
http://www.theideabox.com
If your preschoolers are bored of *Teletubbies* already, try this site for
activities to keep them entertained.

Kid's Domain
http://www.kidsdomain.com
Huge array of stuff here for kids and their parents: brain-builders, games
(both online and downloadable), tips on safe surfing, Pokémon, crafts,
desktop icons, etc. A similar service is provided by atkidz
(http://www.atkidz.com).

Kids' Games
http://dmoz.org/Kids_and_Teens/Games
http://www.wicked4kids.com
http://www.kidsdomain.com/games/
http://www.randomhouse.com/seussville/games/
http://games.yahoo.com/games/yahooligans.html/
Give the babysitter a break.

Kids' Jokes
http://www.kidsjokes.co.uk
http://www.users.bigpond.com/lander/
Reams of clean jokes, riddles and knock-knocks.

Kids-Party
http://www.kids-party.com
Ideas to prevent your child from crying at their own birthday party.

Kids' Space
http://www.kids-space.org
Hideout for kids to swap art, music and stories with new friends across
the world.

Liana's Paper Doll Boutique
http://www-personal.umich.edu/~lsharer/paperdolls/
If you've got a printer you've now got a rather large paper doll collection, with costumes ranging from ballerina outfits to Scarlett O'Hara.

The Little Animals Activity Centre
http://www.bbc.co.uk/education/laac/
The second the music starts and the critters start jiggling you know you're in for a treat. Let your youngest heir loose here after breakfast and expect no mercy until afternoon tea. As cute as it gets.

Magic Tricks
http://www.magictricks.com
http://www.trickshop.com
http://www.magicweek.co.uk
Never believe it's not so.

Neopets
http://www.neopets.com
Nurture a "virtual pet" until it dies.

Roper's Knots
http://www.realknots.com
It's not what you know; it's what knots you know.

Secret Languages
http://www.yahooligans.com/content/ka/almanac/language/lan00010.html
Learn Double Dutch, Pig Latin and Skimono Jive.

Seussville
http://www.randomhouse.com/seussville/
The online home of the Cat in the Hat, Sam-I-Am, Horton, The Grinch and The Whos.

Sing Along Midis and Lyrics
http://www.niehs.nih.gov/kids/musicchild.htm/
Gather round for a spot of keyboard karaoke.

StarChild
http://starchild.gsfc.nasa.gov
Nasa's educational funhouse for junior astronomers. See also
http://www.earthsky.com and http://www.starport.com

Star Wars Origami
http://www.ftmax.com/ArtLife/Origami.html
Graduate from flapping birds onto Destroyer Droids and Tie Fighters.
Prefer something that will actually fly? See: http://www.aricraft.com. For
more paperfolding, try: http://www.origami.com

Teen Advice
http://www.teenadvice.net
Part of the enormous Student Center Network, this site has loads of
forums and experts for advice on anything from acne to (surprise, surprise) sex. For more advice on tricky subjects, try Embarrassing
Problems (http://www.embarrassingproblems.co.uk).

Law and Crime

Toy Stores
http://www.faoschwartz.com
http://www.imaginarium.com
http://www.toysrus.co.uk
It's just like Christmas all year round.

The Unnatural Museum
http://www.unmuseum.org
Lost worlds, dinosaurs, UFOs, pyramids and other mysterious exhibits from the outer bounds of space and time.

The Yuckiest Site on the Internet
http://www.yucky.com
Fun science with a leaning towards the icky-sticky and the creepy-crawly. But if you want to get thoroughly engrossed in the gross, slither right along to: http://www.grossology.org

Law and Crime

For legal primers, lawyer directories, legislation and self-help:
Compact Law http://www.compactlaw.co.uk
Delia Venables http://www.venables.co.uk
FindLaw http://www.findlaw.com
InfoLaw http://www.infolaw.co.uk
UKLegal http://www.uklegal.com

For more on criminal activities, trends, arrests and law enforcement, rustle through the following guides:
About Crime http://crime.about.com
Crime Spider http://www.crimespider.com
Open Directory http://dmoz.org/Society/Crime/

A–Z Guide to British Employment Law
http://www.emplaw.co.uk
Get the upper hand on your boss.

The Absolute Worst Things to Say to a Police Officer
http://www.geocities.com/Heartland/Prairie/7559/copjokes.html/
"Aren't you the guy from The Village People?"

APBnews.com
http://www.apbonline.com
Highly acclaimed network news service focusing on crime, justice and safety.

Brutal.com
http://www.brutal.com
Bad news from around the world, as it breaks.

Burglar.com
http://www
.theburglar.com
Profit from stolen goods that some-how happened to be in your posses-sion.

Copyright Myths
http://whatiscopyright.org
http://www.templetons.com/brad/copyright.html
Just because it's online doesn't make it yours.

The Court Service
http://www.courtservice.gov.uk
In amongst all the dull information and legalese is a collection of recent judgements handed down by the country's Justices.

Crime Magazine
http://www.crimemagazine.com
Encyclopedic collection of outlaw tales.

Cybercrime
http://www.cybercrime.gov
http://www.cybersnitch.net
How to report online crooks.

Law and Crime

Desktop Lawyer
http://www.desktoplawyer.net
Cut legal costs by doing it online.

Divorce Online
http://www.divorce-online.co.uk
DIY D.I.V.O.R.C.E. for residents of England and Wales.

Dumb Crooks
http://www.dumbcrooks.com
Let the masters teach you how not to do it.

Dumb Laws
http://www.dumblaws.com
Foreign legislation with limited appeal.

ECLS
http://www.e-commercelawsource.com
Global monitor and directory of online business law.

The Evidence Store
http://www.evidencestore.com
"Need a hand for your day in court? How about a foot or a skull? ... Accident reconstructions? The Evidence Store's experts will create all the visual exhibits you'll need to educate even the toughest jury."

Famous Mugshots
http://www.mugshots.org
Lifestyles of the rich and famous.

FBI Files
http://foia.fbi.gov/alpha.htm/
Download the FBI's reports released by the Freedom of Information Act on the Black Panthers, Al Capone, Pablo Picasso, Elvis and Winston Churchill.

Law and Crime

Freelawyer
http://www.freelawyer.co.uk
Ask a legal question and get a jargon-free response from a qualified solicitor with a list of local specialists as well as no-obligation estimates.

Gang Land
http://www.ganglandnews.com
This amazing site from former New York *Daily News* reporter Jerry Capeci has just about everything you could want to know about Salvatore "Sammy Bull" Gravano, John Gotti, Wing Yeung Chan and their ilk.

Guide to Lock Picking
http://www.lysator.liu.se/mit-guide/mit-guide.html/
Never climb in through the window again.

Legal Services Commission
http://www.legal-aid.gov.uk
Information on Community Legal Service and Criminal Defence Service from the public body that oversees their administration.

Police Officer's Directory
http://www.officer.com
http://www.cops.aust.com
http://www.crimespider.com
Top of the pops cop directory with more than 1500 baddy-nabbing bureaux snuggled in with law libraries, wanted listings, investigative tools, hate groups, special ops branches and off-duty homepages. To see who's in Scotland Yard's bad books: http://www.met.police.uk

Police Scanner
http://www.policescanner.com
Listen in on busts in progress by the NY, LA, Dallas and San Diego police departments.

PursuitWatch
http://www.pursuitwatch.com
Get paged when there's a live police chase on TV.

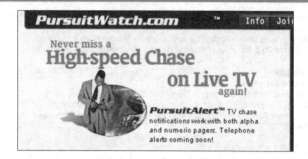

Rate your risk
http://www.nashville.net/~police/risk/
See if you're likely to be robbed, stabbed, shot or beaten to death in the near future.

Society of Will Writers
http://freespace.virgin.net/society.willwriters/
Information on wills and bequests from the will writers' professional body.

Speedtrap.com
http://www.speedtrap.com
Ironically, this site is rather slow, but still a great resource for drivers who want to know, umm, where traffic flashpoints might occur. See also UK Speed Traps (http://www.ukspeedtraps.co.uk).

Video Vigilante
http://www.videovigilante.com
If you lived in Oklahoma City, what else would you do but wander the city streets with a video camera looking for guys picking up prostitutes?

Museums and Galleries

Homepages of bricks-and-mortar museums

British Museum http://www.thebritishmuseum.ac.uk
Guggenheim http://www.guggenheim.org
The Hermitage http://www.hermitagemuseum.org
Louvre http://www.louvre.fr
Metropolitan Museum of Art http://www.metmuseum.org
Museo Del Prado http://museoprado.mcu.es
Museum of Modern Art http://www.moma.org
National Gallery http://www.nationalgallery.co.uk
National Portrait Gallery http://www.npg.org.uk
Natural History Museum http://www.nhm.ac.uk
Tate Gallery http://www.tate.org.uk
Uffizi Gallery http://www.uffizi.firenze.it
Victoria & Albert Museum http://www.vam.ac.uk

Artists

Leonardo da Vinci http://sunsite.dk/cgfa/vinci
Matisse http://www.ocaiw.com/matisse.htm
Michelangelo http://www.ibiblio.org/wm/paint/auth/michelangelo
Monet http://webpages.marshall.edu/~smith82/monet.html
Picasso http://www.tamu.edu/mocl/picasso/
Rembrandt http://www.ibiblio.org/wm/paint/auth/rembrandt
Van Gogh http://www.vangoghgallery.com

ArtMuseum
http://www.artmuseum.net
Infrequent exhibitions of modern US classics.

Museums and Galleries

Bad Art
http://www.badart.com

Di With Sty, Orange Maiden and *Still Life With Agony Faces* are just some of the masterpieces enshrined here – you won't see them anywhere else but your local charity shop. Meanwhile, http://www.glyphs .com/moba is the Web presence of Boston, Massachusetts' bricks-and-mortar shrine to good artists gone bad.

Bitstreams
http://www.whitney.org/bitstreams/

A fine exhibit of minimal digital art from New York's Whitney Museum, with downloadable art.

British Lawnmower Museum
http://www.lawnmowerworld.co.uk

SEE: the world's fastest lawnmower. SEE: Prince Charles's lawnmower. SEE: the water-cooled egg boiler lawnmower. SEE: Vanessa Feltz's lawnmower.

Dia Center for the Arts
http://www.diacenter.org

Web exclusives from "extraordinary" artists, plus the lowdown on the NY Dia Center's upcoming escapades.

The Exploratorium
http://www.exploratorium.edu

No substitute for visiting this great San Francisco museum in the flesh, but The Exploratorium's Website is filled with fun and educational sections on sports medicine, the solar system, the Hubble Telescope and the Panama Pacific Exposition.

Isometric Screenshots
http://whitelead.com/jrh/screenshots/
An online exhibition by artist Jon Haddock in which he has rendered some of the 20th century's defining moments (the protests at Tianamen Square, the beating of Rodney King, the assassination of Martin Luther King) in the visual style of video games.

Museum of Menstruation and Women's Health
http://www.mum.org
Its curator may be a man, but this is a rather weird and wonderful site that takes its subject pretty seriously.

Sulabh International Museum of Toilets
http://www.sulabhtoiletmuseum.org/
There goes the neighbourhood.

24 Hour Museum
http://www.24hourmuseum.org.uk
Portal for British museums, with an excellent search feature which allows you to look for museums with food, baby changing facilities or that tie in with national curriculum requirements. Also try MuseumNetwork (http://www.museumnetwork.com) or Museums Around the World (http://www.icom.org/vlmp/world.html/). For galleries as well as museums see The Art Guide (http://www.artguide.org) or The Gallery Channel (http://www.thegallerychannel.com).

Unusual Museums of the Internet
http://www.unusualmuseums.org
Homepage of the Unusual Museums Webring, your gateway to such exotic destinations as the Toilet Paper Museum, World of Crabs, Cigar Box Art and the Toilet Seat Art Museum.

Washington Banana Museum
http://www.geocities.com/NapaValley/1799/
The world's greatest collection of banana ephemera. No plantains, please.

Web Gallery of Art
http://gallery.euroweb.hu
For fans of everything from Giotto frescoes to Rembrandt's *The Nightwatch*, this fantastic site houses digital reproductions of some 8000 works from between 1150 and 1750.

Web Museum
http://www.southern.net/wm/
Easily one of the best sites on the Web, the Web Museum hosts a fantasy collection of art – like having the Louvre, the Metropolitan Museum of Art, the Hermitage and the Prado all right around the corner. There is also an extensive glossary of terms, artist biographies and enlightening comment on each of the works displayed.

Music

If you're at all into music you've certainly come to the right place. Whether you want to hear it, read about it or watch it being performed you'll be swamped with options. If you're after a specific band, label or music genre, the Ultimate Band List on Artists Direct should be your first port of call:

Ultimate Band List http://www.ubl.com

Then try these directories:

About.com http://about.com/arts
Open Directory http://dmoz.org/Arts/Music/

SonicNet http://www.sonicnet.com/allmusic/
Yahoo http://launch.yahoo.com

As ever, if these fail to satisfy, try:
Google http://www.google.com

For an astoundingly complete music database spanning most popular genres, with bios, reviews, ratings, and keyword crosslinks to related sounds, sites, and online ordering, see:
All Music Guide http://www.allmusic.com

And don't overlook our own printed guides to Rock, Reggae, Drum & Bass, Jazz, Classical, House, Techno, Soul, World and Opera:
Rough Guides to Music http://www.roughguides.com

Much of the mainstream music press is already well established online. For the latest music news:

Artists Direct http://artistsdirect.com

You'll find thousands of archived reviews, charts, gig guides, band bios, selected features, shopping links, news, and various sound artefacts courtesy of these familiar beacons:
Billboard http://www.billboard.com
Blues and Soul http://www.bluesandsoul.co.uk
Dirty Linen http://kiwi.futuris.net/linen/
Folk Roots http://www.frootsmag.com
Mojo http://www.mojo4music.com
NME http://nme.com
Q http://www.q4music.com
Rolling Stone http://www.rollingstone.com
Spin http://www.spin.com
Vibe http://www.vibe.com

Buying records online

Shopping for music is another area where the Net not only equals but outshines its terrestrial counterparts. Apart from the convenience of not having to tramp across town, you can find almost anything on current issue, whether or not it's released locally, and in many cases preview album tracks in RealAudio. You might save money, too, depending on where you buy, whether you're hit with tax and how the freight costs stack up. Consider splitting your order if duty becomes an issue.

The biggest hitch you'll find is when stock is put on back order. Web operators can boast a huge catalogue simply because they order everything on the fly, putting you at the mercy of their distributors. The trouble is your entire order might be held up by one item. The better shops check their stock levels before confirming your order and follow its progress until delivery.

As far as where to shop goes, that depends on your taste, but, unless your tastes are very esoteric, you can't go too far wrong with most of the blockbusters:

Amazon **http://www.amazon.co.uk**
AudioStreet **http://www.audiostreet.co.uk**
BOL **http://www.uk.bol.com**
CDNow **http://www.cdnow.com**
HMV **http://www.hmv.com**
101 CD **http://www.101cd.com**
Tower Records **http://uk.towerrecords.com**
Virgin Megastore **http://www.virginmega.com**

Or, if you're after something more obscure, you'll find no shortage of options under the appropriate Yahoo categories or at: **http://www.offitsface.com/links.html/**

Like these, for example:
Aquarius **http://www.aquariusrecordssf.com**
The online presence of one of America's best record shops is perhaps even better than visiting its hallowed halls in person. Simple to navigate and constantly updated, the selection (everything from

Sounds of North American Frogs to *Super Duck Breaks*) is hard to beat and the reviews are funny, engaging and informative.

CDEmusic http://www.cdemusic.org
This American site carries not only electronic music from a time when it was made only by men in white labcoats but specialist books, music software and seriously sexy musical equipment like the Moog Moogerfooger processor.

CD Wow http://www.cd-wow.com
Cheap chart CDs (£9 at press time). See also Play 247 (http://www.play.com).

CyberCD http://www.cybercd.de • http://www.musicexpress.com
German outfits with enormous catalogues, though not so cheap.

Desscarga http://www.descarga.com
If you are a fan of Latin music, you must, must check out this site. ¡Sabroso!

Dusty Groove http://www.dustygroove.com
The Website of this renowned Chicago record shop created the blueprint for Internet-based record mail order services, and they're

still doing it better than anyone else. If you're interested in hip-hop, funk, soul, reggae, Latin or obscure soundtracks, it's nearly impossible to leave the site empty-handed.

Buying records online (continued)

Forced Exposure http://www.forcedexposure.com
This Massachusetts distributor is the colossus of underground music, and its informative, easy-to-use Website is another jewel in its crown. Along with an excellent search feature (which, unlike too many mail order sites, searches the personnel lists as well as the main artist name), the reviews are opinionated and informative.

Global Electronic Music Market http://gemm.com
One-point access to over two million new and used records from almost two thousand sources. See also: http://www.secondspin.com

Hard to find records http://www.htfr.com
Record-finding agency that specializes in house, hip-hop, soul and disco vinyl.

Other Music http://www.othermusic.com
Since opening in 1996 opposite Tower Records, New York City's bastion of the weird, wacky and just plain great has made a name for itself as one of America's best record emporia. Divided into sections like "Out" (avant-garde music from this world and others), "In" ('90s indie rock) and "Le Decadanse" (sophisto pop), its site embodies the virtues that made it so good in the first place: friendly, helpful and attitude-free.

Penny Black http://www.pennyblackmusic.com
Indie pop, punk and electronica.

Record Finder http://www.recordfinders.com
Deleted vinyl, including over 200,000 45s.

Rough Trade http://www.roughtrade.com
The Website of London's underground landmark is housed in a slick designer package. It would benefit from less time-consuming graphics, but the stock is excellent and the prices, while not the bargain level of the giants, ain't bad. Additional bonuses include an old t-shirt section, chat rooms and downloads – plus there's no tricky spiral staircase to navigate.

Sandbox Automatic http://www.sandboxautomatic.com
Without a doubt the best source for independent hip-hop on the Net. There are no bells and whistles, but what a choice.

Secondsounds http://www.secondsounds.com
Buying used CDs online may be even more risky than in an actual shop because you can't check out the merchandise, but if you're after a bargain this site is hard to beat.

Sterns African Records Centre http://www.sternsmusic.com
The UK's number-one retailer of world music does a fine job online as well.

For a listing of price comparison agents, see Shopping (p.302).

Cooking your own CD

Fancy whipping up your own custom CD but don't have the equipment? Simply run through the catalogue, preview what looks good, submit your track listing, and they'll burn it to disc:

CD Now http://www.cdnow.com
Emusic http://www.emusic.com
Razorcuts http://www.razorcuts.co.uk

And if your concentration is up to it, MTV:

Europe http://www.mtveurope.com
UK http://www.mtv.co.uk

Don't buy a stereo component until you've consulted the world's biggest audio opinionbases:

AudioReview.com http://www.audioreview.com
AudioWeb http://www.audioweb.com
What Hi-Fi http://www.whathifi.com

Or if you wouldn't settle for less than a single-ended triode amp:

Audiophilia http://www.audiophilia.com
GlassWare http://www.glass-ware.com
Stereophile http://www.stereophile.com
Triode Guild http://www.meta-gizmo.com

Consult these directories for manufacturers, shops and other audio sites:

AudioWorld http://www.audioworld.com
Hifiheaven.com http://www.hifiheaven.com
UK Hi-Fi Dealers http://hifi.dealers.co.uk

Addicted to Noise
http://www.addict.com
Monthly news and reviews with a heavy bias towards the rowdy end of the pop rock spectrum.

African Music
http://www.africanmusic.org
World Music aficionados should make a beeline for this library, search-able by country or artist, and with an accompanying shopping area.

All About Jazz
http://www.allaboutjazz.com
Don't let the expensive corporate layout fool you, this American site doesn't just cover Kenny G. As its name suggests, it aims to deal with the entire spectrum of jazz from Anthony Braxton to John Scofield. That

it succeeds is down to an easily navigable layout, a wealth of info and contributions from the biggest names in jazz journalism.

Ari's Simple List of Record Labels
http://recordlabels.nu/index.htm
Exactly what it says on the tin.

Art of the Mixed Tape
http://www.artofthemix.org
"If you have ever killed an afternoon making a mix, spent the evening making a cover, and then mailed a copy off to a friend after having made a copy for yourself, well, this is the site for you." Kind of says it all, really.

The Bad MIDI Museum
http://littleitaly.fortunecity.com/vatican/791/midi.htm
Not that even "good" MIDI doesn't suck.

B-Boys.com
http://www.b-boys.com
Hip-hop portal with lots of multimedia content.

Boom Selection
http://boomselection.n3.net
The headquarters of the British bootleg mix scene.

Canonical List of Weird Band Names
http://www.geminiweb.net/bandnames/
Just be thankful your parents weren't so creative. Here's the story behind a few: http://www.heathenworld.com/bandname/

Classical Music on the Net
http://www.musdoc.com/classical/
http://www.gmn.com/classical/
Gateway to the timeless.

Classical Net
http://www.classical.net
An excellent resource for the beginner, with guides to the basic reper-toire and building a CD collection. More adventurous listeners may find it a bit wanting, however.

Music

The Covers Project
http://covers.wiw.org
The musical version of Six Degrees of Kevin Bacon.

The Dance Music Resource
http://www.juno.co.uk
New and forthcoming dance releases for mail order, UK radio slots and a stacked directory.

Dancetech
http://www.dancetech.com
One-stop shop for techno toys and recording tips. For more on synths, try http://www.synthzone.com and http://www.sonicstate.com. For software downloads, guitar tabs and loads of other resources for musicians, try http://www.hitsquad.com

Dave D's Hip-Hop Corner
http://www.daveyd.com
Hip-hop portal, more at http://www.rapstation.com

Desktop Theremin
http://www.bbc.co.uk/science/playground/theremin1.shtml
Re-create the *Forbidden Planet* soundtrack or "Good Vibrations" at home.

Detritus
http://www.detritus.net
An excellent Website devoted to the fringes working on "recycled culture".

Dial-the-Truth Ministries
http://www.av1611.org
So why does Satan get all the good music?

Dictionaraoke
http://www.dictionaraoke.org
Hilarious MIDI/Talking Dictionary versions of all your favourite pop hits.

Digizine
http://www.digidesign.com/digizine
E-zone dedicated to Pro Tools, *the* music editing tool.

Disco-Disco.com

http://www.disco-disco.com/index.html
Where disco is more than just afro wigs and flares. More strobe-lit remembrances at http://www.discomusic.com/index.html

DJ University

http://dju.prodj.com
Become a wedding spinner.

Donna's Long and Short of It

http://www.metal-sludge.com/LongShort.htm/
The most essential music resource on the Net: Donna and her gaggle of groupies give you the lowdown on the vitals of 150+ heavy metal gods.

dotmusic

http://www.dotmusic.com
Top source of UK and global music news, weekly charts, and new releases in RealAudio. See also: http://www.music3w.com

The Droplift Project

http://www.droplift.org
Join in some plunderphonic fun by smuggling some avant-garde sampladelic CDs onto the shelves of major chain retailers.

Electronic Musical Instruments

http://www.obsolete.com/120_years/
From the ondes martenot to the sampler, this online museum is the liveliest, least techie source of information on the rapidly expanding world of music technology.

Everything Starts With an E

http://www.everythingstartswithe.co.uk
Sorted old skool rave site with vintage mixes from the early '90s.

Music

Evil Music
http://www.evilmusic.com
Don't know the difference between Black Metal and Doom Metal, or
what constitutes Original Death Metal as opposed to Brutal Death
Metal? Let Spinoza Ray Prozac be your guide to the dark world of the
Metal underground.

Fat Lace
http://www.fat-lace.com
The Internet presence of the hilarious "Magazine for ageing B-boys" contains mostly copy from the print version which covers hip-hop with an
irreverent slant only possible in the UK. An added bonus is the Random
Old School Name Generator for all the Lord Disco Loves out there.

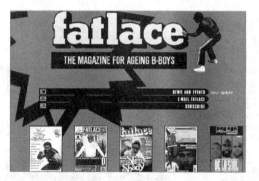

Freestyling
http://www.freestyling.com
Fancy yourself as the next Tupac or Jay-Z? Post your best rhyme here
and wait to be discovered. For more traditional battling, try Ughh
(http://www.ughh.com).

Funk45.com
http://www.funk45.com
A great entrée into the murky world of deep funk collecting. The site is
chock-full of MP3s and RealAudio files of hopelessly obscure funk
records. The only catch is that the files are only one minute long, with

the aim being to introduce people to this arcane world rather than destroying its informal economy.

Funky Groovy Lexicon
http://www.funk.ch/funk-lexikon.htm
Over 322 pages (in PDF format), the FGL catalogues nearly everything that can be construed as funky, from 100 Proof Aged in Soul to Zzebra. There's also a gallery of suave cats in dashikis and killer Afros. Believe it or not, it's from Switzerland.

Garage Music
http://www.garagemusic.co.uk
If you don't live in the East End and want to keep up with what the pirates are playing, click here for the latest news, events and downloads. See also http://www.dubplate.net

Get Out There
http://www.getoutthere.bt.com
Expose your unsung talents or listen to other unsigned acts. More audition opportunities at http://www.aandronline.com. For tips on getting signed try http://www.getsigned.com

Gracenote
http://www.cddb.com
Automatically supplies track listings for the CDs playing in your PC drive.

Gramophone
http://www.gramophone.co.uk
There is no better site for serious classical music aficionados. The Web home of *Gramophone* magazine boasts access to its database of 25,000 CD reviews. Need more reasons to visit? How about audio clips, the option to buy from the site, links, listings, glossary, artist bios and feature articles?

Groupie Central
http://www.groupiecentral.com
More than just a repository of tales of decadence and bad sex, this often eye-popping forum is by turns sly, knowing, empowering, brutal and, of course, risqué.

Harmony Central
http://www.harmonycentral.com
Directory and headspace for musicians of all persuasions.

Hot Concerts
http://www.hotconcerts.com
Performances from everyone from Tricky to Blue Oyster Cult.

Hyperreal
http://www.hyperreal.org
Perhaps the godfather of all music sites, Hyperreal has been going since 1992. It's a one-stop window shop for all things rave and Ambient. Erowid's Psychoactive Vaults host the raver's version of the *Physician's Desk Reference* – a library of info on mind-altering substances.

Independent Underground Music Archive
http://www.iuma.com
Full-length tracks and bios from thousands of unsigned and indie-label underground musicians.

Jazz
http://www.jazzreview.com
http://www.allaboutjazz.com
http://www.downbeat.com
Bottomless drawer of beard-stroking delights.

Kareoke.com
http://www.kareoke.com
Sing along in the privacy of your own home.

Kompaktkiste
http://www.kompaktkiste.de
The bluffer's guide to electronic music: an extensive list of
CDs of electronic music
organized by artist with track
listings and running times. It
makes no judgements, but if
you're looking for that hard to
find Phthalocyanine remix,
come here first.

Large Hot Pipe Organ
http://www.lhpo.org
Thrill to the throb of the world's first MIDI-controlled, propane-powered, explosion organ.

Launch.com
http://launch.yahoo.com
Thousands of music videos, audio channels, record reviews and chat forums.

Libretto List
http://php.indiana.edu/~lneff/libmlist.html/
A fantastic resource for opera buffs, this site has links to just about every public domain libretto available on the Net.

London Musicians Collective
http://www.l-m-c.org.uk
The LMC has been promoting the cause of improvised music in the Big Smoke for over a quarter of a century. Their site features content from their journal, *Resonance*, streaming audio from their radio show and information on studio facilities.

Lyrics Search Engine
http://lyrics.astraweb.com
Finding song lyrics on the Web is a science constantly fraught with difficulty due to copyright laws, but for now this site reigns. See also http://www.thesonglyrics.com

The Manual
http://www.klf.de/online/books/bytheklf/manual.htm/
Think you can do better than Hear'Say? Have a glance at the essential guide to pop superstardom, written by the ace pranksters in The KLF.

Metal Sudge
http://www.metal-sludge.com
Heavy metal portal that treats the genre with the dignity and respect it deserves.

MIDI Farm
http://www.midifarm.com
Synthesized debasements of pop tunes, TV themes, and film scores. More cheesy listening at MIDI Buddy (http://johnsworld.com/midi/) and MIDI World (http://www.midi-world.net/).

Minidisc.org
http://www.minidisc.org
Keep in tune with Sony's troubled Minidisc format.

Mr Lucky
http://www.mrlucky.com
Get smooth with rhythm 'n' booze.

Niceup
http://www.niceup.com
Probably the most irie reggae site on the Net, Niceup contains discographies, articles on topics like "Studio One Riddims", a lyrics archive, histories, news and a Patois dictionary.

Online Guitar Archive
http://www.olga.net
A truly awesome site for guitarists and bassists. No more scurrying through back issues of *Guitar Player* for tablature for Blue Öyster Cult's "Godzilla" – OLGA boasts some 40,000 tabs.

Opprobrium
http://www.info.net.nz/opprobrium/
No longer printed on paper, the legendary *Opprobrium* has been strictly digital ever since editor Nick Cain moved to London. Nevertheless, its coverage of avant jazz, Japanoise, Improv and radical minimalism remains almost peerless.

Original Hip Hop Lyrics Archive
http://www.ohhla.com
Mind-blowingly complete archive of all of your favourite rhymes.

Perfect Sound Forever
http://www.furious.com/perfect/
Calling itself "the online magazine with the warped attitudes", PSF is

one of the best music sites on the Net. Although most of the articles are straight interview transcripts and don't take advantage of the Web format, the writing on leftfield heroes is passionate and informative.

Rap Dictionary
http://www.rapdict.org
Can't understand your teenage son anymore? Log on here, dun, and you'll get the 411.

Roadie.net
http://www.roadie.net
No backstage pass necessary.

The Sample FAQ
http://members.accessus.net/~xombi/intro.html/
Ever wondered what beat The Beastie Boys ripped off for "Shadrach" or who's sampled Isaac Hayes? This whistle-blowing Website tears the lid off the record crates of hip-hop's most famous producers.

Scratch Simulator
http://www.turntables.de
Can't afford a pair of SL 1200s? Practise your reverse orbit scratches and beat juggling here, or at Infinite Wheel (http://www.infinitewheel.com), Live Jam (http://livejam.com) or ScratchOMatic (http://www.fm-productions.com/scratch.html/).

Music

Shareware Music Machine
http://www.hitsquad.com/smm/
Tons of shareware music players, editors and composition tools, for every platform.

Show and Tell Music
http://www.showandtellmusic.com
Albums much cooler than anything you own.

Smithsonian Institution
http://www.si.edu
Although this site is as gigantic as the famous American museum itself, if you're interested in folk music (from both America and the rest of the world) it's an absolute paradise, with info on their Folkways record label, Webcasts, galleries and articles (augmented with RealAudio files).

Songplayer
http://www.songplayer.com
Can't read music and still want to play guitar like Hendrix or keyboards like Keith Emerson? Try this music tuition site which has some 4000 songs in its files, and there are no cumbersome staves, bars or clefs to wrestle with.

Sonic Net
http://www.sonicnet.com
Big-name live cybercasts, streaming video channels, chats, news and reviews.

Sony
http://www.sony.com
Think about everything that Sony flogs. Now imagine it all squeezed under one roof.

Soul City
http://www.soulcity.ndo.co.uk
Listen to hundreds of '60s and Northern Soul clips.

Bizarre Records

American Song Poem Archives http://www.aspma.com
Archive of the bizarre mid-century phenomenon where studio
hacks set music to the lyrics of ordinary Joes – resulting in some of
the weirdest records ever.

Collecting Crap Records
http://www.78rpm.sonow.com/002/Crmain.htm
The what, why, where and hows of collecting records like Rolf
Harris's "Pukka Chicken" and King Uszniewicz & His
Uszniewicztones' "She Won't Turn Over for Me".

Frank's Vinyl Museum
http://franklarosa.com/$spindb.query.new.vinyl/
Exhibition of charity shop flotsam, including such timeless classics
as *Ken Demko Live at the Lamplighter Inn* and an album of Beatles
covers done by dogs.

The Internet Museum of Flexi/Cardboard/Oddities
http://www.wfmu.org/MACrec/
Records made out of metal, souvenirs from the Empire State
Building and other curios.

Songs in the Key of Z http://www.keyofz.com/keyofz/
Irwin Chusid's fantastic introduction to the world of outsider music.
More at http://www.incorrectmusic.com

Soulman's World of Beats
http://www.worldofbeats.com/old_site
E-zine for all the crate diggers, with articles focusing on the samples
from all of your favourite hip-hop records. More vinyl obsession at
http://www.breakz4dayz.com and http://www.samplehead.com

Sounds Online
http://www.soundsonline.com
Preview loops and samples, free in RealAudio. Pay to download studio
quality. If it's effects you're after, try: http://www.sounddogs.com

Music

SS7x7 Sound System
http://www.ss7x7.com
Mix your own tracks in Shockwave. Or have a bit of a scratch:
http://www.turntables.de

Taxi
http://www.taxi.com
Online music A&R service. And guess what? You and your plastic kazoo
are just what they're looking for.

This Day in Music
http://www.thisdayinmusic.com
Find out which member of the Bay City Rollers shares your birthday and
other essential music trivia.

Uncensored Celebrity Outtakes
http://www.fadetoblack.com/outtakes
Priceless recordings by William Shatner and the legendary tape of Linda
McCartney singing "Hey Jude".

Urban Sounds
http://www.urbansounds.com
Excellent, well-planned and designed electronica site from the US. The
Minimalism issue features hot names on the underground and is sexily
intercut with Rem Koolhaas sketches and Donald Judd reproductions.

WholeNote
http://www.wholenote.com
Guitar resources and chat boards. For live lessons, see:
http://www.riffinteractive.com

The Wire
http://www.thewire.co.uk
Subtitled "Adventures in Modern Music", the online home of the British
avant-garde music magazine *The Wire* features in-depth articles from
past issues on a pantheon of underground gods and goddesses and a
comprehensive set of links to set you exploring the labyrinthine demi-
monde of experimental music.

MP3s

Unlike every music delivery system since the development of $33^{1/3}$ and 45rpm records, MP3 is the first format not forced upon consumers by the record industry. Short for "MPEG-1 audio layer 3", MP3 is a format that compresses digital music files without a significant degradation in sound quality and has become the standard way of storing music on the Internet. In order to take advantage of MP3 you need some up-to-date kit: at least 32MB of RAM, a 56K modem, lots of room on your hard drive and, if you have an older PC, a sound card. You will also need to download MP3 player software like Soundjam for Macintosh or Winamp or RealJukebox for PC which are usually available in basic, free versions or more advanced versions for $29.95.

The best place to start is MP3.com (**http://www.mp3.com**) which has links to all the downloadable MP3 player software, lots of information for beginners and a vast catalogue of files. The software allows you to download MP3 files (which you can also do using your browser) and play them through the speakers on your computer. Many of the software programs have "ripping" options which allow you to convert a track on a CD into an MP3 file. This is where the rub comes. Peer-to-peer file-sharing programs that use the Gnutella platform (**http://www.gnutellanews.com**) — Morpheus (**http://www.morpheus-os.com**), LimeWire (**http://www.limewire.com**), BearShare (**http://www.bearshare.com**), KaZaA (**http://www.kazaa.com**), Gnucleus (**http://www.gnucleus.com**), eDonkey (**http://www.edonkey2000.com**) and Mactella (**http://www.cxc.com**) — or programs like Madster (**http://www.madster.com**), which take advantage of AOL's Instant Messenger software, allow people to trade files with one another — without any record company mediation. Other sites like Audio Galaxy (**http://www.audio-galaxy.com**) require you to download their own software in order to share files. The Record Industry Association of America, of course, doesn't like this and has tried to put a stop to free file exchanges, and at the time of writing the state of music on the Net is very much up in the air. ⇨

MP3s (continued)

The most likely answer to the conundrum is a subscription service like:

Emusic **http://www.emusic.com**

For $10 a month you can download MP3s from established artists.
Wippit **http://www.wippit.com**
Unlimited downloads for £30 a year.
Rhapsody **http://www.listen.com**
Full access for $9.95 a month.

For more MP3 options, try:
Lycos MP3 Search **http://music.lycos.com/downloads**
MP3 Board **http://www.mp3board.com**

Many of the industry players' sites weren't ready as this book went to press, but the names to look out for are:
Burnitfirst **http://www.burnitfirst.com**
Joint MP3 subscription venture from EMI and LiquidAudio. It's the only major label service that allows you to keep downloaded songs permanently and to burn them onto CDs. The catch ... the only music offered is from EMI Christian Music Group.

MusicNet http://www.musicnet.com
MusicNet represents the online interests of BMG, EMI and the Warner Music Group, and is also working to establish a subscription version of Napster (http://www.napster.com), the file-sharing service that kicked off the furore a couple of years ago.

Pressplay http://www.pressplay.com
The joint venture of Sony and Universal, Pressplay also features music released by EMI, Matador, Jive, Rounder, TVT, Razor & Tie, Roadrunner and more. The service limits the number of downloads and burns a user can do — and it even limits the number of streams you can access from the site. As of press time, it was only available in the US.

For some of the copyright issues involved, go to Free Music Philosophy (http://www.ram.org/ramblings/philosophy/fmp.html/).

Advanced Audio Coding http://www.aac-audio.com
Learn the news on the audio compression format destined to replace MP3.

Coalition for the Future of Music http://www.futureofmusic.org
Run by riot grrl Jenny Toomey, this organization campaigns for the rights of the independent musician in the file-sharing furore and is a good place to get to grasp with what's at stake for both the musician and label.

To discover the next Hear'Say or Slipknot, try:
Clickmusic http://www.clickmusic.co.uk
Get Signed http://www.get-signed.co.uk
Peoplesound http://www.peoplesound.com
Vitaminic http://www.vitaminic.co.uk

Nature

3D Insects
http://www.ento.vt.edu/~sharov/3d/3dinsect.html/
Whizz around a selection of 3D bugs. They're not real insects but at least they don't have pins through their backs. For a bigger range of bug bios, see: http://insects.org

African Wildlife Foundation
http://www.awf.org
Great site covering everything from the aardvark to the zebra.

Animal Diversity Web
http://animaldiversity.ummz.umich.edu
Database of animal history, classification, distribution and conservation from the University of Michigan. More at Natureserve (http://www.natureserve.org).

Aquatic Network
http://www.aquanet.com
A good site promoting sustainable aquaculture, with some great photography and solid information saving it from being too earnest.

ARKive
http://www.arkive.org.uk
Electronic archive of the world's endangered species.

Birding
http://birding.about.com
http://www.camacdonald.com/birding/
http://dmoz.org/Recreation/Birdwatching/
Birds are such regional critters that one site couldn't hope to cover them all. Use these to find the chirpiest one on your block.

Birds of Britain
http://www.birdsofbritain.co.uk
Webzine devoted to our fine feathered friends, with an illustrated guide to some 100 species.

Cetacea.org
http://www.cetacea.org
Excellent encyclopedic source of information on whales, dolphins and porpoises.

Dinosaur Interplanetary Gazette
http://www.dinosaur.org
It may be as slow and cumbersome as a Brontosaurus stuck in the LaBrea tar pits, but patience does pay off with a wealth of information and features.

The Electronic Zoo
http://netvet.wustl.edu/e-zoo.htm/
Up and running since 1993, this virtual menagerie is the best collection of animal-related links on the Web.

EMBL Reptile Database
http://www.embl-heidelberg
.de/~uetz/LivingReptiles.html
Slither through for info on everything from turtles to amphisbaenae.

female

Khanom,
Nakhon Si Thammarat,
Peninsular Thailand
© U. Manthey

eNature.com
http://www.enature.com
Vibrant field guides to North American flora and fauna.

Field Trips
http://www.field-guides.com
A neat idea, if not perfectly executed: visit this site and take virtual field trips involving deserts, oceans, hurricanes, sharks, fierce creatures, salt marshes, volcanoes and other natural wonders of the world.

Forces of Nature
http://library.thinkquest.org/C003603/
Thinkquest's student-designed Website devoted to avalanches, droughts, landslides, earthquakes and other natural disasters.

Nature

ForestWorld
http://www.forestworld.com
http://forests.org
Timber tales from both sides of the dozer.

Great Cats of the World
http://www.greatcatsoftheworld.com
The homepage of the Bridgeport Nature Center in Texas functions as a
mini-encyclopedia of lions, tigers, leopards and cougars.

Insects on the Web
http://www.insects.org
Definitely not one for your
little girl, this excellent educational resource of
creepy-crawlies features
some rather too detailed
photography of everyone's
least favourite bugs.

Mr Winkle
http://www.mrwinkle.com
Okay, so how cute is Mr Winkle? But is he really real?

Nessie on the Net
http://www.lochness.co.uk
Watch the Loch Ness Webcam, spot the monster and win £1000.

Predator Urines
http://www.predatorpee.com
Bewitch neighbouring Jack Russells with a dab of bobcat balm or true
blue roo poo: http://www.roopooco.com

Sea turtle migration-tracking
http://www.cccturtle.org/satwelc.htm/
Adopt a bugged sea reptile and follow its trail.

World Wildlife Fund
http://www.worldwildlife.org.uk
Teach your kids that the WWF isn't all about pile drivers and steroid
cases in skimpy shorts. More animal lovers at the World Society for the

Protection of Animals (http://www.wspa.org.uk) and the Royal Society for the Protection of Animals (http://www.rspca.org).

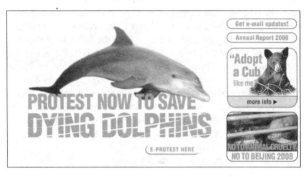

ZooNet
http://www.zoonet.org
Perhaps the best virtual zoo on the Web.

News, Newspapers and Magazines

Now that almost every magazine and newspaper on the globe from *Ringing World* (http://www.ringingworld.co.uk) to the *Falkland Island News* (http://www.sartma.com) is discharging daily content onto the Net, it's beyond this guide to do much more than list a few of the notables and then point you in the right direction for more. The simplest way to find your favourite read would be to look for its address in a recent issue. Failing that, try entering its name into a subject guide or search engine. If you don't have a title name and would prefer to browse by subject or region, try:

Open Directory http://dmoz.org/News/

Yahoo http://dir.yahoo.com/News_and_Media/

News, Newspapers and Magazines

Newspapers rarely replicate themselves word for word online, but they often provide enough for you to live without the paper edition. Not bad considering they're generally free online before the paper even hits the stands. Apart from whatever proportion of their print they choose to put online, they also tend to delve deeper into their less newsy areas such as travel, IT, entertainment and culture. Plus they often bolster this with exclusive content such as breaking news, live sports coverage, online shopping, opinion polls and discussion groups. In most cases they'll also provide a way to search and retrieve archives, though this might incur a charge. There are also a few sites that index multiple news archives, again usually at a price. Such as:

Electric Library http://www.elibrary.com
FindArticles.com http://www.findarticles.com
NewsLibrary http://www.newslibrary.com
Northern Light http://www.nlsearch.com

A few of the more popular news bugles, to get you started:
Arab News http://www.arabnews.com
Christian Science Monitor http://www.csmonitor.com
Daily Mail http://www.dailymail.co.uk
Daily Mail & Guardian http://www.mg.co.za
Economist http://www.economist.com
Evening Standard http://www.thisislondon.co.uk
Express http://www.express.co.uk
Financial Times http://www.ft.com
Guardian http://www.guardian.co.uk
The Hindu http://www.hinduonline.com
Independent http://www.independent.co.uk
International Herald Tribune http://www.iht.com
Irish News http://www.irishnews.com
LA Times http://www.latimes.com
Mirror http://www.mirror.co.uk

News, Newspapers and Magazines

Le Monde http://www.lemonde.fr
National Enquirer http://www.nationalenquirer.com
National Geographic News http://news.nationalgeographic.com
News of the World http://www.newsoftheworld.co.uk
Newsweek http://www.newsweek.com
NY Times http://www.nytimes.com
Observer http://www.observer.co.uk
El País http://www.elpais.es
Scotsman http://www.scotsman.com
South China Morning Post http://www.scmp.com
La Stampa http://www.lastampa.it
Sun http://www.thesun.co.uk
Tehelka http://www.tehelka.com
Telegraph http://www.telegraph.co.uk
Time Daily http://www.time.com
Times http://www.thetimes.co.uk
Times of India http://timesofindia.indiatimes.com
USA Today http://www.usatoday.com
Village Voice http://www.villagevoice.com
Washington Post http://www.washingtonpost.com
Weekly World News http://www.weeklyworldnews.com

Like much you do online, reading news is addictive. You'll know you're hooked when you find yourself checking into newswires throughout the day to monitor moving stories. Try these for a fix:

Breaking News

Ananova http://www.ananova.com
Associated Press http://wire.ap.org
BBC http://news.bbc.co.uk
CNN http://www.cnn.com
ITN http://www.itn.co.uk

News, Newspapers and Magazines

NBC http://www.msnbc.com
Reuters http://www.reuters.com
Sky http://www.sky.com
Wired News http://www.wired.com

While most magazines maintain a site, they're typically more of an adjunct to the print than a substitute. Still, they're worth checking out, especially if they archive features and reviews or break news between issues. Again, check a recent issue or one of the directories for an address. If you'd rather subscribe to the paper edition, try:

http://www.magsuk.com

AlterNet
http://www.alternet.org
Roundup of almost all of America's alternative weekly papers.

American Newspeak
http://www.scn.org/news/newspeak/
Celebrating the arts of doublethink, spin, media coaching and other ways to mangle meaning.

Clique
http://clique.org.uk
Roundup of stories that didn't get coverage from the mainstream news sources, whether because they were too controversial, too bizarre or just too stupid.

Crayon
http://www.crayon.net
Most of the major portals such as Excite, Yahoo and MSN also allow you to create a custom news page that draws from several sources – though none does it quite so thoroughly as Crayon. Infobeat (http://www.infobeat.com) does similar things but delivers by email.

Electric Library
http://www.elibrary.com

A great resource that allows you to view full text versions of some seven million articles, books, pictures, TV and radio transcripts. Unfortunately you have to pay $59.95 a year for the privilege.

Inside
http://www.inside.com
Media news with a heavy US slant.

A Journalist's Guide to the Internet
http://reporter.umd.edu
No design whatsoever, but a useful set of links to resources for journalists.

Moreover
http://www.moreover.com/news/
The best free service for searching current or recent stories across hundreds of international news sources. Also try News Index (http://www.newsindex.com) and What the Papers Say (http://www.whatthepaperssay.co.uk). Like someone to monitor the Web and assorted newswires for mention of your product or misdeeds? Try Webclipping.com (http://www.webclipping.com).

MyVillage
http://www.myvillage.com
Online community with a heavy emphasis on local news. Best in and around London, but slowly increasing their profile across the country.

NewsNow
http://www.newsnow.co.uk
News aggregators allow you to tap into several sources simultaneously. This one might be the best: it has more UK-specific content than any of the others and is apparently updated every five minutes. For more, try:

Arts & Letters Daily http://www.aldaily.com

Asia Observer http://www.asiaobserver.com

FastAsia (Asia) http://www.fastasia.com

NewsHub http://www.newshub.com

Russian Story http://www.russianstory.com

TotalNews http://www.totalnews.com

Yahoo News http://dailynews.yahoo.com

E-zines

"E-zines" are magazines that only exist online or are delivered by email. But because almost any regularly updated Web page fits this description, the term has lost much of its currency. Although most e-zines burn out as quickly as they appear, a few of the pioneers are still kicking on.

For more, try browsing one of the directories listed at:
http://dmoz.org/News/Ezines/Directories/

The Chap http://www.artfink.demon.co.uk/chap/
"Dressing for Golf" and other essential manners guides for the modern male.

Drudge Report http://www.drudgereport.com
The shock bulletin that set off the Lewinsky avalanche. A one-hit wonder perhaps, but still a bona fide tourist attraction on the info goat track.

Future File http://futurefile.com
Thought-provoking e-zine portal from technocrat Todd Maffin, featuring ideas and trends to look for in the next decade.

Gurl.com http://www.gurl.com
Zine dedicated to hip young things pitched somewhere between the original *Sassy* and *Jane*.

IGN http://www.ign.com /affiliates/index.html
IGN (Internet Gaming Network) treads similar – though generally tamer – ground to UGO, partnering mostly with high-quality gaming, sci-fi, wrestling and comic sites.

NTK http://www.ntk.net
Sarcastic high-tech media magazine. For geeky Popbitch (see Gossip) fans.

Salon http://www.salon.com
The real e-zine suc-
cess story. It spans
the arts, business,
politics, lifestyle and
technology in a style
that's both smart and
breezy.

Slate
http://slate.msn.com
Microsoft's long-suffering Slate marks similar territory to Salon, but succeeds more in being terribly dull.

Spiked http://www.spiked-online.com
Caustic, political e-zine from former Living Marxism supremo Mick Hume.

Suck http://www.suck.com
Arguably the only e-zine that ever mattered, Suck sat in a smug class all by itself. Its archives are still worth reading, if not for its cocked eye on all that's wired and painfully modern then at least for Terry Colon's cartoons.

Underground Online http://www.ugo.com
Big men's magazine-style network devoted to music, wrestling, film, TV, books, technology and so on.

The Onion
http://www.theonion.com
News the way it was meant to be.

Blogs

"Blogs", or Weblogs, are essentially diaries — logs of a person's thoughts, what they did, what's interesting them, and news. They are getting a lot of coverage at the moment because they represent the latest development in the Web's democratization of culture: due to their immediacy and their liberation of the means of production, blogs are being hyped as the next publishing revolution. Here are some blogging resources and some of the best blogs on the Net:

Adam Curry's Weblog
http://live.curry.com
Blog of former MTV VJ; go straight to the MTV Chronicle for all the dirt.

Blogger.com
http://www.blogger.com
Links, news and everything you need to create your own blog.

Boom Selection
http://boomselection.n3.net/
The headquarters of the British bootleg mix scene.

The Daily Report
http://www.zeldman.com/coming.html
Web guru Jeffrey Zeldman dishes up

The Paper Boy
http://www.thepaperboy.com
This site is perhaps the best specialist directory of newspapers and news organizations on the Web, with links to everything from Bulgarian

tech advice and links, and the wickedly funny "If the great movies had been Websites".

Eatonweb Portal
http://portal.eatonweb.com
A huge list of blogs.

Librarian.net
http://www.librarian.net
A model blog, with a crucial insight on the subterranean world of the librarian.

MetaFilter
http://www.metafilter.com
A community blog.

Pop Culture Junk Mail
http://www.popculturejunkmail.com
Your guide to the flotsam of post-industrial society.

Talking Points Memo
http://www.talkingpointsmemo.com
All the dirt from the Washington DC Beltway.

Weblogs: A History and Perspective
http://www.rebeccablood.net/essays/weblog_history.html
A history of the phenomenon.

National Radio to eight different papers from Zambia. Other directories to check out include NewsLink (http://newslink.org), Editor & Publisher (http://www.mediainfo.com), Metagrid (http://www.metagrid.com), NewsDirectory (http://www.newsdirectory.com), Online Newspapers (http://www.onlinenewspapers.com) and Publist (http://www.publist.com). To find magazines, try The Magazine Boy (http://www.themagazineboy.com).

Tech News
http://www.news.com
Computing and technology newswire. Of course, there's no shortage of similar sites: NewsLinx (http://www.newslinx.com), SiliconValley (http://www.siliconvalley.com), TechWeb (http://www.techweb.com) and ZD Network News (http://www.zdnet.com) are some of the best. For e-business news: InternetNews (http://www.internetnews.com).

This Is True
http://www.thisistrue.com
Randy Cassingham's weekly column of preposterous-but-true news stories and headlines collated from the major wire services.

Wireless Flash News Service
http://www.flashnews.com
News service specializing in pop culture stories, featuring some of the least newsworthy headlines in history.

World Press Review
http://www.worldpress.org
Keeping tabs on the people who keep tabs on us. Also keep an eye on News Watch (http://www.newswatch.com).

News, Newspapers and Magazines

News Tickers

A news ticker is like having a wire service on your desktop, complete with scrolling headlines. Click on one and you'll be taken to the full story. You have to be online in order to receive the news, so they are best for those with ADSL or ISDN connections. Usually, all getting a news ticker entails is downloading the software (sometimes at a cost) and installing it on your computer. Tickers range from the very basic to customizable ones with loads of options; some can even be placed in the Windows taskbar.

BBC Newsline http://www.bbc.co.uk/newsline/
A straightforward but very good news ticker.

Desktop News http://www.desktopnews.com
Powerful, customizable ticker with plenty of different channels to choose from.

FT Desktop News Ticker
http://globalelements.ft.com/NewsAndAnalysis/Ticker
/downloadinterface.html
All the breaking news from the City.

InfoGate http://www.infogate.com
One of the best tickers for business news.

Moreover NewzTop http://www.moreover.com/dev/ticker.html
Customizable ticker utilizing any of Moreover's categories.

WorldFlash http://www.worldflash.com
Extensive ticker with a keyword alert feature allowing you to keep track of stories of particular interest.

Outdoor Pursuits

Birdlinks

http://www.birdlinks.co.uk
Gateway to the world of birdwatching. More to look at on:
http://birding.about.com
http://www.camacdonald.com/birding/
http://dmoz.org/Recreation/Birdwatching/
http://www.birdsofbritain.co.uk

The Butterfly Website

http://www.butterflywebsite.com
The Monarch of butterfly sites, with galleries, lists of gardens and butterfly gardens and loads of information on biology, conservation and behaviour.

Camp Sites

http://www.camp-sites.co.uk
Find a place to pitch your tent in the UK.

Go Fishing

http://www.go-fishing.co.uk
Your compleat angling resource. Other sites that would make Isaak Walton proud: Angler's Net (http://www.anglersnet.co.uk), Angling News (http://www.angling-news.co.uk) and Sea Angler (http://sea-angler.org).

Great Outdoor Recreation Pages

http://www.gorp.com
Ignore all the multivitamin and SUV adverts and the American bias because this is the best outdoors site on the Web. The superlative how-to pages

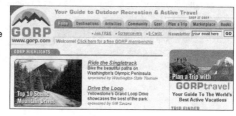

alone make it worth navigating the pop-up ads, plus there are good articles, trail finders, destination guides, discussion groups, photo galleries and you can book holidays and buy gear from the site.

Ramblers' Association
http://www.ramblers.org.uk
All the latest news on walking and other pedestrian pursuits. For more info, take your browser on a stroll over to Walking World (http://www.walkingworld.com) or Walking Britain (http://www.walkingbritain.co.uk).

Rock Climbing in the UK
http://www.ukcrags.com
Great resource for British rock climbers, with news, articles, Webcams, events listings, routes and crag descriptions. More handholds can be found at Climb Guide (http://www.climb-guide.com).

Pets

About Veterinary Medicine
http://vetmedicine.about.com
About's vet pages are an excellent resource for pet owners worried about their moggie or pet lizard and are filled with advice, news, disease indexes and forums.

The Aviary
http://www.theaviary.com/ci.shtml/
Everything you'd ever want to know about companion birds – and then some.

Barbara's Canine Café
http://www.k9treat.com
Only In America part 346: If your mutt's got a food allergy or you just want to get your hound a "celebration gift basket" made from all-natural ingredients, look no further.

Cat Tips
http://www.cat-tips.com
"Understanding kitty psychology", "Litterbox blues" and other feline facts.

Chazhound
http://www.chazhound.com
Resources for dog lovers as well as screensavers, games and doggie greeting cards.

The Dogpatch
http://www.dogpatch.org
Advice on training your pooch, plus the best canine links on the Web.

Dogs Online
http://www.dogsonline.co.uk
Directory pages for British dog owners, including lost and found, breeders, puppies for sale and dog-friendly accommodation.

Equine World
http://www.equine-world.co.uk
Great site covering all things equestrian. See also Equiworld (http://www.equiworld.net).

FishDoc
http://www.fishdoc.co.uk
All the information you need if your goldfish is looking a bit green around the gills. For aquarium links go to Fish Link Central (http://www.fishlinkcentral.com).

House Rabbit Society
http://www.rabbit.org
Online community and resource for rabbit owners. Also try the Rabbit Welfare Association (http://www.rabbitwelfare.co.uk/index.htm).

Kingsnake.com
http://www.kingsnake.com
A mind-bogglingly enormous portal for reptile and amphibian enthusiasts.

Museum of Non-Primate Art
http://www.monpa.com
Online home of the people behind the "Why cats paint" caper, with special exhibitions devoted to dancing with cats and "bird art".

New Pet.com

http://www.newpet.com

Friendly and informative site for new or soon-to-be owners of a cat or dog.

Pet Cat

http://www.petcat.com

In addition to the usual information and advice, this feline resource allows you to create a virtual cat and even offers horoscopes for Tiddles. See also Moggies (http://www.moggies.co.uk).

Pet Mad

http://www.petmad.com

Despite first appearances, this Irish site is probably the best (and cheapest) online pet shop for UK surfers. For organic food and alternative remedies try Pets' Park (http://www.petspark.com).

Pet Planet

http://www.petplanet.co.uk

Not to be confused with the American site listed below, this site houses one of the UK's best online pet shops, with special features like a lost pet service and rehoming facilities.

The Pet Project

http://www.thepetproject.com

There's a whiff of New Age aromatherapy here ("the special bond between human and animal") and the focus is firmly on the US, but this is surely the most comprehensive pet resource on the Web, with all manner of advice on everything from canine nutrition to interpreting the sounds your chinchilla makes. Other good resources are Acme Pet (http://acmepet.petsmart.com) and Pet Planet (http://www.petplanet.com).

Photography

Rodent Fancy
http://www.rodentfancy.com
With information on everything from African rock rats to Mongolian gerbils, rodent fanciers shouldn't look anywhere else.

RSPCA Online
http://www.rspca.co.uk
The RSPCA's homepage offers advice, allows the kids to adopt a cyberpet before getting the real thing and features news and information on campaigns for animal welfare.

Tubcat
http://www.tubcat.com
Fat cats.

Photography

American Museum of Photography
http://www.photographymuseum.com
Exhibitions from back when cameras were a novelty.

Black & White World
http://www.photogs.com/bwworld/
A celebration of black-and-white photography.

British Journal of Photography
http://www.bjphoto.co.uk
Homepage of the venerable magazine and a valuable resource for the professional photographer.

Digital Camera Resource Page
http://www.dcresource.com
A simple, easy-to-use site, offering reviews of loads of digital cameras and equipment as well as product news and information on issues like Mac OS X compatibility.

Digital Photography Review
http://www.dpreview.com
Considering a new digital camera? Read on.

Digital Truth: Photo Resource
http://www.digitaltruth.com
Perhaps the best photographic resource for the advanced photographer, with loads of tips, downloadable f-stop calculation software and "the world's largest" film development chart.

Exposure
http://www.88.com/exposure/
A beginner's guide to photography, whose neatest feature is the simulated camera which mimics the effects of adjustments in shutter speed and aperture on pictures.

Invisible Light
http://www.atsf.co.uk/ilight/photos/index.html
Your complete guide to infrared photography.

Photography

Life
http://www.lifemag.com
View *Life* magazine's Picture of the Day then link through to some of the world's most arresting photographs. There's even more over at *Time*'s Picture Collection (http://www.thepicturecollection.com) and Australia's Newsphotos (http://www.newsphotos.com.au).

Masters of Photography
http://www.masters-of-photography.com
An excellent collection of the works of some of history's greatest snappers, from Berenice Abbott to Garry Winogrand. In addition to the images there are links to articles and other Websites with biographical and technical information.

Photodisc
http://creative.gettyimages.com/photodisc
Plunder these photos free, or pay for the hi-res versions.

PhotoWave
http://www.photowave.com
Portal for professional photographers. Amateurs should try PhotoNet (http://www.photo.net), PhotoLinks (http://www.photolinks.net), Still Journal (http://www.stilljournal.com) or About's photography pages (http://photography.about.com).

PhotoZone
http://www.photozone.de
This site offers comparative analysis of cameras and lenses, and loads of technical information on all sorts of equipment.

Pinhole Visions
http://www.pinhole.com
A great site devoted to the art of pinhole photography, a primitive form of picture-taking that creates a dreamlike effect unattainable with conventional photography. There are two gallery spaces, discussion groups, news and links to other resources.

Online Photo Albums

Got some snaps you'd like to show the world – or just your friends (through selective password access)? Upload them here:

Album Pictures http://www.albumpictures.com
Club Photo http://www.clubphoto.com
MSN Photos http://photos.msn.com/home.aspx
Photobox http://www.photobox.co.uk
PhotoLoft http://www.photoloft.com
Picture Trail http://www.picturetrail.com
Web Shots http://www.webshots.com
Yahoo! Photos http://photos.yahoo.com

Shutterbug
http://www.shutterbug.net
The online home of the American *Shutterbug* magazine includes a massive archive of past articles, product reviews, news, hints, galleries, competitions and more. Digital photographers should focus on eDigital Photo (http://www.edigitalphoto.com).

Take Better Photos
http://betterphotos.cjb.net
No-nonsense site offering tricks and tips on correcting common photographic errors, picking the best viewpoint, compensating for parallax, computer enhancement, etc, etc. For more serious (really serious) tuition at a cost, try Photo Seminars (http://www.photo-seminars.com). For an online database of British photography courses click http://www.photo-college.net

Year in the Life of Photojournalism
http://www.digitalstoryteller.com/YITL/
Tag along with pros and see what they do day to day.

24 Hours in Cyberspace
http://www.cyber24.com
One thousand photographers save the day.

Politics and Government

Politics and Government

Most governmental departments, politicians, political aspirants and causes maintain Websites to spread the word and further their various interests. To find your local rep or candidate, start at their party's homepage. These typically lie dormant unless there's a campaign in progress, but can still be a good source of contacts to badger. Government departments, on the other hand, tirelessly belch out all sorts of trivia right down to transcripts of ministerial radio interviews. So if you'd like to know about impending legislation, tax rulings, budget details and so forth, skip the party pages and go straight to the department. If you can't find its address through what's listed below, try:

Yahoo http://dir.yahoo.com/Government/
Open Directory http://dmoz.org/Society/Government/

For the latest election night counts, check the breaking news sites (p.241). Below is a selection of the most useful starting points.

British Politics Links http://www.ukpol.co.uk
Government Portal http://www.ukonline.gov.uk
Green Party http://www.greenparty.org.uk
Labour http://www.labour.org.uk
Liberal Democrats http://www.libdems.org.uk
National Assembly for Wales http://www.wales.gov.uk
Natural Law http://www.natural-law-party.org.uk
Northern Ireland Assembly http://www.ni-assembly.gov.uk
Plaid Cymru http://www.plaidcymru.org
Prime Minister http://www.pm.gov.uk
Scottish National Party http://www.snp.org
Scottish Parliament http://www.scottish.parliament.uk
Sinn Féin http://www.sinnfein.ie
Social Democratic and Labour Party http://www.sdlp.ie

Politics and Government

Socialist Party http://www.socialistparty.org.uk
Socialist Workers Party http://www.swp.org.uk
Tories http://www.conservatives.com
Ulster Unionist Party http://www.uup.org

Adopt-A-Minefield
http://www.adoptaminefield.com
Help clear war-torn communities of deadly explosives.

Amnesty International
http://www.amnesty.org
Join the battle against brutal regimes and injustice.

Animal Concerns Community
http://animalconcerns.netforchange.com
Online community for animal rights advocates.

Antiwar
http://www.antiwar.com
http://www.iacenter.org
Challenges US intervention in foreign affairs, especially the Balkans and Middle East.

The Big Breach
http://www.thebigbreach.com
Download a free copy of the British MI6 spy-and-tell book.

Bilderberg Group
http://www.bilderberg.org
Read about the people who really rule the world.

The British Monarchy
http://www.royal.gov.uk
Tune into the world's best-loved soap opera.

British Politics Pages
http://www.ukpolitics.org.uk
News and history for politicos, with a great links page.

Politics and Government

Center for the Moral Defense of Capitalism

http://www.moraldefense.com

http://www.aynrand.org

Is greed still good in the Y2Ks? Maybe not good but legal, says Microsoft's last bastion of sympathy.

Central Intelligence Agency

http://www.cia.gov

Want the inside on political assassinations, arms deals, Colombian drug trades, spy satellites, phone tapping, covert operations, government-sponsored alien sex cults and the X-files? Well, guess what? Never mind, you won't go home without a prize see http://www.copvcia.com and http://www.magnet.ch/serendipity/cia.html/

Communist Internet List

http://www.cominternet.org

http://www.yclusa.org

Angry intellectuals and workers unite.

The Complete Bushisms

http://slate.msn.com/default.aspx?id=76886

The subliminable wit and wisdom of George Dubya.

Conspiracies

http://www.mt.net/~watcher/

http://www.conspire.com

Certain people are up to something and, what's worse, they're probably all in it together. If these exposés of the sixty biggest cover-ups of all time aren't proof enough, then do your bit and create one that's more convincing: http://www.turnleft.com/conspiracy.html/

Council for Aboriginal Reconciliation
http://www.reconciliation.org.au
Unfinished business in the Lucky (for some) Country.

Disinformation
http://www.disinfo.com
The dark side of politics, religious fervour, new science, along with current affairs you won't find in the papers.

Doonesbury
http://www.doonesbury.com
Over thirty years of Gary Trudeau's legendary political cartoon.

Electronic Frontier Foundation
http://www.eff.org
Protecting freedom of expression on the Internet.

ePolitix
http://www.epolitix.com
British politics portal.

Fax Your MP
http://www.faxyourmp.com
Pester your local member through an Internet-to-fax gateway.

FBI FOIA Reading Room
http://foia.fbi.gov
FBI documents released as part of the Freedom of Information Act. Includes a few files on such celebrities as John Wayne, Elvis, Marilyn and the British Royals. Check out who's most wanted now at:
http://www.fbi.gov

Federation of American Scientists
http://www.fas.org
Heavyweight analysis of science, technology and public policy including national security, nuclear weapons, arms sales, biological hazards, secrecy and space policy.

Foreign Report
http://www.foreignreport.com
Compact subscription newsletter with a track record of predicting international flashpoints well before the dailies.

Free Tibet
http://www.freetibet.org
Favourite Website of the Beastie Boys and Richard Gere.

Freedom Forum
http://www.freedomforum.org
Organization dedicated to free-speech issues, newsroom diversity and freedom of the press.

The Gallup Organization
http://www.gallup.com
Keep track of opinion trends and ratings.

Gates Foundation
http://www.gatesfoundation.org
See where the world's second richest man is spreading it around.

Gay & Lesbian Alliance against Defamation
http://www.glaad.org
Stand up against media stereotyping and discrimination of those deviating from the heterosexual norm. For more news, advice and dispatches from the activist front, try Gay Men's Health Crisis (http://www.gmhc.org), Stonewall (http://www.stonewall.org.uk) and Act Up New York (http://www.actupny.org).

Gendercide
http://www.gendercide.org
Investigates mass killings where a single gender is singled out.

German Propaganda Archives
http://www.calvin.edu/cas/gpa/
Who did you think you were kidding, Mr Hitler?

Grassroots.com (US)
http://www.grassroots.com
Tracks political action and election policies across the board, aided by
TV Nation champ Michael Moore: (http://www.michaelmoore.com).

Greenpeace International
http://www.greenpeace.org
Rebels with many a good cause.

GW Bush Art
http://gwbushart.port5.com
Distort the American president to your heart's content.

Hate Monitor
http://www.hatemonitor.org
http://www.publiceye.org
http://www.splcenter.org
Shining the public flashlight on hate groups and political forces that
threaten to undermine democracy and diversity.

Hindu Holocaust Museum
http://www.mantra.com/holocaust/
Contends that the massacre of Hindus during Muslim rule in India was
of a scale unparalleled in history, yet an event that has largely gone
undocumented.

Illuminati Links
http://www.newnetizen.com/illuminati/illuminatilinks.htm/
All the Web resources you need on the elitist One World government.
For a more jovial version, play Illumiati: New World Order The Game
(http://www.sjgames.com/inwo/).

InfoWar
http://www.infowar.com
Warfare issues from prank hacking to industrial espionage and military
propaganda.

Jane's IntelWeb
http://intelweb.janes.com
Brief updates on political disturbances, terrorism, intelligence agencies
and subterfuge worldwide. For a full directory of covert operations, see:
http://www.virtualfreesites.com/covert.html/

Politics and Government

Liberty
http://www.liberty-human-rights.org.uk
Championing human rights in England and Wales.

MediaAttack
http://www.mediaattack.com
Video clips of talking heads and their celebrity guests put on the spot
with awkward questions.

National Charities Information Bureau
http://www.ncib.org
http://www.charity-commission.gov.uk
Investigate before you donate.

National Forum on People's Differences
http://www.yforum.com
Toss around touchy topics such as race, religion, and sexuality with a
sincerity that is normally tabooed by political politeness.

One World
http://www.oneworld.net
Collates news from over 350 global justice organizations.

Open Secrets
http://www.opensecrets.org
Track whose money is oiling the wheels of US politics.
More keeping 'em honest at: http://www.commoncause.org

Oxfam
http://www.oxfam.org
Pitch in to fight poverty and inequality.

Political Arena
http://www.planetquake.com/politicalarena/c2k.htm
Stage American elections on Quake.

The Political Graveyard
http://www.politicalgraveyard.com
Find out where over 81,000 politicians, diplomats and judges are
buried.

Political Leanings of Selected Cartoon Characters

http://www.unknown.nu/cartoon

Uncover the ideologies of those seemingly innocent Saturday morning fixtures.

Political Leanings of Selected Cartoon Characters

Porky Pig

New Deal-era liberal. Big on farm subsidies. Supported Humphrey, Stevenson, Muskie, etc..

Not terribly political, but she was around leftists most of the time, having grown up in a Jewish family in Brooklyn. In the 1930's, she sang at a fundraiser for the Spanish Republicans (at her brother's request). This came back to haunt her in the 1950's, when it made it difficult for her to get gigs due to the tenor of the McCarthy era. She ended up having to move to France to support herself, where she became an even bigger star than she had been in America.

Political Wire

http://politicalwire.com

In-depth political news aggregator that is US-heavy but which does cover international politics as well.

Politics Online

http://www.PoliticsOnline.com

It may be subtitled "Fundraising and Internet tools for politics", but this is actually a good general political site, with an emphasis on how connectivity is changing the face of the game.

The Progressive Review

http://www.prorev.com

Washington dirt dug up from all sides of the fence. For darker soil, try: http://www.realchange.org

Protest.net – A Calendar of Protest Worldwide

http://protest.net

Find a nearby riot you can call your own.

Politics and Government

Spin On
http://www.spinon.co.uk
Play games such as "Stay to the Right of Jack Straw", "Egg Prescott" and the Hague Goes Trucking Simulator.

Spunk Press
http://www.spunk.org
http://www.infoshop.org
All the anarchy you'll ever need, organized neatly and with reassuring authority.

This Modern World
http://www.thismodernworld.com
Archive of Tom Tomorrow's scathing political cartoon.

Trinity Atomic Web Site
http://www.fas.org/nuke/trinity/
See what went on, and what went off, fifty-odd years ago, then file into the archives of high-energy weapon testing and see who else has been sharpening the tools of world peace.

UK Census
http://www.statistics.gov.uk
More statistics on the UK and its citizens than you'd care to know.

UK Online
http://www.ukonline.gov.uk
Not to be confused with the ISP, this UK Online aims to be the place where people interact with the government. Like most governmental policies, it seems pretty hazy and to get anywhere you have to dig far too hard.

US Presidential Candidates and their Evil Genes
http://www.nenavadno.com/usaelections2000.html/
Biocybernetic criminals from the 33rd dimension take America.

YouGov
http://www.yougov.com
A good attempt at using the Internet to make government more account-
able. There are columns and comment from John Humphrys, Fay Weldon
and Ian Hargreaves, plus constantly updated political news. The best
features, though, are the People's Parliament, which allows users to vote
on the same issues as parliament, a service to create e-petitions and
GovDoctor, which identifies MPs, councillors and service managers.

Property

British Association of Removers
http://www.barmovers.com
Search for a mover who meets the BAR's standards of service.

FinanCenter
http://www.financenter.com
Figure out your monthly payments or what you can't afford.

Help I Am Moving
http://www.helpiammoving.com
Tries to remove the hassle from moving. Also try The Move Channel
(http://www.themovechannel.com) and Really Moving
(http://www.reallymoving.com).

Home Check
http://www.homecheck.co.uk
An excellent service for prospective home buyers: type in your future postcode and it will tell you if you need to worry about subsidence, pollution,
air quality, flood risk or if the Triads are likely to firebomb the flat below.

Homewatch & Neighbourhood Watch Directory
http://www.localhomewatch.co.uk
Join with your neighbours to keep property values high.

Property

HouseWeb
http://www.findaproperty.com
http://www.houseweb.co.uk
http://www.propertyfinder.co.uk
http://www.propertylive.co.uk
http://www.property-sight.co.uk
http://www.vebra.com

Rent, buy or sell property within the UK. More properties at Accommodation Directory (http://www.accommodation.com), Assertahome (http://www.assertahome.com), Easier (http://www.easier.co.uk), Homefile (http://www.homefileuk.co.uk), Home Free Home (http://www.homefreehome.co.uk), Homepages (http://www.homepages.co.uk), Home Sale (http://www.home-sale .co.uk), HouseNet (http://www.housenet.co.uk), Let's Direct (http://www.letsdirect.co.uk), LondonHomeNet (http://www .londonhomenet.com), Mooov (http://www.mooov.com), Pavilions of Splendour (http://www.heritage.co.uk), Property World (http://www.propertyworld.com), Property Watch (http://www .propwatch.com) and UK Property Gold (http://www.ukpg.co.uk). For commercial property, try Comproperty (http://www.comproperty.com).

ihavemoved.com
http://www.ihavemoved.com
Bulk-notify UK companies of your new address.

International Real Estate Digest
http://www.ired.com
Locate real estate listings, guides, and property-related services world wide.

Islands for Sale
http://www.islandsforsale.com
Get away from it all.
For more opportuni-
ties for isolation, try
Tropical Islands
(http://www.tropical-
islands.com) or World
of Private Islands
(http://www.vladi-private-islands.de).

NACOSS

http://www.nacoss.org
Homepage of the National Approval Council for Security Systems: keep tabs on the guys installing your alarm. Check out http://www.locksmiths.co.uk) to make sure your lock doesn't get picked.

Property Broker

http://www.propertybroker.co.uk
If you live within the M25 you can avoid the middleman and advertise your property here for a flat fee of £78.

UpMyStreet

http://www.upmystreet.com
Astounding wealth of house prices, health, crime, schools, tax and other statistics on UK neighbourhoods. Mighty useful if you're shifting base.

Web Guide to Household Packing

http://www.avatar-moving.com/support/doc_packing_guide.html/
Stock up on bubblewrap.

Radio and Webcasts

Not only do almost all radio stations have a Website, most now pipe their transmissions online. However, as of press time the state of Internet radio was in perilous shape due to the American CARP (Copyright Arbitration Royalty Panel) substantially increasing the royalty rates that Internet broadcasters have to pay. Tune into http://www.saveinternetradio.com for the latest information on the campaign to protect this vital resource. The stations that are still online broadcast (Webcast) in RealAudio and/or Windows Media Format, so grab the latest copies of both before setting out. Both players come with in-built station directories along with Web-based event guides which are fine for starting out, but nowhere near complete.

RealGuide http://realguide.real.com
Windows Media Guide http://windowsmedia.com

Radio and Webcasts

Not enough? Then buy the *Rough Guide to Internet Radio* or try one of the specialist radio directories, which list physical radio stations with Websites along with full-time stations that only exist online, normally lumped together by country or genre. If they don't provide a direct link to the live feed, visit the station's site and look for a button or link that says "live" or "listen".

Internet Radio Directories

BRS Web Radio http://www.web-radio.fm
ComFM http://www.comfm.fr/live/radio/
Live Radio http://www.live-radio.net
Radio Crow http://www.radiocrow.com
Radio Jump http://www.radiojump.com
Radio Locator http://www.radio-locator.com
RadioNow http://www.radio-now.co.uk
RadioWise http://www.radiowise.com.au/stations_live.htm/
Shoutcast http://www.shoutcast.com
Sunset Radio http://sunsetradio.com
Virtual Tuner http://www.virtualtuner.com

Apart from the traditional single-stream broadcasters, dozens of sites host multiple feeds. These might be live, on demand, on rotation, archived or one-off events. They tend to work more like inflight entertainment than radio.

Multistream Webcasters

Air Bubble http://www.airbubble.com
Anime Hardcore http://animehardcore.gamesquad.net/ahr/index.shtml
Betalounge http://www.betalounge.com
CD Now http://www.cdnow.com/radio/
Groovetech http://www.groovetech.com

House of Blues http://www.hob.com
Interface http://interface.pirate-radio.co.uk
Live 365 http://www.live365.com
Online Classics http://www.onlineclassics.net
Spinner http://www.spinner.com
Yahoo! Radio http://radio.yahoo.com

There are thousands upon thousands of Webcasters sending their signals into the ether. These are some of the more familiar names and some of the oddest:

BBC Radio

http://www.bbc.co.uk/radio1/
http://www.bbc.co.uk/radio2/
http://www.bbc.co.uk/radio3/
http://www.bbc.co.uk/radio4/
Auntie online, with something for everyone.

BitBop Turner

http://www.audiomill.com
Stupid name, but a great tool: download the software and it monitors online radio stations most likely to play your favourite songs, then records them for playback at your leisure.

De Concertzender

http://www.omroep.nl/concertzender/
A real boon for lovers of "highbrow" music: jazz, classical and New Music from this Dutch terrestrial station.

Dance Portal

http://www.danceportal.co.uk
Can't get out on Friday night? Put on your dancing shoes and point your browser here for Webcasts from, as Pete Tong would probably say, "the most upfront clubs" in the UK. Also check out CNSoho (http://www.cnsoholive.co.uk).

Gaialive

http://www.gaialive.co.uk
Trance, House, Techno and Hard House 24/7.

MTV

http://www.mtv.com
It may not be radio, but it does have hundreds of video streams available.

On the Wire

http://onthewire.hypermart.net
The best reggae on the Web from BBC Lancashire's Steve Barker, with an extra-special 24-hour dub loop for echo fanatics. Try also Black Ark (http://www.blackark.com).

Solid Steel

http://www.ninjatune.net/solidsteel/
Coldcut have been airing their essential mixes since 1988 on various terrestrial stations; you can listen to almost all of them (with playlists) here.

Swank Radio

http://www.swankradio.com
Spaceage bachelor pad muzak for cocktail enthusiasts and Tiki lovers everywhere.

Van Halen Radio Network

http://www.vhradio.com
Yup, all Van Halen, all the time.

WFMU

http://www.wfmu.org
Lucky residents of the New York metropolitan area have been able to call this treasure theirs for thirty-odd years. Now you can listen to the best freeform radio station on earth no matter where you live.

WNUR

http://www.wnur.org
Another great American station (from Chicago) covering experimental and local music better than nearly anyone else.

Xfm
http://www.xfm.co.uk
Catch London's indie station live online, all the time.

If you fancy setting up your own station or listening to the online equivalent of pirate radio, try:

Icecast.org http://www.icecast.org

Live365 http://www.live365.com

Shoutcast http://www.shoutcast.com

-- Over 38,000 internet radio stations broadcasting now on Live365 --

Welcome!

Whether you're looking for **music** to accompany you at work, an **obscure talk show** about UFOs, or **live mixes** by underground DJs to play at your next party, Live365 offers the most diverse selection of **internet radio stations** you'll find anywhere.

Welcome to the Radio Revolution!

To promote your own station or search for a song or artist currently playing across thousands of others:

RadioSpy http://www.radiospy.com

Crystal Radio
http://www.midnightscience.com
Build a simple wireless that needs no battery.

Interface Pirate Radio
http://www.pirate-radio.co.uk
Attempting to bring the aural ambience of east London to the Net.

Phil's Old Radios
http://www.antiqueradio.org
If you've ever drifted to sleep bathed in the soft glow of a crackling Bakelite wireless, Phil's collection of vacuum-era portables may instantly flood you with childhood memories.

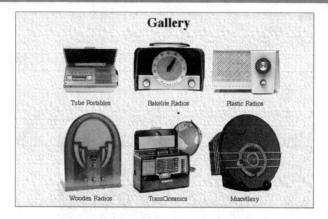

Gallery

Tube Portables | Bakelite Radios | Plastic Radios

Wooden Radios | TransOceanics | Miscellany

Pirate Radio
http://pirateradio.about.com
Stake your claim on the airwaves. More piracy info at How to Be a
Radio Pirate (http://www.irational.org/sic/radio/).

Police Scanner
http://www.policescanner.com
http://www.apbnews.com/scanner/
http://www.javaradio.com
Live emergency scanner feeds piped into RealAudio. Eavesdrop on
busts in progress. More on scanners at: http://www.strongsignals.net

Reference

With the Net threatening the very foundations of the encyclopedia industry, it should come as no surprise to find most of the
household names well entrenched online. While they're not all
entirely free, they're certainly cheaper and more up to date than
their bulky paper equivalents.

Britannica http://www.eb.com
Columbia http://www.bartleby.com/65/
Encarta http://www.encarta.com
Macquarie http://www.macquariedictionary.com.au

The premier Web encyclopedia
Now just $5 a month

Acronym Finder
http://www.acronymfinder.com
http://www.ucc.ie/info/net/acronyms/acro.html/
Before you follow IBM, TNT and HMV into initializing your company's name, make sure it doesn't mean something blue.

All Experts
http://www.allexperts.com
http://www.askme.com
http://www.abuzz.com
Ask any question and let unpaid experts do the thinking.

Alternative Dictionary
http://www.notam.uio.no/~hcholm/altlang/
Bucket your foreign chums in their mother tongue.

American ASL Dictionary
http://www.handspeak.com
http://www.bconnex.net/~randys/
Learn sign language through simple animations.

Anagram Genius
http://www.anagramgenius.com
Recycle used letters.

Reference

Aphorisms Galore
http://www.ag.wastholm.net
Sound clever by repeating someone else's lines.

Babelfish Translator
http://babelfish.altavista.com/translate.dyn/
Translate text, including Web pages, in seconds. Though run some text back and forth a few times (http://www.telalink.net/~carl/multibabel/) and you'll end up with something that wouldn't look out of place on a Japanese T-shirt. If you can't pick the language, try: http://www.dougb.com/ident.html/

Bartleby Reference
http://www.bartleby.com/reference/
Free access to several contemporary and classic reference works such as the American *Heritage* dictionaries, *Columbia Encyclopedia*, Fowler's *King's English*, Emily Post's *Etiquette*, the *Cambridge History of English and American Literature* and Gray's *Anatomy*.

Biography
http://www.biography.com
Recounting more than 25,000 lives.

Calculators Online
http://www-sci.lib.uci.edu/~martindale/RefCalculators.html/
Awesome directory of some 10,000 online tools to calculate everything from how much sump-oil one puts in soap to the burden of bringing up brats.

Cliché Finder
http://www.westegg.com/cliche/
Submit a word or phrase to find out how not to use it.

Earthstation1
http://www.earthstation1.com
The 20th century captured in sound and vision.

eHow
http://www.ehow.com
Make yourself useful through step-by-step tutorials.

Encyclopedia Mythica
http://pantheon.org/mythica/
Hefty album of mythology, folklore and legend.

Famous Quotations Network
http://www.famous-quotations.com
Perk up essays and letters with a witticism from Oscar Wilde or a
Senegalese proverb. For more quotes, try The Quotations Page
(http://www.quotationspage.com) or Silly Quotes
(http://www.sillyquotes.com) or Motivational Quotes
(http://www.motivational-quotes.com).

Find Articles
http://www.findarticles.com
No fuss, no muss search engine of more than 300 magazines and journals. The results are all printable and free.

How Stuff Works
http://www.howstuffworks.com
Learn the secrets behind fake tans, animal camouflage and cable modems.

How to Speak to an Extraterrestrial
http://adrr.com/lingua/alien.htm/
Crash course in ET101.

InfoPlease
http://www.infoplease.com
Handy, all-purpose almanac for stats and trivia.

Ka-BOOM! A Dictionary of Comic Book Words
http://www.geocities.com/Athens/Marathon/5150/dictionary/
Become fluent in the language favoured by leading superheroes.

Learn a language

Arabic http://i-cias.com/babel/arabic/
The French Tutorial http://www.frenchlesson.com
German For Travellers http://www.germanfortravellers.com
The Japanese Tutor http://www.japanese-online.com
Spain Is Moving http://www.spainismoving.com

Librarian's Index
http://www.lii.org
Naturally there are oodles of reference portals brimming with helpful reference tools. These are some of the best:

LibrarySpot http://www.libraryspot.com

Open Directory http://dmoz.org/Reference/

Refdesk.com http://www.refdesk.com

Yahoo http://dir.yahoo.com/reference/

Megaconverter 2
http://www.megaconverter.com/mega2/
Calculate everything from your height in angstroms to the pellets of lead per ounce of buckshot needed to bring down an overcharging consultant.

Nonsensicon
http://www.nonsensicon.com
Non-existent words and their meanings.

Nupedia
http://www.nupedia.com
Nupedia is a new open content encyclopedia project collated by volunteers. You're invited to contribute.

Oxford Reference
http://www.oxfordreference.com
Mind-blowing reference library of some 100 titles now online.
Unfortunately, you have to subscribe.

Rap Dictionary
http://www.rapdict.org
Hip-hop to English. Parental guidance recommended.

RhymeZone
http://www.rhymezone.com
Get a hoof up in putting together a classy love poem.

Roget's Thesaurus
http://www.thesaurus.com
New format; useless as ever.

Skeptic's Dictionary
http://www.skepdic.com
Punch holes in mass media funk and pseudosciences such as
homeopathy, astrology and iridology.

Slang dictionaries

Playground Slang http://www.odps.cyberscriber.com
Bridge the generation gap.

A Prisoner's Dictionary http://dictionary.prisonwall.org
Shhh, a 5-0 is coming.

Silicon Valley Slang Page
http://www.sabram.com/Slang/slang.html
For your next meeting with Bill Gates.

Twists, Slugs and Rocoes
http://www.miskatonic.org/slang.html/
Talk like Mike Hammer.

Wizard's Gay Slang Dictionary
http://www.hurricane.net/~wizard/19a.html/
For adults only.

Spellweb
http://www.spellweb.com
Compare two words or phrases and see which gets more hits in a search engine. If it demonstrates anything, it's that the Web is strung together with a lot of bad spelling.

The Straight Dope
http://www.straightdope.com
Cecil Adams's answers to hard questions. Find out how to renounce your US citizenship, what "Kemosabe" means and the difference between a warm smell of colitas and colitis.

Streetmap.co.uk
http://www.streetmap.co.uk
Find a location anywhere in the UK with a postcode, phone number, street name or latitude and longitude. If you're planning a US road trip, try Mapquest (http://www.mapquest.com).

Strunk's Elements of Style
http://www.bartleby.com/141/
The complete classic of English usage in a nutshell, though unfortunately not the latest edition. For more on grammar and style:

alt.usage.English FAQ http://homepages.tcp.co.uk/~laker/faq/
Education Finder http://www.edunet.com/english/grammar/
Garbl's Writing Resources http://www.garbl.com
Montreal Gazette Style Guide http://www.canada.com/montreal /montrealgazette/specials/styleguide

Symbols
http://www.symbols.com
Ever woken up with a strange sign tattooed on your buttocks? Here's where to find what it means without calling in Agent Mulder.

What is?
http://www.whatis.com
http://www.webopedia.com
Unravel cumbersome computer and Internet jargon without having even more thrown at you.

Whoohoo
http://www.whoohoo.co.uk
If you come from Berwick and find yourself in the East End unable to understand a word anyone says, this site may be of help.

The Why Files
http://whyfiles.org
The science behind the headlines.

World Atlas
http://www.worldatlas.com
Maps, flags, latitude and longitude finder, population growth and so on – though you might prefer the maps on paper. For more maps, geography and GPS resources, try About Geography (http://geography.about.com), National Geographic (http://www.nationalgeographic.com/mapmachine) and the Open Directory (http://dmoz.org/Reference/Maps/).

World Factbook
http://www.odci.gov/cia/publications/factbook/
Information for spies from the CIA.

Xrefer
http://www.xrefer.com
Consult this site to query a broad selection of prominent reference works from Oxford University Press, Houghton Mifflin, Penguin, Macmillan, Bloomsbury and Market House Books.

Yellow Pages
http://www.yell.com
If you're too lazy to flip through the book.

YourDictionary.com
http://www.yourdictionary.com
For one-point access to over a thousand dictionaries across almost every language. Try also Dictionary.com (http://www.dictionary.com) and One Look (http://www.onelook.com).

Relationships, Dating and Friendship

The Internet is the biggest singles bar humankind has ever created: with millions and millions of users from around the world, even the most lovelorn are bound to find someone worth cyber-flirting with. However, it's worth bearing in mind that the World Wide Web is no different from the real world and there are plenty of scam artists, hustlers, leeches and other unsavoury characters lurking in unsuspected corners. By all means enjoy dropping virtual handkerchiefs to perspective suitors, but keep your wits about you. Before engaging in any social intercourse on the Net, go to Wildx Angel (http://www.wildxangel.com) for advice on the safest way to go on the pull online.

To help you on your way, here are some of the Web's biggest dating agencies:

Dateline http://www.dateline.uk.com
Dating Direct http://www.datingdirect.com
Elite Dating http://www.elite-dating.co.uk
Friendfinder http://www.friendfinder.com
Lavalife http://www.lavalife.com
Lovefinder http://www.lovefinder.co.uk
Match.com http://www.match.com
SocialNet http://www.relationships.com
The Switch http://www.theswitch.co.uk
UDate http://www.udate.com
UK Singles http://www.uksingles.co.uk
Where's My Date? http://www.wheresmydate.com
WooWho http://www.woowho.co.uk

To find a chat room, try a chat portal like:
The Chat Room Directory http://www.webarrow.net/chatindex/
Chatseek http://chatseek.com
Chat Shack Network http://chatshack.net

Relationships, Dating and Friendship

The Ultimate Chatlist http://www.chatlist.com

For more, try the Open Directory's chat portal list:
http://dmoz.org/Computers/Internet/Chat/Link_Lists/

Coincidence Design
http://www.coincidencedesign.com
For a mere $78,000 the "professionals" at this site will engineer a meeting with the girl/boy of your dreams.

Crazy Bitch
http://www.crazy-bitch.com
What happens when men have affairs with their secretaries.

Cyberspace Inmates
http://www.cyberspace-inmates.com
Strike up an email romance with a prison inmate – maybe even one on death row.

Dating
http://dating.about.com
About's dating advice page hosts a motherload of sensible information on dating both on- and offline.

Dating Directories
http://www.singlesites.com
http://www.100hot.com/directory/lifestyles/dating.html/
Come aboard, they're expecting you.

The Divorce Support Page
http://www.divorcesupport.com
Lots of friendly ears and shoulders to cry on.

Friends Reunited
http://www.friendsreunited.co.uk
You haven't forgotten. Now track them down one by one. More people who teased you in the common room are at
http://www.classmates.com. If you were behind bars rather than in school http://www.convictsreunited.com might help.

Relationships, Dating and Friendship

Gentle, Romantic Woman Seeks Agnostic or Atheist for Strong Attraction, Friendship, Eventual Marriage and Deepest Love
http://hometown.aol.com/mary1777/index.htm
Middle-aged divorcée lays down the law.

Hot or Not?
http://www.hotornot.com
http://www.ratemyface.com
Submit a flattering photo and have it rated by passing chumps. So popular it has spawned a string of spoofs, such as: http://www.
amigothornot.com; http://www.amigeekornot.com;
http://www.amifuglyornot.com; http://www.amipotornot.com;
http://www.amiallyourbaseornot.com. To sort by rating, see:
http://log.waxy.org/hot/. To instantly create your own custom Am I
page: http://www.iamcal.com/ami/l/

The Hugging Site
http://members.tripod.com/~hugging/
The history of embracing, hugging stories and tips to improve your cuddling technique.

Javina's Prostitution FAQ
http://www.javina.com/JJ3/faq.html/
Learn the truth behind the *Pretty Woman* fantasy.

Love Calculator
http://www.lovecalculator.com
Enter your respective names to see if you're compatible.

Meg's Boyfriend of the Week
http://www.drizzle.com/~knuckles
In which Meg rates TV stars by their proximity to that paragon of perfection: MacGyver.

Pen Pal Directory
http://dir.yahoo.com/Social_Science/Communications/Writing/Correspondence/Pen_Pals/
Exchange email with strangers.

Relationships, Dating and Friendship

PlanetOut
http://www.planetout.com
http://www.rainbownetwork.com
http://www.qrd.org
http://www.datalounge.com
http://www.queertheory.com
Directories to all that's that way inclined.

The Rejection Line
http://www.lazystudent.co.uk/rejectline.html
Let the professionals break it to that not so special someone.

Romance 101
http://www.rom101.com
Chat-up lines, compatibility tests and advice from men to women like "Never buy a 'new' brand of beer because 'it was on sale'."

Secret Admirer
http://www.secretadmirer.com
http://www.ecrush.com
Find out whether your most secret crushed one digs you back.

So There
http://www.sothere.com
A place to post your parting shots.

Swoon
http://www.swoon.com
Dating, mating, and relating. Courtesy of Condé Nast's *Details*, *GQ*, *Glamour*, and *Mademoiselle*. For dessert, try:
http://dating.about.com

Things My Girlfriend and I Have Argued About
http://homepage.ntlworld.com/mil.millington/things.html/
Add this page to that list.

Tips for Dating Emotional Cripples
http://www.grrl.com/bipolar.html/
The site all women must visit.

Tips for Dating

Emotional Cripples

Vampire Exchange
http://www.vein-europe.demon.co.uk
http://www.sanguinarius.org
Give blood as an act of love.

Way Too Personal
http://www.waytoopersonal.com
Wild and woolly adventures in Internet dating.

Weddings in the Real World
http://www.theknot.com
http://www.nearlywed.com
Prepare to jump the broom – or untie the knot:
http://www.divorcesource.com

Religion

If you haven't yet signed up with a religious sect or are unhappy with the one passed down by your folks, here's your opportunity to survey the field at your own pace. Most are open to newcomers, though certain rules and conditions may apply. For a reasonably complete and unbiased breakdown of faith dealerships, try:

BeliefNet http://www.beliefnet.com
Comparative Religion http://www.academicinfo.net/religindex.html/
Religious Tolerance http://www.religioustolerance.org

But don't expect such an easy ride from those demanding proof:
Atheism http://atheism.miningco.com
Christian Burner http://www.christianburner.com
The Secular Web http://www.infidels.org

Adherents.com
http://www.adherents.com
Statistical ranking of the world's religions from the Aaronic Order to Zurvanism.

Religion

Anglicans Online
http://anglicansonline.org
A gentle catapult into the Church of England worldwide.

Avatar Search
http://www.AvatarSearch.com
Search the occult Net for spiritual guidance and lottery tips.

The Bible Gateway
http://bible.gospelcom.net
Set your table with the Good Book.

A Brief History of the Apocalypse
http://www.chrisnelson.net/end1.htm
It takes a lickin' and keeps on tickin'.

The British Druid Order
http://www.druidorder.demon.co.uk
Dance around Stonehenge, make potions and meet fellow wizards.

BuddhaNet
http://www.buddhanet.net
Take a ride on the wheel of dharma and download the Diamond Sutra.

Catholic Church – God's One and Only Church
http://www.truecatholic.org
More troops armed with the truth.

Catholic Online
http://www.catholic.org
Saints, Angels, shopping, discussion and a portal to the online territory occupied by Catholics.

Celebrity Atheist List
http://www.celebatheists.com
Big names you won't spot in Heaven.

Cheesy Jesus
http://www.cheesyjesus.com
http://www.ship-of-fools.com/Gadgets/
Buy gadgets to bring you closer to God.

Finally, an action figure representing the greatest man of all! This 5" tall plastic figure has poseable arms and gliding actions—perfect for blessing Barbie and guiding GI Joe through the line of fire! Each action figure comes attractively blister carded with fun Jesus facts on the back. Hours of biblical fun!

Price: $7.95

Chick
http://chick.com
Hardcore Christian pornography.

Christian Answers
http://christiananswers.net
Movies and computer games reviewed and hard questions answered, by Christians who know what's good for you and your family.

Christian Naturists
http://home.vistapnt.com/markm/
Frolic with other Christian funseekers, the way God intended.

Christians v Muslims
http://debate.org.uk
http://www.rim.org/muslim/islam.htm/
http://members.aol.com/AllahIslam/
http://www.answering-islam.org
http://www.muslim-answers.org
http://www.biblicalchristianity.freeserve.co.uk
Put your faith on the line.

Church of England

http://www.cofe.anglican.org

The home of Anglicanism online. Presbyterians should head north of the border at Church of Scotland (http://www.churchofscotland.org.uk).

Church of the Subgenius

http://www.subgenius.com

Find the truth through slackness.

(Click HERE to become an ORDAINED SUBGENIUS MINISTER.)

CrossSearch

http://www.crosssearch.com

Set sail through safe waters to find Christian groups of all denominations.

Crosswalk

http://www.crosswalk.com

Catch up with the latest on Jesus.

Demon Possession Handbook

http://diskbooks.org/hs.html/

Train for a job with the Watcher's Council.

Exorcism

http://www.logoschristian.org/exorcism.html

Don't try this at home.

Free Deliverance

http://www.demonbuster.com

Use Jesus's teachings to cast out demons, wage spiritual warfare and overcome bipolar disorder, depression, addiction, obesity and other modern ailments.

The Greatest Truth Ever Revealed

http://www.sevenseals.com

Revelations from survivors of the Waco siege.

The Hindu Universe

http://www.hindunet.org

Hindu dharma – the philosophy, culture and customs.

Religion

The Holy See
http://www.vatican.va
Official hideout of the pope and his posse.

Islamic Gateway
http://www.ummah.net
http://www.musalman.com
http://www.fatwa-online.com
Get down with Muhammed (*sallallahu `alaihi wa sallam*).

Jah Rastafari
http://www.webcom.com/nattyreb/rastafari/everlasting.html/
A packed site devoted to worshipping Haile Selassie as the living god.

Jesus, a Historical Reconstruction
http://www.concentric.net/~Mullerb/
Getting to the truth about the man from Nazareth.

Jesus of the Week
http://www.jesusoftheweek.com
The original Mr Nice Guy in 52 coy poses per year. Catch him winking
at: http://www.winkingjesus.com

The Miraculous Winking Jesus

On April 23rd 1996, this picture of Jesus
Christ miraculously winked at me. This
experience has changed my life. Over six
hundred and thirty thousand people have
come to witness this miracle. Many people
have had a lot to say about their
experience. If you are fortunate enough to
witness this image of Jesus Christ wink,
please tell your friends and family about
this miracle!
- Rev. Jonathan C. Chance (Internet Field
Missionary)

Jesus winked at me!   Jesus did not wink at me!

Winking Jesus   Super Store   Reflections   Donate   Contact

Latter Day Designs Vinyl Figures
http://www.lehi.com/vin1.html/
Action figures from The Book of Mormon.

The Mark of the Beast
http://www.greaterthings.com/essays/666mark.htm
Did you know that "Holy Bible" is "666" in ASCII code?

Miracles Page
http://www.mcn.org/1/miracles/
Spooky signs that point towards a cosmic conspiracy.

The 93 Current
http://www.93current.de
The magick of Aleister Crowley. Do more of what thou wilt at An Introduction to Crowley Studies (http://www.maroney.org/ Crowley Intro/) and The Works of Aleister Crowley (http://www.netropic.org/crowley).

Not Proud
http://www.notproud.com
Confess your most entertaining sins.

OrishaNet
http://www.seanet.com/Users/efunmoyiwa/
Learn about the Cuban religion of Santeria and consult with Oshun, Ifá and Elegba.

The Pagan Library
http://www.paganlibrary.com
Pagan and Wiccan texts and other information on the mysteries of the Craft.

Peyote Way Church of God
http://www.peyoteway.org
Unless you're Native American or live in select southern US states, you stand to be locked up for finding God through the psychedelic cactus. Otherwise, feel free to fry your brain; just don't drive home from church.

Religion

Prophecy and Current Events
http://www.aplus-software.com/thglory/
http://www.prophezine.com
You'll never guess who's coming to dinner. Don't bother cooking, though; he's supposed to be a real whizz with food.

Religious Frauds
http://religiousfrauds.50megs.com
Esteemed reptile slayer David Icke sniffs out Christian cons.

Roy Taylor Ministries
http://www.roytaylorministries.com
"American Pie" is God's song and other examples of questionable hermeneutics.

Saint John Coltrane African Orthodox Church
http://www.saintjohncoltrane.org
Branch of the One Holy Catholic and Apostolic Church whose patron saint is the great jazz saxophonist.

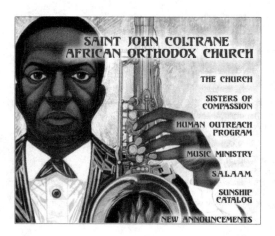

Satanism 101
http://www.satanism101.com
Enter this address and go straight to Hell:
http://www.what-the-hell-is-hell.com
http://www.virtualhell.org

Scientology
http://www.scientology.org.uk
The favoured religion of Hollywood stars.

Shamanism
http://deoxy.org/shaman.htm/
Entheogens, plant sacraments and other ecstatic vehicles.

Ship of Fools: the Magazine of Christian Unrest
http://ship-of-fools.com
The lighter side of Christianity.

Sikh Museum
http://www.sikhmuseum.org
The teachings and history of the main religion of the Punjabi region of
India.

Skeptics Annotated Bible
http://www.skepticsannotatedbible.com
Contends that the Good Book is a misnomer.

Spirit Web
http://www.spiritweb.com
Pass the joss-sticks, stroke some crystals, get in touch with your past
lives and hitch a ride on a passing UFO.

Stories of the Dreaming
http://www.dreamtime.net.au
Selection of enchanting bedtime stories in text, video and audio that
explain creation from an Aboriginal perspective. Don't believe in creation? Go tell it to the jury: http://www.talkorigins.org

Totally Jewish
http://www.totallyjewish.com
http://www.maven.co.il
http://judaism.about.com
http://aish.com
Spiritual guidance and community portals for the chosen people
(http://www.chosen-people.com) and curious goyim. More good mozel
at JewishNet (http://www.jewishnet.co.uk).

24 Hour Church of Elvis
http://www.churchofelvis.com
No spiritual advice here, just the gift shop.

Universal Life Church
http://ulc.org
Become a self-ordained minister.

The Vodou Page
http://members.aol.com/racine125/
Learn how to convene with the loas.

The Witches' Voice
http://www.witchvox.com
Expresses a burning desire to correct misinformation about witchcraft, a
legally recognized religion in the US since 1985.

Zen
http://www.do-not-zzz.com
Take a five-minute course in meditation.

Science

To keep abreast of science news and developments stop by
Scitech, which aggregates stories from the leading scientific
media:

Scitech Daily Review http://www.scitechdaily.com

Or go straight to one of the many science journals:

Archeology http://www.archaeology.org
Beyond 2000 http://www.beyond2000.com
British Medical Journal http://www.bmj.com
Bulletin of Atomic Scientists http://www.bullatomsci.org
Discover http://www.discover.com
Discovery Channel http://www.discovery.com
Earth Times http://www.earthtimes.org
Edge http://www.edge.org
Highwire Press http://highwire.stanford.edu
The Lancet http://www.thelancet.com
National Geographic http://www.nationalgeographic.com
New Scientist http://www.newscientist.com
Popular Mechanics http://www.popularmechanics.com
Popular Science http://www.popsci.com
Science à GoGo http://www.scienceagogo.com
Science Magazine http://www.sciencemag.org
Science News http://www.sciencenews.org
Scientific American http://www.scientificamerican.com
The Scientist http://www.the-scientist.com
Skeptical Inquirer http://www.csicop.org/si/
Technology Review http://www.techreview.com

Looking for a something specific or a range of sites within a strand? Try browsing or searching a directory:

Hypography http://www.hypography.com
Open Directory http://dmoz.org/Science/
SciSeek http://www.sciseek.com
Treasure Troves of Science http://www.treasure-troves.com
Yahoo http://dir.yahoo.com/science/

Albert Einstein Online

http://www.westegg
.com/einstein/

In essence an Albert
Einstein portal, with
links to biographies,
quotes, articles and
essays, photos and
other pages related to
Time magazine's Man
of the Century.

Pictures of Albert Einstein
(Click for larger pictures)

The oldest picture | Patent clerk | 1920 | ca. 1900
1931 | Radio talk | Barcelona, 1923 | Berlin 1922

Amusement Park Physics

http://www.learner.org/exhibits/parkphysics/

If your kid has absolutely no interest in potential and kinetic energy,
send them to this fantastic site for the coolest science lesson on the
Web and give them the chance to design their own rollercoaster.

AnthroNet

http://www.anthro.net

Gateway to the world of anthropology, archeology and other social sciences.

Battlebots

http://www.battlebots.com

Robots kick ass.

KICK BOT!

ROBOT DEATHTRAP

Biology
http://biology.about.com
Vast array of life-science links and articles.

Bizarre Stuff You Can Make in Your Kitchen
http://freeweb.pdq.net/headstrong/
A really fun archive of classic home science experiments from the 1930s to the 1960s. Brings out the Magnus Pike in everyone.

The Braintainment Center
http://www.brain.com
http://www.mensa.org
http://www.iqtest.com
http://www.mind-gear.com
http://www.mindmedia.com
Start with a test that says you're not so bright, then prove it by buying loads of self-improvement gear. Short on brains? Try:
http://www.brains4zombies.com

Bunny Survival Tests
http://www.pcola.gulf
.net/~irving/bunnies/

Determining whether marshmallow bunnies can survive lasers, flames, hot tubs, coyotes, radiation and oxygen deprivation. For more rabbit "science", go to The Bunnies Strike Back (http://marks.networktel.net).

Chemistry.org.uk
http://www.liv.ac.uk/Chemistry/Links/link.html/
The chemistry section of the WWW Virtual Library has some 8500 links to chemistry sites. Advanced chemists should check out ChemWeb (http://www.chemweb.com) and its Available Chemical Directory of 278,000 compounds (you need to subscribe to gain access).

The Constants and Equations Pages
http://tcaep.co.uk
A great reference resource for students of maths and science, metric identities, Avogadro's Number, SI units and other m
headaches.

Cool Robot of the Week
http://ranier.hq.nasa.gov/telerobotics_page/coolrobots.html/
Clever ways to get machines to do our dirty work. For a directory of
simulators, combat comps, clubs and DIY bots, direct your agent to:
http://www.robotcafe.com

Dangerous Laboratories
http://www.dangerouslaboratories.org
Definitely don't try this at home.

Documentation and Diagrams of the Atomic Bomb
http://serendipity.magnet.ch/more/atomic.html
...oe this doesn't fall into the wrong hands; imagine the effect on
...hbourhood:
...pbs.org/wgbh/amex/bomb/sfeature/mapablast.html

...ety
Darth.org
...of science wrong.

...rg
...ingerprints.

Gray's Anatomy Online
http://www.bartleby.com/107/
The complete edition of the essential anatomical text.

History of Mathematics
http://www-groups.dcs.st-andrews.ac.uk/~history/
The life and times of various bright sparks with numbers.

HotAir – Annals of Improbable Research
http://www.improbable.com
Science gone too far, or around the bend. Includes the Ig Nobel awards for achievements that cannot, or should not, be reproduced.

How Does a Thing Like That Work?
http://www.pitt.edu/~dwilley/hdatltwmenu.html
Entertaining physics demonstration experiments.

How Stuff Works
http://www.howstuffworks.com
Unravel the mysterious machinations behind all sorts of stuff from Christmas to cruise missiles.

Institute of Physics
http://www.iop.org
Fast, well-designed physics portal. For articles like "The Industrial Physicist Who Has it All" (http://physicsweb.org), check out PhysicsWeb (http://physicsweb.org); for the history of the second superstring revolution, try Physics.org (http://www.physics.org).

Interactive Frog Dissection
http://teach.virginia.edu/go/frog/
Pin down a frog, grab your scalpel and follow the pictures.

The Lab
http://www.abc.net.au/science/
ABC science news and program info with Q&As from Aussie pop-science superstar, Dr Karl Kruszelnicki.

MadSciNet: 24-hour Exploding Laboratory
http://www.madsci.org
Collective of more than a hundred scientific smarty-pantses set up specifically to answer your dumb questions. More geniuses for hire at:
http://www.ducksbreath.com
http://www.wsu.edu/DrUniverse/
http://www.sciam.com/askexpert/
http://www.sciencenet.org.uk

MIT Media Labs
http://www.media.mit.edu
If you've read *Being Digital* or any of Nicholas Negroponte's *Wired* columns, you'll know he has some pretty tall ideas about our electronic future. Here's where he gets them.

Museum of Dirt
http://www.planet.com/dirtweb/dirt.html/
Celebrity dirt of an entirely different nature.

National Inventors Hall of Fame
http://www.invent.org
Homepage of a museum based in Akron, Ohio dedicated to the world's most important inventors. Includes short biographies and pictures of luminaries like Thomas Edison, Enrico Fermi and Louis Pasteur. For more modern inventions, go to Inventions And Technologies (http://www.inventions-tech.com/epanel.htm/), and for questionable inventions see Patently Absurd!
(http://www.patent.freeserve.co.uk).

Netsurfer Science
http://www.netsurf.com/nss/
Subscribe to receive weekly bulletins on science and technology sites.

Nobel e-Museum
http://www.nobel.se
Read all about Nobel Prize winners.

Rocketry Online
http://www.rocketryonline.com
Take on NASA at its own game.

Skeptics Society
http://www.skeptic.com
http://www.csicop.org
Don't try to pull a swift one on this crowd.

The Soundry
http://library.thinkquest.org/19537
A fun introduction to the science of acoustics.

Strange Science: The Rocky Road to Modern Paleontology and Biology
http://www.strangescience.net
A great site exploring the fallout of science's paradigm wars.

Time Travel
http://freespace.virgin.net/steve.preston/
"We discuss many of the common objections to time travel and we show that these objections are without foundation."

USGS National Earthquake Info Center
http://gldss7.cr.usgs.gov
http://www.gps.caltech.edu/~polet/recofd.html/
Stats and maps of the most recent quakes worldwide.

Virtual Autopsy 2
http://www.le.ac.uk/pathology/teach/va/welcome.html
Definitely not for the squeamish, this site gives you the opportunity to fish around the insides of eight cadavers and try to determine the cause of death from their case histories.

Volcano World
http://volcano.und.nodak.edu
Monitor the latest eruptions, see photos of every major volcano in the world, and virtually tour a Hawaiian smoky without choking on sulphur fumes.

VoltNet
http://www.voltnet.com
Celebrate the power of electricity by blowing things up.

WebElements
http://www.webelements.com
http://www.chemsoc.org/viselements/
Click on an element in the periodic table and suss it out in depth. Now crosscheck its comic book reference:
http://www.uky.edu/Projects/Chemcomics/ and recite its poem:
http://www.superdeluxe.com/elemental/

Weird Science and Mad Scientists
http://www.eskimo.com/~billb/weird.html/
http://www.student.nada.kth.se/~nv91-asa/mad.html/
Free energy, Tesla, anti-gravity, aura, cold fusion, parapsychology and other strange scientific projects and theories.

Why Files
http://whyfiles.news.wisc.edu
Entertaining reports on the science behind current news.

Shopping

BizRate
http://www.bizrate.com
Shopping sites rated and reviewed.

Bottom Dollar
http://www.bottomdollar.com
One of the biggest comparison engines or shopping bots: enter a product name or keyword here and it'll return a listing of prices and availability across a range of retailers. Of course, a bargain-finder is only as good as its sources, so the best ones scour a broad range of sites. For more deals, try: Checkaprice (http://www.checkaprice.com), Dealtime

(http://www.dealtime.com), Easy Value (http://www.easyvalue.com),
Kelkoo (http://uk.kelkoo.com), Price Checker
(http://www.PriceChecker.co.uk), The Price Guide UK
(http://www.price-guide.co.uk) and ShopSmart
(http://uk.shopsmart.com).

Buy.co.uk
http://www.buy.co.uk/Personal/Calculators/
Price and service comparisons of mobile phones, credit cards, electricity, water and gas suppliers. For more info on mobile phone and utilities suppliers try uSwitch (http://www.uswitch.com). To compare the price of landline phone bills, go to http://www.phonebills.org.uk. For energy suppliers try http://www.ukenergy.co.uk

Buyersview
http://www.buyersview.co.uk
Similar in some senses to Productopia (see p.304) and other shopping review sites in that it houses consumer reviews and rankings of shopping sites. But it also has added features like Get Me the Manager, an online complaints service, and Abandoned Trolley, which aims to discover why potential online shoppers decided to go elsewhere.

Catalogue City
http://uk.uk.catalogcity.com
If you're unconvinced by online shopping and would prefer it on paper, drive your postie crazy by ordering every catalogue in the world. For even more junk mail, try Buyers' Index (http://www.buyersindex.com), Catalink (http://www.catalink.co.uk) and Catalog Site
(http://catalogsite.catalogcity.com).

Consumer World
http://www.consumerworld.org
Not all of the information here may be appropriate because it's an American site, but this should be an automatic bookmark for anyone intending to do any shopping either on- or offline. Aside from the comparison engines, bargain listings and product reviews, it has alerts on the latest scams and annoying marketing practices.

How to Complain
http://www.howtocomplain.com
Let the professionals do it for you.

LetsBuyIt.com

http://www.letsbuyit.com
This site uses collaborative buying power to clinch lower prices for its members across Europe.

MyGeek

http://www.mygeek.com
Type in your shopping request here and they will approach several different merchants looking for the best price.

PriceWatch

http://www.pricewatch.com
If you're after computer products, this shopping bot is one of the best comparison engines on the Web. Also try Shopper.com (http://www.shopper.com).

Productopia

http://www.productopia.com
The most thorough collection of buying guides, customer opinions, ratings and links to external reviews. More consumer advice is available at: Amazon (http://www.amazon.co.uk), Consumer Review (http://www.consumerreview.com), Dooyoo (http://www.dooyoo.com), Epinions (http://www.epinions.com), eSmarts (http://www.esmarts.com), Google Groups (http://groups.google.com) and Rateitall.com (http://www.rateitall.com). Of course, there's always Which? (http://www.which.net) for trustworthy consumer advice.

Recall Announcements

http://www.recallannouncements.co.uk
Stay up-to-date on the consumer safety front.

ShittyGift.com

http://www.shittygift.com
Like any provincial high street but magnified a million times,

The Bar Stool Racer

the Internet is a minefield of tack and bad ideas. This site is a reminder that taste and bandwidth don't always go hand in hand.

ShopSmart

http://uk.shopsmart.com

UK directory of shopping sites. Since it's impossible to be complete, if you can't find what you're after here, try: Buyers' Guide (http://www.buyersguide.to), My Taxi (http://www.mytaxi.co.uk), Shop Finger (http://www.shopfinger.com), UK Shopping (http://www.ukshopping.com) and UK Shop Search (http://www.ukshopsearch.com).

Silver Surfers

ARP/050

http://www.arp.org.uk

News, information and forums from the Association of Retired and Persons Over 50.

BBC Health: Health at 50

http://www.bbc.co.uk/health/50plus/

Easily among the best of the BBC sites, largely because – unlike most of the Beeb's pages – it's not dependent on Auntie's programming. The advice is honest and trustworthy and there are no bells or whistles.

Better Government For Older People

http://www.bettergovernmentforolderpeople.gov.uk

Unfortunately, this governmental site is as dull, tedious and cumbersome as its domain name.

FiftyOn

http://www.fiftyon.co.uk

A portal for 50-pluses, with its best and most laudable feature being the advice and vacancies database it maintains for older jobseekers.

Hell's Geriatrics

http://www.hellsgeriatrics.co.uk

Grow old disgracefully.

Silver Surfers

I Don't Feel 50
http://www.idf50.co.uk
A fun, irreverent site run by Graham Andrews, with topics like "Is Age Concern too Old?" and "Mind the Generation Gap".

National U3A UK
http://www.u3a.org.uk
Continuing adult education from the Third Age Trust and the University of the Third Age.

Retirement Matters
http://www.retirement-matters.co.uk
Online magazine specializing in news, reviews and information for over-50s.

Saga Magazine
http://www.saga.co.uk/magazine/
Homepage of the magazine for over 50s, with content from the current issue, although there is no archive of past articles.

See How They Grow
http://www.seehowtheygrow.com
A guide to grandparenting, with chat boards, advice and plenty of stories about little monsters.

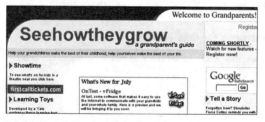

Senior Site
http://www.seniorsite.com
American online community for grown-ups, with Pat Boone as the entertainment correspondent and an excellent section on protecting yourself against "senior scams".

Seniority.co.uk
http://www.seniority.co.uk
Like all online communities, this one for senior citizens is only as good
as its contributors. While some of Seniority is hit-and-miss, it does have
an impressive community spirit.

SeniorsSearch
http://www.seniorssearch.com
Search engine dedicated to resources for silver surfers.

Third Age
http://www.thirdage.com
This American online magazine for older women may look like some terrible advert for feminine hygiene products, but underneath the terrible
design is an informative, friendly e-zine.

Write a Senior Citizen
http://www.writeseniors.com
Penpals for seniors.

Space

If you have more than a passing interest in space, skip the popular science mags (p.295) and newswires (p.239), and go straight
to the source:

British National Space Centre http://www.bnsc.gov.uk
European Space Agency http://www.esrin.esa.it
NASA http://www.nasa.gov
Royal Greenwich Observatory http://www.rog.nmm.ac.uk

Or try any of these specialist space ports:
About Space http://space.about.com
Amateur Astronomy Magazine http://www.amateurastronomy.com
Astronomy.com http://www.astronomy.com
Astronomy Now http://www.astronomynow.com
Explorezone http://explorezone.com
Human Spaceflight http://spaceflight.nasa.gov

Space

Jet Propulsion Lab http://www.jpl.nasa.gov
Planetary Society http://planetary.org
Sky & Telescope Magazine http://www.skypub.com
Space.com http://www.space.com
Space Daily http://www.spacedaily.com
SpaceRef http://www.spaceref.com
SpaceScience http://www.spacescience.com
Universe Today http://www.universetoday.com

Alien Bases on Earth
http://www.earth-today.com
See, in great detail, where the Gods have parked their chariots.

Alien Scalpel
http://www.alienscalpel.com
Protect yourself against abduction.

Area 51
http://www.terraserver.com/Area51.asp/
Inspect the first public satellite photos of the infamous no-fly zone.

Artemis Project
http://www.asi.org
Join a queue to go to the moon.

AstroCapella
http://www2.smart.net/~ksmale/astrocapella/idea.html/
Learn astronomy through great tunes such as "Doppler Shifting" and "Habitable Zone".

Astronomy Picture of the Day
http://antwrp.gsfc.nasa.gov/apod/astropix.html/
Enjoy a daily helping of outer space served up by a gourmet astrochef.

Auroral Activity
http://www.sec.noaa.gov/pmap/
Instantly see the current extent and position of the auroral oval above each pole.

Auroras: Paintings in the Sky
http://www.exploratorium
.edu/learning_studio
/auroras
http://www.alaskascience
.com/aurora.htm

If you're ever lucky enough
to see the Aurora during a
solar storm, you'll never
take the night sky for granted again. The Exploratorium
does a commendable job in
explaining a polar phenomenon that very few people understand.
Except maybe these champs: http://www.haarp.alaska.edu

Bad Astronomy
http://www.badastronomy.com
Ditch your lifetime's supply of space misconceptions and clichés.

Chandra X-Ray
http://www.chandra.harvard.edu
Telescope's-eye view of black holes and supernovas.

Clickworkers
http://clickworkers.arc.nasa.gov
Wangle a NASA job onto your résumé by counting craters on Mars.

Comets & Meteor Showers
http://comets.amsmeteors.org
Be on the lookout for falling rocks.

Darksky
http://www.darksky.org
Join the campaign against wanton street lighting. You'll see why in the
gallery.

Deep Cold
http://www.deepcold.com
Artistic mockups of chic space racers that never left the hangar.

Space

DEEPCOLD

Earth Viewer
http://www.fourmilab.ch/earthview/
View the Earth in space and time.

Eclipse Cam
http://eclipse.span.ch/liveshow.htm/
You don't even need a special box designed by your science teacher to view this site.

Galactic Information Service
http://home.c2i.net/galactic/torealf/
"Here you will find information about the technology of the spacepeople. UFO pictures. Spacelanguage and pictures from other dimensions/planets."

Geocentricity
http://www.biblicalastronomer.org
Dedicated to proving the sun revolves around the earth.

Heavens Above
http://www.heavens-above.com
Correctly identify nearby satellites and space stations.

Hubblesite
http://hubble.stsci.edu
Intergalactic snapshots fresh from the Hubble telescope.

Hypothetical Planets
http://seds.lpl.arizona.edu/nineplanets/nineplanets/hypo.html/
Paul Schylter's history of planets that have vanished or perhaps existed only in the minds of pre-Hubble scientists.

Inconstant Moon
http://www.inconstantmoon.com
http://www.spacescience.co.uk
Click on a date and see what's showing on the Moon.

Intelligent Life on Mars
http://go.to/intelligentlifeonmars
The little green men know quantum physics.

International Star Registry
http://www.starregistry.co.uk
Raise your flag in outer space.

Mars Home Page
http://mpfwww.jpl.nasa.gov
Get a bit more red dirt live from NASA's space safari before you stake out your first plot at http://www.marsshop.com. For the latest news, see: http://www.marsnews.com

Mars Society UK
http://www.marssociety.org.uk
British chapter of an organization dedicated to get humans to visit Mars.

The Martian Archives
http://www.infocom.com/~thomil/welcome.htm
Prepare yourself for the coming global superstorm.

MrEclipse
http://www.mreclipse.com
Dabble in the occultations.

Net Telescopes
http://www.telescope.org/rti/
http://denali.physics.uiowa.edu
Probe deep space by sending requests to remote telescopes.

Space

The Nine Planets
http://www.ex.ac.uk/Mirrors/nineplanets/
Bill Arnett's impressive multimedia tour of our solar system.

Planet Search
http://exoplanets.org
Info on planets in and outside our solar system.

Retro Aerospace
http://www.retro.com
Recycling simpler, sturdier rockets to make space travel more accessible to the common man.

Rocket Guy
http://www.rocketguy.com/
The homepage of Brian Walker who plans to shoot himself thirty miles into the atmosphere. Wish him luck.

Scope Reviews
http://www.scopereviews.com
Read first, buy later – or maybe build your own:
http://www.atmjournal.com

Seti@home
http://setiathome.ssl.berkeley.edu
http://setifaq.org
Donate your processing resources to the non-lunatic end of the search for extraterrestrial intelligence by downloading a screensaver that analyses data from the Arecibo Radio Telescope. Progress reports at:
http://www.seti.org
http://planetary.org
http://seti.uws.edu.au

Solar System Simulator
http://space.jpl.nasa.gov
Shift camp around the solar system until you find the best view.

Space Adventures
http://www.spaceadventures.com
If you've got $20 million lying around you could become the next

Dennis Tito. For the more modest of means, this site offers zero gravity flights and personalized spacesuits just in case.

Space Calendar

http://www.jpl.nasa.gov/calendar/
Guide to upcoming anniversaries, rocket launches, meteor showers, eclipses, asteroid and planet viewings and other happenings in the inter-galactic calendar.

Space Weather

http://www.spaceweather.com
http://www.windows.ucar.edu/spaceweather/
Monitor the influence of solar activity on the Earth's magnetic field.

SpaceWeather.com

Science news and information about the Sun-Earth environment.

SPACE WEATHER
**Current
Conditions**

Solar Wind
velocity:337.0 km/s
density:6.6 protons/cm³

What's Up in Space -- 2 Jul 2001
Subscribe to Space Weather News!

QUIET SUN: The Sun is sprinkled with a half-dozen small sunspots today, but none pose a threat for powerful flares. Forecasters expect solar activity to remain low for the next 48 hours.

Star Stuff

http://www.starstuff.com
Beginner's guides to astronomy for kids.

Sport

For live calls, scores, tables, draws, teams, injuries and corruption enquiries across major sports, try the newspaper sites (p.239), breaking news services (p.241) or sporting specialists like:

Eurosport http://www.eurosport.com
SkySports http://www.skysports.com
Sportal (INT) http://www.sportal.com
Sporting Life http://www.sporting-life.com
Sports.com (Euro) http://sports.com

But if your interest even slightly borders on obsession you'll find far more satisfaction on the pages of something more one-eyed. For clubs and fan sites, drill down through Yahoo and the Open Directory. They won't carry everything, but what you'll find will lead you to the right forces:

Open Directory http://dmoz.org/Sports/
Yahoo Sports http://dir.yahoo.com/recreation/sports/

If you can't get to the telly or are looking for Webcasts of that crucial Ryman's League derby, check Sport On Air (http://www.sportonair.com) for listings of streaming audio coverage of sport on the Web.

For the darker side of sport, check out Hofstetter's Sports Jerk of the Week (http://jerkoftheweek.com/) which keeps tabs on all the stories clubs would prefer stayed buried.

American Football

NFL
http://www.nfl.com
http://www.nfluth.com
http://www.nfleurope.com
Media schedules, chats, news, player profiles, stats and streaming highlight videos from the National Football League's past and current seasons.

Athletics

The Athletics Site
http://www.athletix.org
Almost everything you could want to know about athletics – other than how to run as fast as Maurice Greene.

Aussie Rules

Australian Football League
http://www.afl.com.au
Men in tight shorts playing aerial ping-pong.

Baseball

Major League Baseball
http://www.mlb.com
Home of the second most boring sport on earth.

The Baseball Archive
http://www.baseball1.com
The most outrageous complete statistical analysis of sport anywhere. For more lunatic scholarship, see Big Bad Baseball (http://www.bigbadbaseball.com).

Basketball

NBA.com
http://www.nba.com
Pro basketball news, picks, player profiles, analyses, results, schedules and highlight videos.

Boxing

Seconds Out
http://www.secondsout.com
With its merger with Boxing News, this site is effectively a pugilism portal, linking up to just about everything related to the sweet science.

Cricket

Click Cricket
http://www.clickcricket.com
This site may be a bit heavy on coverage of cricket in the Indian subcontinent, but it's one of the few cricket sites that feature tips and advice on playing the game.

Sport

CricInfo
http://www.cricinfo.com
Perhaps a bit like cricket itself this site is a bit creaky and not exactly flashy, but it has all the news and information anyone who hasn't memorized *Wisden* could ever need – from Test level down to local leagues.

Don Bradman bowled by Bill Bowes for a duck in his first Test innings at Melbourne (2nd Test)

334 Not Out
http://www.334notout.com
The "Bodyline Series", the exploits of Donald Bradman and the rest of the history of the Ashes are enshrined at this fun site, along with current news.

Wisden
http://www.wisden.com
The Bible of the cricket establishment has finally embraced the potential of the Net, but you have to pay (£37.50 a year) to get the most out of it.

Cycling

Cycling News
http://www.cyclingnews.com
Tour de force coverage of the Tour De France.

Darts

Toe the Oche
http://www.toetheoche.co.uk
Complete coverage of the professional darts scene, plus a campaign to bring *Bullseye* back to British TV screens.

Extreme Sports

Adventure Sports Directory
http://www.adventuredirectory.com
http://dmoz.org/Sports/Extreme_Sports/
For all that falls under the banner of "extreme sports" – from taking your

pushbike offroad to the sort of sheer recklessness that would get you cut from a will. For something more flashy, check out http://www.pie.com and http://expn.go.com

Goals – Global Online Adventure Learning Site
http://www.goals.com
Chase adventurous lunatics like Mick Bird, who's circling the globe in a canoe.

Fishing

Anglers Net
http://www.anglersnet.co.uk
The best British fishing portal on the Web. For more try http://www.fishing4fun.co.uk

Fishing Directories
http://www.thefishfinder.com
http://fishsearch.com
Trade tips and generally exaggerate about aquatic bloodsports.

Fitness

Abdominal Training
http://www.timbomb.net/ab/
Build "abs ripped liked ravioli".

Fitness Online
http://www.fitnessonline.com
Log your training and nutrition regime online.

Football

Football Ground Guide
http://www.footballgroundguide.co.uk
Comprehensive guide to the homes of all 92 league clubs.

Football365
http://www.football365.com
Everything you need to know about the Premiership and beyond. Not enough news? Try:

Sport

FA Premier http://www.fa-premier.com
Nationwide http://www.football.nationwide.co.uk
One Football http://www.onefootball.com
Planet Football http://www.planetfootball.com
Rivals Network http://www.rivals.net
Soccer Association http://www.soccerassociation.com
SoccerNet http://www.soccernet.com
When Saturday Comes http://www.wsc.co.uk

Soccerbase
http://www.soccerbase.com
For game, club and player stats.

Team Talk
http://www.teamtalk.com
The latest news from every club in Britain constantly updated.

Golf

GolfWeb
http://www.golfweb.com
Unbeatable coverage of the American PGA. For European golf, try
Europeantour.com (http://www.europeantour.com). For women's golf,
your clubhouse of choice should be the LPGA site (http://www.lpga.com).

OnlineGolf
http://www.onlinegolf.co.uk
Very good all-round shopping site for clubs, shoes, fleeces and balls,
plus tips for beginners and experts alike.

Gymnastics

International Gymnast
http://www.intlgymnast.com
Peerless news and views from the competitive gymnastics world. For
training tips and advice on routines, try Gymnastics Routine Directory
(http://www.gym-routines.com).

Hockey

Fieldhockey.com
http://www.fieldhockey.com
Sticks and stuff.

Ice Hockey

The A to Z Encyclopedia of Ice Hockey
http://www.azhockey.com
Complete coverage of ice hockey throughout the world. For results and stats from the best league in the world, go to NHL.com (http://www.nhl.com). For the real reason people watch ice hockey, check out:
http://zeroreality.com/fights/
http://www.BroadStreetBully.com
http://www.ChicagoFighters.com

Ice Skating

Recreational Figure Skating FAQ
http://www.cyberus.ca/~karen/recskate
Figure-eights, Hammil Camels, Triple toe-loops and more.

SkateWeb
http://www.frogsonice.com/skateweb/
News, pics and bios of your favourite stars on ice.

Martial Arts

Martial Arts Network
http://www.martial-arts-network.com
All you need to become the next Chuck Norris or Jet Li.

Motorsport

Atlas F1
http://www.atlasf1.com
Extensive coverage of Formula 1.

Sport

Indy Car Racing
http://www.indyracingleague.com
All the news from the Brickyard.

Monster Truck Racing
http://www.ushra.com/m_trucks.html/

Put a pinch of chewing tobacco between your cheek and gum and watch Grave Digger and cohorts squash some bugs.

Motograndprix.com
http://www.motograndprix
.com
Just about every motorcycle event in the world is covered here.

NASCAR
http://www.nascar.com
Dixie's favourite stock cars.

World Motorsport Index
http://www.worldmotorsport.com
Start here for your gasoline-induced pleasure. More revs at Auto Sport (http://www.autosport.com). For more specific pleasures, try:

World Rallying
http://www.worldrally.net
Small cars sliding into trees and skidding in the mud.

Rugby

Planet Rugby
http://www.planet-rugby.com
http://www.rleague.com
http://www.ozleague.com
http://www.scrum.com
http://www.rugbyheaven.com
Up-to-the-minute coverage of hard men trotting in and out of the blood bin, plus columnists, a historical archive, rules and a shop.

Sailing

Sailing Index
http://www.smartguide.com
http://www.madforsailing.com
Everything seaworthy: from swapping yachts to choosing a GPS.

Skiing

SkiCentral
http://www.skicentral.com
http://www.skiclub.co.uk
Indexes thousands of ski-
related sites covering such
things as snow reports, resort
cams, snowboard gear,
accommodation and coming
events in resorts across the
world. For snowboarding, see:
http://www.twsnow.com
http://www.board-it.com

Snooker

110 Snooker
http://www.110sport.com/snooker
All the news from the bays.

Surfing

Surf Link
http://www.surflink.com
Articles, numerous Webcams, tips and surfing forecasts for the entire
world – alerting you when a killer wave is headed to your local break.

World Surfing
http://www.goan.com/surflink.html/
Every day's like Big Wednesday. For daily breaks and Aussie seaboard
cams, see: http://www.coastalwatch.com

Sport

Swimming

Swimmersworld.com
http://www.swimmersworld.com
Coverage of the competitive swimming scene.

WebSwim
http://www.webswim.com
The FAQ of the rec.sport.swimming newsgroup, with information on training, suits, etc.

Tennis

Tennis.com
http://www.tennis.com
All the news from the pros, plus instructional sections, racquet and shoe reviews, pro endorsements and fitness tips.

Wrestling

For the official line, go to WWF (http://www.wwf.com), but for the unofficial line and the bottom line, try:

The DDT Digest
http://www.ddtdigest.com
Great wrestling zine, with the history of blading, the downfall of the WCW in pictures, vintage programmes and other crucial tidbits of wrestling ephemera.

1Wrestling.com
http://www.1wrestling.com
For coverage of the grappling world beyond the WWF and for the most influential coverage of the big boys, this should be your first wrestling bookmark.

Solie's Vintage Wrestling
http://www.solie.org
Do you remember grappling before Vince McMahon's delusions of grandeur or do you have no idea who Kerry Von Erich, Magnum TA or Bruno Sammartino are? Either way you need to visit this shrine to the squared circle's old school.

You call that a sport?

British Minigolf Association http://members.aol.com/MiniGolf98/
You won't be laughing when you find out that tournament prize
money can reach $100,000.

Canadian Amateur Tug of War Association
http://www.tugofwar.ca
You're just pulling my leg.

Disc Golf World http://www.discgolfworld.com
The latest news from the frisbee golf scene, plus all the "drivers"
and "putters" you'll ever need.

International Beltsander Drag Racing Association
http://www.beltsander-races.com
All the news and highlights from the fast-paced, laugh-in-the-face-
of-death world of beltsander drag racing.

PaintBall.com http://www.paintball.com
All the information you need to make life hell for the groom-to-be.

World Elephant Polo Association http://elephantpolo.com
How is it that a team from Iceland is the best in the world?

Telecoms

Campaign for Unmetered Telecommunications
http://www.telecom.eu.org
Rail against the call-charging system that's making Europe an Internet
backwater.

Directory Enquiries
http://www.bt.com/directory-enquiries/dq_home.jsp
BT's directory enquiries site. For other British phone searches,
try 192.com (http://www.192.com), Thomson Directories
(http://www.infospace.com/uk.thomw), UK Phone Book
(http://www.ukphonebook.com) and the Yellow Pages
(http://www.yell.com).

Eat My Phone
http://www.eatmyphone.com
Create your own logos for your mobile.

Efax
http://www.efax.com
http://www.j2.com
Free up a phone line by receiving your faxes by email.

Free Fax Services
http://www.tpc.int
Transmit faxes via the Internet free.

MobileWorld
http://www.mobileworld.org
http://www.unwin.co.uk/phonez.html/
Assorted info on mobile phones and cellular networks.

Oftel
http://www.oftel.gov.uk
Keep a watch on the telephone watchdog.

The Payphone Project
http://www.payphone-project.com
An utterly bizarre site devoted to that near-extinct dinosaur of 20th-century technology, the payphone. Includes payphone news, history of the payphone, photos and numbers. For more payphone numbers, try the Pay Phone Directory (http://www.payphone-directory.org).

Postcode Pages
http://www.grcdi.nl/linkspc.htm/
Find a postcode in almost any country.

Reverse Phone Directory
http://www.reversephonedirectory.com
Key in a US phone number to find its owner. To find a UK location see:
http://www.warwick.ac.uk/cgi-bin-Phones/nng/

SMS Text Messages
http://sms.lycos.co.uk/mobile
Send free text messages to mobile phones worldwide.

Splash Mobile
http://www.SplashMobile.com
Ring tones, logos, games and other essential accessories for your
mobile. The site pays fees to the MCPS, so you can rest assured that
the composer of the *Knight Rider* theme will get his just royalties. Other
ring tone sites:

Jippii! http://www.jippii.co.uk

Mobile Tones http://www.mobiletones.com

Monstermob http://www.monstermob.com

Phoneringsong http://www.phoneringsong.com

Phunky Phones http://www.phunkyphones.com

Ringtones Online http://www.ringtones.co.uk

Your Mobile http://www.yourmobile.com

Telecoms

WAP Sites

If you've got a WAP phone or just like to pretend that you do (get a WAP emulator which enables your PC to read WML encoded script at http://updev.phone.com), these are some of the best sites:

Ananova www.ananova.com
Get breaking news sent as customized WAP pages to your phone.

Ents24 www.ents24.co.uk
What's-on listings for the entire country.

Genie http://www.genie.co.uk
Get up-to-the-minute sports results.

Mail2Wap http://www.mail2wap.com
Collect your POP3 mail on a WAP phone.

Mobile WAP www.mobilewap.com
The largest WAP search engine.

Pocket Doctor http://www.pocketdoctor.co.uk/wap
Never forget to take your medicine, or get symptom descriptions sent to your mobile.

Railtrack http://railtrack.kizoom.co.uk
Why talk to an operator at the National Rail Enquiries line when you can have the info zapped to your phone instead? To check out how long your delay on the Tube will be, go to http://www.tflwap.gov.uk

Retrotopia Wireless Intellivison
http://www.intellivisionlives.com/retrotopia/wireless.shtml
Play '80s classics like Astrosmash and Night Stalker on your mobile phone.

WAP Translator http://langues.ifrance.com/langues/index.wml
Translate to and from English, French, Italian, Spanish, German and Dutch with your phone.

The Telegraph Office
http://fohnix.metronet.com/~nmcewen/tel_off.html/
http://www.navyrelics.com/tribute/bellsys/
Trip through the history of wired communications from Morse telegraphy to the Bell System.

UK STD Codes
http://www.brainstorm.co.uk/utils/std-codes.html
Keep up to date with the labrynthine complexities of the UK's phone exchanges.

UK.Telecom FAQ
http://www.gbnet.net/net/uk-telecom/
Satisfy your curiosity about the British phone network.

UK Telecom Tariff Comparisons
http://www.magsys.co.uk/telecom/
http://www.phonebills.org.uk
Compare the prices of leading landline phone service providers for free, but if you want business-rate comparisons or to view the results in spreadsheet format you've got to subscribe. For mobile phone rates, try uSwitch (http://www.uswitch.com/Mobiles/) or Buy.co.uk (http://www.buy.co.uk/Personal/Calculators/mobiles.asp/).

What Does Your Phone Number Spell?
http://www.phonespell.org
Enter your phone number to see what it spells. The reverse lookup might help you choose a number.

World Time & Dialing Codes
http://www.whitepages.com.au/wp/search/time.html/
International dialling info from anywhere to anywhere, including current times and area codes.

Television

Most TV stations maintain excellent sites with all kinds of extras such as live sports coverage and documentary follow-ups. We won't need to give you their addresses because they'll be flashing them at you at every opportunity. In any case, you'll find them all at: http://www.tvshow.com

For personalized listings, perhaps delivered by email, try your local Yahoo or:
http://www.ananova.com/tv
http://www.cableguide.co.uk
http://www.onthebox.com

The best of these, however, might be: Digiguide (http://www.digiguide.co.uk) which is a customizable listings database that covers terrestrial, cable, digital and satellite. You download the site's free software, tell the program which region you live in or whether you have cable or digital and then download the next two week's worth of listings.

To be notified when something's on:

Spyonit http://www.spyonit.com

asSeenonScreen
http://www.asseenonscreen.com
Buy stuff you've seen on TV or in movies.

Bigglethwaite.com
http://www.bigglethwaite.com
With its comprehensive links page to UK TV Websites, this is a good place to start any search.

Broadcast.com
http://www.broadcast.com/television/
With Yahoo's broadcast site, you can watch local US stations to your heart's delight.

Digi Reels
http://www.digireels.co.uk
If you can't get enough of them on TV, then point your browser here immediately and search a mindblowing database of over 100,000 adverts. Also check out UK Television Adverts (http://www.westwood.u-net.com/ads/).

Donna the Vampire Slayer
http://www.dreamwater.net/nomadsrealm/dtvsmain.htm
Can't get enough of *Buffy* or *West Wing*? Why not combine the two.

Drew's Script-O-Rama
http://www.script-o-rama.com/snazzy/tvscript.html/
A huge set of links to an astonishing array of predominantly American television scripts and episode transcripts. Also try Simply Scripts (http://www.simplyscripts.com).

Epguides
http://epguides.com
If you're serious about TV – really, really serious – this site is your holy grail. Containing complete episode guides for over 1700 shows (mostly American) which are linked to the Internet Movie Database for cross-referencing, this is an amazing research tool for academics, journalists, enthusiasts and general freaks. For similar coverage of Britcoms, try TV Comedy Resources (http://www.phill.co.uk), or Hu's Episode Guides (http://www.episodeguides.com) and Television Without Pity (http://www.televisionwithoutpity.com).

Independent TeleWeb
http://www.itw.org.uk
The history of independent commercial television in the UK.

Jump The Shark
http://www.jumptheshark.com
Named after that episode in *Happy Days* when Fonzie ski-jumped over a shark, starting the show's inexorable downward spiral, this brilliant site is dedicated to documenting the moment when your favourite programme goes south.
Signals of impending doom include same-character-different-actor, puberty, "A very special ..." and the presence of Ted McGinley (aka Jefferson on *Married With Children*).

Like Television
http://www.liketelevision.com
The broadband enabled can watch episodes of classic TV like *I Dream Of Jeannie*, *The Three Stooges* and *Bugs Bunny*.

Live TV
http://www.comfm.fr/live/tv/
Tune into live video feeds from hundreds of real world television stations. To record US cable shows and play them back in Real Video (court case pending) see: http://www.snapstream.com

Sausagenet
http://www.sausagenet.co.uk
Tribute to cult and vintage television shows that babysat for Generation X. It has a reviews section (covering video and DVD releases of old programmes) and downloadable sound files, but is most useful as a portal for retro TV enthusiasts.

Sitcoms Online
http://www.sitcomsonline.com
Very US-focused, but if you're looking for any information on a Yankee comedy, this is the first place to look. There are also games, discussions and polls that are fun for any comedy enthusiast regardless of nationality.

Soap City
http://www.soapcity.com
http://members.tripod.com/~TheSoapBox/
Keep up with who's doing what to whom, who they told and who shouldn't find out in the surreal world of soap fiction.

Test Card Circle
http://www.testcardcircle.org.uk
The homepage of Test Card Circle, an organization of enthusiasts of the music that accompanied the test card sequences that reigned over British TV in the dark days before cable.

The 30 Second Candidate
http://www.pbs.org/30secondcandidate/
A fascinating history of the political TV spot from PBS, America's answer to the BBC.

Transdiffusion
http://www.transdiffusion.org
A truly fantastic resource for anyone interested in the history of British broadcasting, this site hosts the archives of the Transdiffusion Organization, which is dedicated to preserving the history of radio and TV in the UK. Included are screen grabs from TV coverage of historical moments, jingles, theme tunes, in-depth articles on various aspects of broadcasting history and course notes for students and teachers.

TV Ark
http://www.tv-ark.co.uk
With its focus on arcana and minutiae, this online museum of British television is one for true believers. Mostly downloadable sound and video files of station identifications and theme tunes at the moment, but videos and information are promised in the future.

TV Cream
http://tv.cream.org
This is everything the Web is meant to be all about: tons of useless knowledge and remembrances by people who should know better. This one features naff telly from the '60s, '70s and '80s, photos of Henry Kelly, station idents from a time when "digital" meant an LCD watch and maths lessons with Lesley Judd. For less tongue-in-cheek coverage of the same territory, try Spud TV (http://www.spudtv.com) for an American perspective or Whirligig (http://www.whirligig-tv.co.uk) for a trip back to the 1950s.

TV Eyes
http://www.tveyes.com
Informs you when your search term is mentioned on TV.

TV Go Home
http://www.tvgohome.com
Onion-style parodies of *The Radio Times*.

TV Party
http://www.tvparty.com
Irreverent, hilarious and more fun than a barrel of Keith Chegwins, this American site is the hall of fame that the medium truly deserves. Included are an amazing archive of uncensored out-takes, frighteningly in-depth articles about all manner of televisual ephemera and pull-no-punches features on programmes.

Television

Regional TV archives

With big media companies like Carlton and Granada dominating ITV, the halcyon days of regional broadcasting are almost gone. However, since television breeds lunacy like no other medium, there are a number of enthusiasts throughout the country dedicated to preserving the memory of low production values, terrible clothes and hopeless segues.

Border Television Area
http://www.bordertvarea.co.uk
Comprehensive archive of ITV in the North.

Harlech House of Graphics
http://www.hhg.org.uk
Thirty years of ITV in the West and Wales.

ITV Southern England
http://members.tripod.co.uk/Southern_TV/
Independent telly from the South since 1958.

Television Southwest
http://www.televisionsouthwest.com
Dedicated to ITV in the West Country.

Tyne Tees Logo Page
http://www.durge.org/~bods/tv/tynetees/
A wry look at the North East's independent station.

TV Show
http://www.tvshow.com
Everything TV – from schedules of every station worldwide and links to just about every show ever made to the technical aspects of production and broadcasting. Start all your TV-related searches here.

TV Tickets
http://www.tvtickets.com
Secure your chance to clap on cue.

VCR Repair Instructions
http://www.fixer.com
How to take a VCR apart and then get all the little bits back in so it fits easier into the bin.

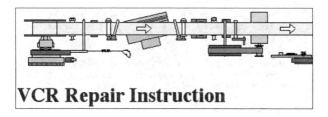

VCR Repair Instruction

Virtue TV
http://www.virtuetv.com
If you're one of the lucky few with broadband access, this virtual channel features independent short films, an archive of music concerts and sports footage, and classic movies like Roger Corman's *Little Shop of Horrors* and Buster Keaton's *Steamboat Bill Jr*.

Who Would You Kill?
http://www.whowouldyoukill.com
So who would you toss into Dawson's Creek?

WWITV
http://wwitv.com
Watch TV stations from around the world, mostly obscure.

TV Programmes

The Web would be nothing without people who have obsessions that transcend rational thought, and television is particularly well-served by fanaticism. Here are some of the best sites devoted to a single show.

Angelic Slayer http://www.angelicslayer.com
Run by a teenage fan from Arizona, this rather amazing site devoted to *Buffy The Vampire Slayer* and *Angel* has attracted over two million hits.

Cookd And Bombd http://www.cookdandbombd.co.uk
Site devoted to the warped comedy and media terrorism of Chris Morris. More at http://www.koekie.org.uk/funnel

Corrie Net http://www.corrie.net
This *Coronation Street* archive has everything everyone could ever want to know about Ken Barlow and Hilda Ogden.

Erinsborough.com http://www.erinsborough.com
Catch up with all the gossip from Ramsay Street.

Frank Butcher's Philosophical Car Lot
http://geocities.com/SunsetStrip/Stadium/1123/page1.html
RealAudio clips of *EastEnders*' philosopher-king.

Friends Place http://www.friendsplace.com
Every script of every episode ever. But if you have that much spare time it might make you wish you had some of your own.

Jupiter Mining http://www.jupitermining.com
Homepage of the *Red Dwarf* fan club.

Time

Calendarzone
http://www.calendarzone.com
Calendar links and, believe it or not, calzone recipes.

DateReminder
http://www.datereminder.co.uk
Remind yourself by email.

The Death Clock
http://www.deathclock.com
Get ready to book your final taxi.

Heroes of Horology
http://www.shadow.net/~bobt/heroes/heroes.htm/
A picture gallery of history's greatest timekeepers.

Horology – The Index
http://www.horology.com
This text-heavy portal to all things pertaining to the science of timekeeping includes information on collecting timepieces, email addresses of "cyber-horologists" and links to horological organizations.

International Earth Rotation Service
http://hpiers.obspm.fr
Ever felt like your bed's spinning? The truth is even scarier.

iPing (US)
http://www.iping.com
Arrange free telephone reminders for one or many.

Martian Time
http://pweb.jps.net/~tgangale/mars/index4.htm
Learn exactly when the little green men will be coming.

Metric Time
http://www.billcollins.com.au/bc/mt/
Decimalized excuses for being late.

Time

Online Planners
http://www.appoint.net
http://www.supercalendar.com
http://www.calendars.net
Maintain your planner online. Excite, Yahoo, MSN, and Netscape offer similar things.

Time and Date
http://www.timeanddate.com
http://old.smh.com.au/media/wtc/smhwtc.html
Instantly tell the time in your choice of cities. Keep your PC clock aligned with a time synchronizer:
http://www.ntp.org/software/index.html

Time Cave
http://www.timecave.com
Schedule an email to be sent at a specific time in the future.

Time Cube
http://www.timecube.com
Disprove God through the simultaneous 4-day Time Cube.

US National Debt Clock
http://brillig.com /debt_clock
Watch your children's future slip away.

USNO Master Clock Time
http://tycho.usno.navy.mil /what.html/
Compute the local apparent sidereal time in your part of the world or listen to a live broadcast of the USNO Master Clock announcer. Get your computer's clock set by modem at:
http://tycho.usno.navy.mil/modem_time.html/

Trains

End of the Line

http://www.wigancrdc.co.uk

Site devoted to the faded (and rusting) glory of withdrawn locomotives lying on the scrap heap.

Loco Watch

http://www.locowatch.com

This detailed news magazine for enthusiasts of both modern and historical railways includes regular updates on which locomotives are being serviced, news and listings of rail tours, photos and resources for spotters.

Rail Britain

http://www.railbritain.com

A big site aimed at both the traveller and the enthusiast, including news, chat rooms, timetables, maps, rolling stock guides and fleet information.

Steam Locomotive

http://www.steamlocomotive.com

This impressive American site is a storehouse of information on steam trains geared towards the serious, tech-minded enthusiast. Includes detailed information on wheel arrangements, horsepower and hundreds of locomotives from the golden age of rail travel.

Trains

Steamy Affairs

Railway preservation may not have the hippest image in the world, but steam engines are enjoying a renaissance throughout the world. The UK currently boasts around 430 miles of track (more than the London Underground) used by the country's 1200 steam engines. Here are a few sites devoted to historical railways both in Britain and abroad.

Richard Leonard's Steam Locomotive Archive
http://members.aol.com/rlsteam/
Nostalgia-sodden photos of North American railroads in the '50s.

Mainline Steam Tours Index
http://www.march.demon.co.uk/tours
Listings of steam locomotive journeys in the UK.

Steam Central
http://www.steamcentral.com
Steam locomotion from an American perspective.

Steam Dreams
http://www.steamdreams.co.uk
The Cathedrals Express.

UK Heritage Railways
http://ukhrail.uel.ac.uk
Guide to the UK's heritage railway scene.

Vintage Trains
http://www.vintagetrains.co.uk
A collection of steam engines preserved by the Birmingham Railway Museum Trust.

Track Bed
http://www.trackbed.com
An impressive site aiming to become the online authority on British rail history. The database includes comprehensive histories of the UK's main rail companies, routes, maps, an in-depth (100K) glossary and photos.

Train Orders
http://www.trainorders.com

Railway hobby site hosting lots of discussion groups, rail cams covering two Californian main lines, quizzes and an archive of over 1000 loco photos.

Train Web
http://www.trainweb.org

This portal is a train-spotter's paradise. In addition to a site catalogue cleverly organized as both white and yellow pages, Train Web hosts chat rooms, forums, photo collections, the Rail Search search engine and the ever-popular Railcams.com so you can catch the Flying Scotsman without ever leaving your armchair. More Internet junctions at http://www.railserve.com and http://communities.prodigy.net/trains

Travel

Whether you're seeking inspiration, planning an itinerary, shopping for a ticket or already mobile, there'll be a tool online worth throwing in your box. You can book flights, reserve hotel rooms, research your destination, monitor the weather, convert currencies, learn the lingo, locate an ATM, scan local newspapers, collect your mail from abroad, find a restaurant that suits your fussy tastes and plenty more. For detailed listings, buy a copy of the *Rough Guide to Travel Online*. If you'd like to find first-hand experiences or travelling companions, hit the Usenet discussion archives at Google (http://groups.google.com) and join the appropriate newsgroup under the rec.travel or soc.culture hierarchies. As with all newsgroups, before you post a question, skim through the FAQs first:

Rec.Travel Library http://www.travel-library.com

Air Travel Handbook http://www.cs.cmu.edu/afs/cs/user/mkant /Public/Travel/airfare.html

You could also try consulting a volunteer "expert".

Abuzz http://www.abuzz.com/category/travel/

Travel

All Experts http://www.allexperts.com/travel/

Then see what the major guidebook publishers have to offer:

Fodors http://www.fodors.com

Frommer's http://www.frommers.com

Insiders http://www.insiders.com

Let's Go http://www.letsgo.com

Lonely Planet http://www.lonelyplanet.com

Michelin http://www.michelin-travel.com

Moon Travel http://www.moon.com

Robert Young Pelton http://www.comebackalive.com

Rough Guides http://www.roughguides.com

Routard http://www.club-internet.fr/routard/

Alternatively, check out online guides such as:

Beachtowel http://www.beachtowel.co.uk

CityVox http://www.cityvox.com

IExplore http://www.iexplore.com

Locals in the Know http://www.localsintheknow.com

World Travel Guide http://www.wtg-online.com

While it might seem like commercial suicide for the Rough Guides to give away the full text of its guides to more than 10,000 destinations, the reality is that books are still more convenient, especially on the road when you need them most. If you'd like to order a guide or map online you'll also find plenty of opportunities either from the above publishers, the online bookshops (p.69), or from travel bookshops such as:

Adventurous Traveler http://shop.gorp.com/atbook

Literate Traveller http://www.literatetraveller.com/index.html

Stanfords http://www.stanfords.co.uk

Many online travel agents also provide destination guides, which might include exclusive editorial peppered with chunks licensed from guidebooks linked out to further material on the Web. For example:

Away.com http://away.com
Escaperoutes http://www.reddirect.co.uk/travel.asp

The biggest problem with browsing the Web for regional information and travel tools is not in finding the sites, but wading through them. Take the following directories for example:

About Travel http://travel.about.com
Budget Travel http://www.budgettravel.com
Excite Travel http://travel.excite.com
Lycos Travel http://travel.lycos.com
Open Directory http://dmoz.org/Recreation/Travel/
My Travel Guide http://www.mytravelguide.com
Traveller Online http://www.travelleronline.com
Trip Advisor (US) http://www.tripadvisor.com
Virtual Tourist http://www.vtourist.com
World Travel Guide http://www.travel-guide.com
World Travel Net http://www.world-travel-net.com
Yahoo Directory http://www.yahoo.com/Recreation/Travel/
Yahoo Travel http://travel.yahoo.com

These are perfect if you want to browse through regions looking for ideas, or find a range of sites on one topic – health, for example. But if you're after something very specific, you might find it more efficient to use a search engine such as Google (see p.6). Keep adding search terms until you restrict the number of results to something manageable. If you'd like to coincide your vacation with a festival or event, go straight to:

What's on When http://www.whatsonwhen.com
What's Going On http://www.whatsgoingon.com

Or for entertainment, eating, and cultural events, a city guide:

Citysearch http://www.citysearch.com
Time Out http://www.timeout.co.uk
Wcities.com http://www.wcities.com

Travel

Yahoo Local http://local.yahoo.com
Zagat (Dining) http://www.zagat.com

If you're flexible, you might find a last-minute special. These Net exclusives are normally offered directly from the airline, hotel, and travel operator sites, which you'll find through Yahoo. There are also a few Web operators that specialize in late-notice and special Internet deals on flights, hotels, events, and so forth, such as:

Bargain Holidays http://www.bargainholidays.com
Best Fares http://www.bestfares.com
Lastminute.com http://www.lastminute.com
Lastminutetravel.com http://www.lastminutetravel.com
Smarter Living http://www.smarterliving.com
Travel Zoo http://www.travelzoo.com

Then there are the reverse-auction sites like Priceline.com where you bid on a destination and wait. You might strike up a good deal if you bid shrewdly and don't mind the somewhat draconian restrictions (see: http://www.angelfire.com/nt/priceline/). Hotwire offers similar discounts on undisclosed airlines but names the price up front. If you're super-flexible, you could try Airhitch or a courier company:

Air Courier Assoc. http://www.aircourier.org
Airhitch http://www.airhitch.org
Hotwire http://www.hotwire.com
IAATC Air Courier http://www.courier.org
Priceline.com http://www.priceline.com

Booking a flight through one of the broad online ticketing systems isn't too hard either, but bargains are scarce. Unless you're spending someone else's money you'll want to sidestep the full fares offered on these major services:

Expedia http://www.expedia.co.uk
Travelocity http://www.travelocity.co.uk
Travel Select http://www.travelselect.co.uk

Although they list hundreds of airlines and millions of fares, the general consensus is that they're usually better for research, accommodation and travel tips than cheap fares and customer service. So if you think it's worth the effort, drop in and check which carriers haul your route, offer the best deals and still have seats available. You can then use their rates as a benchmark. Compare them with the fares on the airline sites and discount specialists such as:

Bargain Holidays http://www.bargainholidays.com

Cheap Flights http://www.cheapflights.com

Deckchair http://www.deckchair.com

Ebookers.com http://www.ebookers.com

Flight Centre http://www.flightcentre.com

OneTravel.com http://www.onetravel.com

Or compare the prices across several agencies simultaneously using these sites:

Farechase http://www.farechase.com

Hotwire http://www.hotwire.com

QIXO http://www.qixo.com

Sidestep http://www.sidestep.com

Finally, see if your travel agent can better the price. If the difference is only marginal, favour your agent. Then at least you'll have a human contact if something goes wrong.

12Degrees
http://www.12degrees.com
Rope in a guidebook author to plan your adventure holiday.

A2Btravel.com (UK)
http://www.a2btravel.com
http://www.ferrybooker.com
http://www.webweekends.co.uk
Resources for getting into, around, and out of the UK, such as car-rental comparison, airport guides, train timetables and ferry booking.

Maps and Atlases

You can generate road and airport maps for most cities worldwide, driving directions for North America and Europe, US traffic reports, world maps and more at:

Expedia http://maps.expedia.com
MapBlast http://www.mapblast.com
MapQuestUK http://www.mapquest.co.uk
Easymap http://www.easymap.co.uk
Mappy http://www.mappy.co.uk
Multimap http://www.multimap.com
Ordnance Survey http://www.ordsvy.gov.uk
Shell Geo Star Route Planner http://www.shellgeostar.com

To create UK street and road maps from postcodes or addresses, see:
Streetmap (UK) http://www.streetmap.co.uk

If you require highly detailed US topographic maps, try:
TopoZone http://www.topozone.com

For more maps, geographical and GPS resources see:
http://geography.about.com
http://dmoz.org/Reference/Maps/

Africam
http://www.africam.com
Sneak a peek at wild beasts going about their business.

The Africa Guide
http://www.africaguide.com
Good, general guides of a region that nearly all the major guide books
and travel services ignore. Try also Africa Net
(http://www.africanet.com).

Art of Travel
http://www.artoftravel.com
How to see the world on $25 a day.

ATM Locators
http://www.visa.com/atms
http://www.mastercard.com/cardholderservices/atm
Locate a bowser willing to replenish your wallet.

Backpacker.com
http://www.backpacker.com
Excellent site for wilderness trekkers, including destination guides, tips
on keeping your boots in shape and the real dope on DEET-free insect
repellents.

The Bathroom Diaries
http://www.thebathroomdiaries.com
One of the most essential sites on the Web: You're in Bamako, Mali
when nature calls and you're after a good, clean Western-style toilet,
click here to find out the nearest one. A wireless version is promised
soon, so you'll have to hang on until then.

Travel

Bed & Breakfast.com
http://www.bedandbreakfast.com
http://www.babs.com.au
http://www.innsite.com
Secure your night's sleep worldwide.

BizTraveler.org
http://www.biztraveler.org
Looking after commercial travellers.

British Waterways
http://www.britishwaterways.co.uk
All you ever wanted to know about canal barging.

Bugbog
http://www.bugbog.co.uk
Nice, compact, easy-to-navigate miniguides for people wanting to go somewhere a bit out of the ordinary. Good features include the best beaches in the world by month, and a destination finder giving you options like colourful culture, festivals and weather.

Caravan Sitefinder
http://caravan-sitefinder.co.uk
Where to hitch your rusting hulk of steel without looking like hippy scum. For places to pitch your tent, try Camp Sites (http://www.camp-sites.co.uk).

CIA World Factbook
http://www.cia.gov/cia/publications/factbook
Vital stats on every country. For the score on living standards: http://www.undp.org

Concierge.com
http://www.concierge.com
Get packing with advice from *Traveler* magazine.

Danger Finder
http://www.comebackalive.com/df/
Adventure holidays that could last a lifetime.

Days Out

http://www.virgin.net/daysout/

You might not want to use their trains to get you there, but Virgin does at least provide an excellent service with this site, which is crammed with ideas for successful day-trips. For more ideas, try About Britain (http://www.aboutbritain.com) and DaysOutUK (http://www.daysoutuk.com).

Electronic Embassy

http://www.embassy.org

Directory of foreign embassies in DC plus Web links where available. Search Yahoo for representation in other cities.

Eurotrip

http://www.eurotrip.com
http://www.ricksteves.com

Look out Europe, here you come.

Family Travel Files

http://www.thefamilytravelfiles.com

Look here for help on what to do when the little monsters start asking, "Are we there yet?" For more UK-specific destinations, try PlanIt4Kids (http://www.planit4kids.com). For holidays with toddlers, try http://www.babygoes2.com

Flight Arrivals & Departures

http://www.flightarrivals.com

Stay on top of takeoffs and touchdowns across North America.

FrequentFlier.com

http://frequentflier.com

The information here is definitely more useful for Americans, but it's nevertheless a great resource for frequent travellers after the best deal for their miles. See also Web Flyer (http://www.webflyer.com).

Gap Year

http://www.gapyear.com

Excellent site dedicated to students about to take a year out, with loads of travel tips and stories.

Global Freeloaders
http://www.globalfreeloaders.com
Take in a globetrotting dosser in exchange for some return hospitality.

HolidayComplaint.com
http://HolidayComplaint.com
Vent some steam about a disappointing holiday here, and read others' complaints before you book.

Hotel Discount
http://www.hoteldiscount.com
http://www.hotelnet.co.uk
http://www.hotelwiz.com
Book hotels around the world. For backpacker rates, try:
http://www.hostels.com

How far is it?
http://www.indo.com/distance/
Calculate the distance between any two cities.

IgoUgo
http://www.igougo.com
Packed full of travellers' photos and journals, this roughguides.com partner site offers candid firsthand information.

Incredible Adventures
http://www.incredible-adventures.com
Convert your cash into adrenaline.

Infiltration
http://www.infiltration.org
Confessions of a serial trespasser.

plan a trip

share experiences

earn rewards

International Home Exchange Network
http://www.homexchange.com
http://www.sunswap.com
http://www.homebase-hols.com
Trade your dreary digs for a palatial beach house.

International Student Travel Confederation
http://www.istc.org
Save money with an authentic international student card.

Journeywoman
http://www.journeywoman.com
Reporting in from the sister beaten track.

Mail2Web
http://www.mail2web.com
Collect and send your POP3 mail instantly from any Web browser.
Faster than Hotmail.

My Travel Rights
http://mytravelrights.com
Disgruntled? Maybe you'll be reimbursed. More at
http://www.passengerrights.com

No Shitting in the Toilet
http://www.noshit.com.au
Delighting in the oddities of low-budget travel.

OAG
http://www.oag.com
Largest database of flight schedules on the Net, which can then be
downloaded to your Palm or mobile.

The Original Tipping Page
http://www.tipping.org
Make fast friends with the bell-hop.

Railtrack
http://www.railtrack.co.uk

Travel

Depress yourself at the state of the country's railways by looking at corporate reports or the timetable details. To book tickets online try The Train Line (http://www.thetrainline.com) or Q Jump (http://www.qjump.co.uk), and for general public transport information try Public Transport Info (http://www.pti.org.uk).

Resorts Online
http://www.resortsonline.com
Your way through 3000 resorts throughout the world categorized by beach, golf, spa, ski, etc.

Roadside America
http://www.roadsideamerica.com
Strange attractions that loom between squished animals on US highways.

Sahara Overland
http://www.sahara-overland.com
Leave the city in a cloud of dust.

Satellite and Aerial Imaging
http://www.terraserver.com
http://terra.nasa.gov
http://www.crworld.co.uk
http://www.photolib.noaa.gov
http://www.globexplorer.com
http://www.multimap.com
See why nine out of ten Martian honeymooners prefer your planet.

Subway Navigator
http://www.subwaynavigator.com
http://www.manhattanaddress.com
Estimate the travelling times between city stations worldwide, or find the right stop in NY.

Taken on the Road: American Mile Markers
http://www.kodak.com/US/en/corp/features/onTheRoad/home/index.shtml
Photographer Matt Frondorf travelled across the USA from New York to San Francisco and took a photo every mile, all 3304 are here.

Theme Parks of England
http://tpoe.virtualave.net
Reviews and info on all the major high G-force thrills to be had without leaving the country.

Tips4Trips
http://www.tips4trips.com
More than 1000 tips for the traveller, from packing to navigating customs on your way back home.

TNT Live!
http://www.tntmagazine.com
Survive London and venture onward with aid from expat streetmags, *TNT* and *Southern Cross*.

Tourism Offices Worldwide
http://www.towd.com
Write to the local tourist office. They might send you a brochure. For even more propaganda, try Official Travel Info (http://www.officialtravelinfo.com).

Traffic and Road Conditions
http://www.accutraffic.com
http://www.rac.co.uk/check_traffic/?view=Standard&nav
Live traffic and weather updates.

Traffic Signs of the World
http://www.elve.net/rcoulst.htm
Next time you're in Kyrgyzstan, you'll know when to look out for the men at work.

Travel and Health Warnings
http://www.fco.gov.uk
http://www.dfat.gov.au
http://travel.state.gov
Don't ignore these bulletins if you're planning to visit a potential hot-spot or health risk, but seek a second opinion before postponing your adventure. If you're off on business, try a professional advisory such as Kroll: http://www.krollworldwide.com

Travel Doctor
http://www.tmvc.com.au
http://www.cdc.gov/travel/
http://www.masta.org
http://www.travelhealth.co.uk
http://www.who.int

Brace yourself against the bugs eagerly awaiting your arrival. For a list of travel medicine clinics worldwide, see http://www.tripprep.com, and for more travel health information and a WAP service, try Medicine Planet (http://www.medicineplanet.com).

Travelmag
http://www.travelmag.co.uk
Several intimate travel reflections monthly.

Travel News Organization
http://www.travel-news.org
Independent travel news, holiday ideas and bargains for British travellers. For more, point your browser to eTravel (http://www.etravel.org).

Travel Paperwork
http://www.travelpaperwork.com
Sort out the red tape before you hit the border.

Travlang
http://www.travlang.com
Add another language to your repertoire.

Unclaimed Baggage
http://www.unclaimedbaggage.com
You lose it; they sell it.

UK Passport Agency
http://www.ukpa.gov.uk
Speed up your passport application at this streamlined site.

Underbelly
http://www.underbelly.com
Short, sharp, shocked guides to the places tourists rarely ever see.

Universal Currency Converter
http://www.xe.com/ucc
Convert Finnish Markkas into Central African Francs on the fly. More at Oanda (http://www.oanda.com).

Vindigo
http://www.vindigo.com
Is Vindigo the future of travel guides? Download its Palm Pilot or AvantGo city guides and decide for yourself.

Virtual Tourist
http://www.virtualtourist.com
Big database of travel reviews written by ordinary people, not travel journalists on press junkets. The reviews are hooked up to maps and links to other sites.

Visit Britain
http://www.visitbritain.com
http://www.uktravel.com
Understand the British way of doing things.

Walkabout
http://www.walkabout.com.au
Get the lowdown on the land down under.

WebFlyer
http://www.webflyer.com
Keep tabs on frequent-flier schemes.

What Cruise
http://www.whatcruise.co.uk
Great ways to spend your kids' inheritance money, plus a section on last-minute deals if you're feeling guilty.

What's on When?
http://www.whatsonwhen.com
http://www.whatsgoingon.com
Annoyed you've missed *Thaipusam* or the *Turning of the Bones* yet again? Get your dates right here.

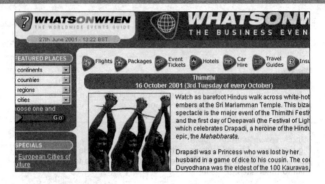

World Heritage Listing
http://www.unesco.org/whc/
Plan your itinerary around international treasures.

Weather

Most news sites report the weather but it's rarely up-to-the-minute. For that you need to go directly to your local weather bureau or a specialist weather reporting service, or check the resources listed in the *Rough Guide to Weather*. For five-day forecasts, charts, storm warnings, allergy reports and satellite photos for thousands of cities worldwide, try:

Accuweather http://www.accuweather.com
CNN Weather http://www.cnn.com/WEATHER/
Intellicast http://www.intellicast.com
Online Weather http://www.onlineweather.com
Weather Channel http://www.weather.com
Weather Organizer http://www.weather.org
Yahoo Weather http://weather.yahoo.com

For more intricate and timely detail, particularly outside the

USA, drop by the Met Office: http://www.metoffice.gov.uk

For amateur observations and the fanatical extremes of weather watching, scan these specialist portals:

About Weather http://weather.about.com

Daniel's Weather Radar Page http://danielwxradar.tripod.com

European Centre for Medium Range Weather Forecasts
http://www.ecmwf.int

Open Directory http://dmoz.org/News/Weather/

The Very Useful UK Weather Page
http://www.maalla.co.uk/uk-weather/

The Weather Resource http://www.nxdc.com/weather/

UM Weather http://cirrus.sprl.umich.edu/wxnet/

WMO Members http://www.wmo.ch/web-en/member.html/

Aviation Digital Data Service
http://adds.aviationweather.noaa.gov
If you're flying to the US, this pilot-orientated site will tell you if you need to pack extra sickbags.

Climate Ark
http://www.climateark.org
Fret about coming changes in the weather.

Everything Weather
http://www.everythingweather.com
The ultimate rainspotter's portal.

Hurricane Hunters
http://www.hurricanehunters.com
The homepage of the 53rd Weather Reconnaissance Squadron features photographs taken from the eye of the storm.

National Environmental Satellite and Data Information Service
http://www.nesdis.noaa.gov
Based in the US, this is the global headquarters of the world's weather trainspotters.

Weather

Ocean Weather
http://www.oceanweather.com
http://www.ssec.wisc.edu/data/sst.html/
Chart the swells and temperatures across the seven seas.

Paul's Weather Satellite and Waffle Page
http://homepage.ntlworld.com/phqfh1
Learn how to build your own weather satellite and meet other climate fanatics.

Snoweye
http://www.snoweye.com
http://www.snow-forecast.com
Spy on thousands of ski resorts worldwide through strategically hidden cameras – or simply have the forecasts beamed directly to your WAP phone.

Space Weather
http://www.spaceweather.com
Monitor the effect of solar activity on the earth's atmosphere.

Tornado and Storm Research Organization
http://www.torro.org.uk
If you're into twisters, this site will spin you right round, baby, right round.

Weather Images
http://www.weatherim-ages.org
Depress yourself with images from Bondi Beach, and then cheer yourself up with the page of weather humour.

Weather Software
http://cirrus.sprl.umich.edu/wxnet/software.html
Stick out a wet thumb from the safety of your swivel chair.

Focused Forecasts

Tired of imprecise regional forecasts? Do you need to know exactly what time of day it will be safe to mow your lawn? Try these sites (most of which have been set up by enthusiasts) offering weather reports right down to your postcode:

Bablake Weather Station
http://bws.users.netlink.co.uk
In-depth forecasts for the Midlands.

BBC Online Weather Centre
http://www.bbc.co.uk/weather/
Forecasts for your postcode.

Meteorological Data From Sussex
http://cpesw3.mols.sussex.ac.uk/es/meteo/
Let the Uni of Sussex help you out.

North West England Weather Site
http://www.argonet.co.uk/users/jim.matt/
From Crewe to Lancaster.

Scottish Weather Information
http://www.geo.ed.ac.uk/home/scotland/scotweather.html/
North of the Border.

Stoke-On-Trent Weather Station
http://www.coyney.demon.co.uk
How specific do you want?

Wild Weather
http://www.wildweather.com
http://australiasevereweather.com
http://www.nssl.noaa.gov
http://www.fema.gov/fema/trop.htm
Set your course into the eye of the storm.

Webcams

World Climate
http://www.worldclimate.com
http://www.weatherbase.com
Off to Irkutzk next August? Here's what weather to expect.

World Meteorological Organization
http://www.wmo.ch
UN division that monitors global climate.

Webcams

Africam
http://www.africam.com
Go on a (virtual) safari without even leaving your armchair.

The Amazing Cooler Cam
http://www.coolercam.com
As if your workplace wasn't boring enough, watch Americans get drinks
from the office water cooler.

Beer Lover Cam
http://www.beerlovercam.com
Watch a couple of guys agonize over whether to grab a can of Bud or
just go for the Miller.

Cat Hospital
http://www.cathospital.co.uk
Join the thousands watching Frank the cat recover from a broken
pelvis.

Earth Cam

http://www.earthcam.com

Links to a vast array of Webcams, usefully organized into categories and subcategories including Traffic, Arts & Entertainment, Metro, Weird and more. Also check Webcam Central (http://www.camcentral.com) and Webcam World (http://www.webcamworld.com).

Electrolux Real Fridge Cam

http://www.electrolux.com/node230.asp/

Discover once and for all whether the light stays on or off when you close the door.

Fly on the Wall

http://www.flyonthewall.com

A portal dedicated to Webcams and streaming video footage of movie premieres and showbiz parties, as well as Times Square, spacecraft landings and, umm, guinea pigs.

Jennicam

http://www.jennicam.org

The most celebrated Webcam of 'em all. The enormous success of Jennicam is partially responsible for that most loathsome aspect of contemporary culture: reality television. But if you want to see where the phenomenon started, log on, pay your membership fee and watch Jenni get drunk and snog strangers ... provided you're an adult.

Pavement Terror

http://www.backfire.co.uk

As if you needed more reason not to trust White Van Man, former delivery man Howard Stone has posted streaming videos of pedestrian horror when his van backfires.

Steve's Ant Farm

http://www.stevesantfarm.com

Watch blurry black punctuation marks build tunnels.

Telerobot

http://telerobot.mech.uwa.edu.au/testing.html

Control a robotic arm in Australia from your Web browser.

Wearcam
http://www.wearcam.org
Your one-stop shop for information on "photoborgs" and wearable computers.

Weird

Absurd.org
http://www.absurd.org
Please do not adjust your set.

Aetherius Society
http://www.aetherius.org
Continue the legacy of the late Sir Dr George King, Primary Terrestrial Mental Channel of the Interplanetary Council.

Aliens and Soul Abduction
http://www.cia.com.au/brough/
Fact: spooky space dudes are stealing our souls. The Bible wouldn't lie: http://aliensinthebible.com. If you think you may be one, see the Alien Counsel at http://www.angelfire.com/md/aliencounsel

American Pie and the Armageddon Prophecy
http://www.roytaylorministries.com
How Madonna testified against the descendants of Israel all the way to number one. But what tragedy awaits her:
http://www.geocities.com/Athens/Atrium/3933/madonna.htm/

Animal Mating Zone
http://www.matings.co.uk
Hardcore sex: the type you only get to see in wildlife documentaries.

Brother Ellis Society
http://www.freespeech.org/besna/besna.html/
Appease God by eating unwanted pets. No details spared. In complete contrast to: http://www.jesusveg.com

Build a Better Batsuit
http://www.geocities.com/thebatguy_99/
Take off on a caped crusade.

Celebrities in Distress
http://www fortunecity.com/lavendar/mockingbird/472/
What's sexier than being gassed, drowned, strangled or blown out into space?

Chemtrails Over America
http://home1.gte.net/quakker/Documents/Chemtrails_Over_America.htm
Those aren't clouds above your head.

Christian Guide to Small Arms
http://www.frii.com/~gosplow/cgsa.html/
"He that hath no sword, let him sell his garment and buy one" – Luke 22:36. It's not just your right; it's your duty, darnit.

Circlemakers
http://www.circlemakers.org
Create crop circles to amuse New Agers and the press.

A Citizen from Hell
http://www.amightywind.com/hell/citizenhell.htm/
If Hell sounds this bad, you don't want to go there.

Clonaid
http://www.clonaid.com
Thanks to the Raelians, we now know all life on earth was created in extraterrestrial laboratories. Here's where you can buy genuine cloned human livestock for the kitchen table. Ready as soon as the lab's finished.

Corpses for Sale
http://distefano.com
Brighten up your guestroom or spoil your pet with a life-sized chew-toy.

The Darwin Awards
http://www.darwinawards.com
Each year the Darwin Award goes to the person who drops off the cen-

sus register in the most spectacular fashion. Here's where to read about the runners-up and er ... winners.

Deep Black Magic
http://www.mindspring.com/~txporter
40 years of CIA research into mind control and ESP. For the perspective of a Finnish immigrant to Canada on mind control see
http://hackcanada.com/canadian/freedom/mylife.html

Derm Cinema
http://www.skinema.com
Know your celebrity skin conditions. But would you recognize them under a gas mask?
http://www.geocities.com/TimesSquare/Alley/8207/

Dolphin Society
http://www.dolphinsociety.org
Driftnet-eating submarines rescue humans who've shape-shifted into dolphins.

Dr MegaVolt
http://www.drmegavolt.com
The Doc sure sparked right up when they switched on the power, but could he cut in the big league?
http://www3.bc.sympatico.ca/lightningsurvivor/

English Rose Press
http://www.englishrosepress.com
Diana sends her love from Heaven.

Fetish Map
http://www.deviantdesires.com/map/map.html/
Join the dots between piggy-players, fursuiters, inflators, crush freaks and where you're standing now.

Flatulence Filter
http://flatulence-filter.com
Because life wasn't meant to be a gas.

Fortean Times
http://www.forteantimes.com
Updates from the print monthly that takes the investigation of strange phenomena more seriously than itself. See also http://www.parascope.com and http://www.bizarremag.com

Future Horizons
http://www.futurehorizons.net
Snap off more than your fair share through solid-state circuitry.

Great Joy In Great Tribulation
http://www.dccsa.com/greatjoy/
Biblical proof that Prince Chuck is the Antichrist and key dates leading to the end of the world. For more enlightenment, including how to debug the pyramids, see: http://members.aol.com/larrypahl/lpahl.htm/

God Channel
http://www.godchannel.com
Relay requests to God via His official Internet channel.

I Can Eat Glass Project
http://hcs.harvard.edu/~igp/glass.html/
Deter excess foreign suitors and carpet dealers with the only words you know in their language.

Illuminati News
http://www.illuminati-news.com
Storm into secret societies and thump your fist on the table.

I Love Leather Pants
http://www.geocities.com/westhollywood/heights/2828/
Don't expect to get André out of his skintight black trousers.

International Ghost Hunters Society
http://www.ghostweb.com
http://www.ghostresearch.org

They never give up the ghost. Nab your own with:
http://www.maui.net/~emf/TriFieldNat.html/

Itz Fun Tew Be Dat Kandie Kid
http://www.angelfire.com/ma/talulaQ/kandie.html/
Mothers – don't let your babies grow up to be ravers.

Lego Death
http://www legodeath.com
Unpleasant death scenes from the guillotine to Elvis dying on the crapper rendered with block toys. For Bible stories illustrated with plastic blocks, go to http://www.thereverend.com/brick_testament

A Mathematical Survey of the English Language
http://www.geocities.com/garywaterbury/
Plot your future through simple arithmetic.

Mind Control Forum
http://mindcontrolforum.com
http://www.mindcontrolmanual.com
http://www.psychops.com
http://www.raven1.net
Unpick Big Brother's evil scheme and then put it to work on the dancefloor.

Mozart's Musikalisches Würfelspeil
http://sunsite.univie.ac.at/Mozart/dice/
Compose a minuet as you play Monopoly.

Mudboy
http://www.mudboyuk.com
Some get their kicks from muddy boots.

Museum of Non-Primate Art
http://www.monpa.com
Become an aficionado of moggy masterpieces.

Neuticles
http://www.neuticles.com
Pick your pet's pocket but leave his dignity intact.

News of the Weird
http://www.newsoftheweird.com
http://www.thisistrue.com
http://www.weirdlist.com
Dotty clippings from the world press.

Nibiruan Council
http://www.nibiruancouncil.com
Stock your bar to welcome the heroic Starseeds, Walkins, and
Lightworkers from the Battlestar Nibiru, who will finally usher in the fifth
dimensional reality.

Non-escalating Verbal Self Defence
http://www.taxi1010.com
Fight insults by acting insane.

PhobiaList
http://phobialist.com
So much to fear, it's scary.

Planetary Activation Organization
http://www.paoweb.com
Prevent inter-dimensional dark forces from dominating our galaxy by
ganging up with the Galactic Federation of Light.

Poop in a Box
http://www.poopinabox.com
Express your gratitude with a gift-wrapped "loaf".

Primate Tips
http://mommensj.web2010.com/ctips3.htm
How to diaper a monkey.

Professional Paranoid
http://www.proparanoid.com
For when no one else will believe
you.

Reincarnation.org
http://www.reincarnation-org.com
Stash your loot with this crowd, then
come back to collect it in your next
life.

Reptoids
http://www.reptoids.com
Was that an alien or merely the subterranean descendant of a
dinosaur?

The Republic of Texas Provisional Government
http://www republic-of-texas.net
Rednecks for liberty, fraternity and
equality.

Rocket Guy
http://www.rocketguy.com
Brian's about to launch himself into
space. Bye-bye, Brian.

The Sacred Geometry Stories of Jesus Christ
http://www.jesus8880.com
How to decode the big J's mathe-
matical word puzzle.

Scrambled Eggs
http://www.callnetuk.com/home/busted/
Nothing a swift kick in the groin won't fix.

Sensoterapia
http://www.sensoterapia.com.co
Master the sex secret you'll never see revealed in this month's *Cleo*.

Sightings
http://www.rense.com
Fishy newsbreaks from talk radio truthferret Jeff Rense. For more real life X-file blather, tune into: http://www.artbell.com

Streakerama
http://www streakerama.com
Get to the bottom of the streaker phenomenon.

Sulabh International Museum of Toilets
http://www.sulabhtoiletmuseum.org
Follow the evolution of the ablution at the world's leading exhibition of bathroom businessware. No need to take it sitting down: http://www.restrooms.org

Terry J Hokanson lives under the Mafia
http://www.geocities.com/terry_tune/
Mild-mannered inventor speaks out against the crime syndicate that controls his life through government hypnotists.

Things My Girlfriend and I Have Argued About
http://homepage.ntlworld.com/mil.millington/things.html/
Add this page to that list.

Time Travel Devices
http://home.inreach.com/dov/tt.htm/
Step back to a time that common sense forgot.

Toe Amputation Project
http://www.bme.freeq.com/spc/toecutter.htm/
No big deal. He still has a couple left.

Toilet-train Your Cat

http://www.karawynn.net/mishacat/
http://susandennis.com

How to point pusskins at the porcelain.

Trapped Angels

http://www.cyberspaceorbit.com/
april.html/

Leading authorities point to evidence that
angels may be alien frauds. Backed up at
http://www.mt.net/~watcher/

WearCam

http://www.wearcam.org

Steve has a Netcam fixed to his head. You
see what he sees. But that won't stop him
having fun.

Why I will never have a girlfriend

http://www.nothingisreal.com/girlfriend/

Derived from first principles, and con-
firmed by his nickname.

World Database of Happiness

http://www.eur.nl/fsw/research/happiness/

Discover where people are happiest and statistically what they mean by
that.

Xenophobic Persecution in the UK

http://www.five.org.uk

If you're below British standards the MI5 will punish you by TV.

ZetaTalk

http://www.zetatalk.com

Nancy's guests today are those elusive aliens that frolic in the autumn
mist at the bottom of her garden.

Rough Guide chronicles series

Chronicles are pocket histories, written by ... illustrated with maps ... recorded history ...

The Rough Guide Chronicle
China
JUSTIN WINTLE

The Rough Guide Chronicle
England
ROBIN EAGLES

The Rough Guide Chronicle
France
IAN LITTLEWOOD

The Rough Guide Chronicle
India
DILIP HIRO

Dip into the past

'Uniquely accessible pocket histories' — History Today
A vital pocket history series for travellers and students alike

Series price £7.99

around the world

in twenty years

London Mini Guide ★ London Restaurants ★ Los Angeles ★ Madeira ★ Madrid ★ Malaysia, Singapore & Brunei ★ Mallorca ★ Malta & Gozo ★ Maui ★ Maya World ★ Melbourne ★ Menorca ★ Mexico ★ Miami & the Florida Keys ★ Montréal ★ Morocco ★ Moscow ★ Nepal ★ New England ★ New Orleans ★ New York City ★ New York Mini Guide ★ New York Restaurants ★ New Zealand ★ Norway ★ Pacific Northwest ★ Paris ★ Paris Mini Guide ★ Peru ★ Poland ★ Portugal ★ Prague ★ Provence & the Côte d'Azur ★ Pyrenees ★ The Rocky Mountains ★ Romania ★ Rome ★ San Francisco ★ San Francisco Restaurants ★ Sardinia ★ Scandinavia ★ Scotland ★ Scottish Highlands & Islands ★ Seattle ★ Sicily ★ Singapore ★ South Africa, Lesotho & Swaziland ★ South India ★ Southeast Asia ★ Southwest USA ★ Spain ★ St Lucia ★ St Petersburg ★ Sweden ★ Switzerland ★ Sydney ★ Syria ★ Tanzania ★ Tenerife and La Gomera ★ Thailand ★ Thailand's Beaches & Islands ★ Tokyo ★ Toronto ★ Travel Health ★ Trinidad & Tobago ★ Tunisia ★ Turkey ★ Tuscany & Umbria ★ USA ★ Vancouver ★ Venice & the Veneto ★ Vienna ★ Vietnam ★ Wales ★ Washington DC ★ West Africa ★ Women Travel ★ Yosemite ★ Zanzibar ★ Zimbabwe

also look out for our maps, phrasebooks, music guides and reference books

THE ROUGH GUIDE TO
Videogaming

Informed, independent advice
on the major gaming platforms

Punchy reviews
of the top games in every genre

Hints, tips and cheats
to crack each game

Directories
of the best Web sites and gaming resources

edenyogi2002@yahoo.co.uk

BLOOMSBURY @ Thistle. Co. UK

Don't bury your head in the sand!

Take cover!

with Rough Guide Travel Insurance